# THE KILLER WITHIN

## PAUL TOOHEY

ALLEN&UNWIN

**FOR J & S**

First published in 2007

Copyright © Paul Toohey 2007

Allen & Unwin
83 Alexander Street
Crows Nest NSW 2065
Australia
Phone: (61 2) 8425 0100
Fax: (61 2) 9906 2218
Email: info@allenandunwin.com
Web: www.allenandunwin.com

National Library of Australia Cataloguing-in-Publication entry:
Toohey, Paul.
    The killer within: inside the world of Bradley John Murdoch.
    1st ed.
    ISBN 9781741143805 (pbk.).
    1. Murdoch, Bradley. 2. Falconio, Peter. 3. Lees, Joanne.
    4. Murderers – Psychology. 5. Criminal behavior. 6.
    Murder – Investigation – Northern Territory. I. Title.
    364.1523099429

Edited by Jo Jarrah
Cover & text design by Phil Campbell
Map by Guy Holt
Typeset by Bluerinse Typesetting
Printed in Australia by Griffin Press

10 9 8 7 6 5 4 3 2 1

# CONTENTS

Darwin

Katherine

Wyndham  Kununurra

NORTHERN
TERRITORY

Derby
Broome
Fitzroy
Crossing

Halls Creek

Wycliffe Well
Roadhouse
Tennant Creek

Wauchope

Barrow Creek

Yuendumu

Tanami Road

Alice Springs

QUEENSLAND

Newman

WESTERN
AUSTRALIA

Kulgera

SOUTH
AUSTRALIA

Carnarvon

Brisbane

Geraldton

Nullarbor Plain

NEW SOUTH
WALES

Kalgoorlie-Boulder

Norsemano

Port Augusta

Perth

Whyalla
Port Pirie
Barossa Valley
Swan Reach
Sedan

Sydney

Adelaide

VICTORIA
Melbourne

Brad Murdoch's preferred
route from Sedan to Broome

TASMANIA

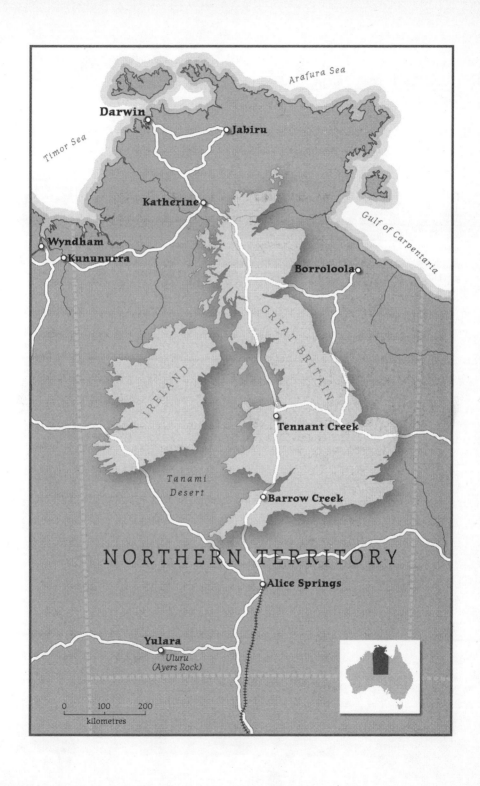

NORTHERN TERRITORY

# PROLOGUE  A SENTIMENTAL GUY

The only time Brad Murdoch ever decked his wife Dianne was just before she left him. It was a good one, right above the eye. But he was never weird. No bent sex, nothing like that. He never forced himself on her.

Dianne met Brad when she was ten. It was at her Aunty Pamela's wedding to Murdoch's older brother, Gary. She never spoke to Brad then; she never really spoke to him for another ten years. Then in 1980, when Dianne was twenty-one, she was visiting Aunty Pam when Brad turned up, with manners. He was neat and tidy. She liked that. In the next year she started seeing him, moving up from Mandurah, 75 kilometres south of Perth, to live with him on the city's outskirts. They started a trucking business, Brad an owner-driver subcontracting to bigger companies. They were declared bankrupt in 1983 and married in 1984. She couldn't remember the date. They didn't ever do wedding anniversaries. They didn't do much, in fact. Brad was always away, driving, hauling.

A son was born in 1986. The relationship was over by then. They passed as strangers in the small rooms of their home. She didn't like the drunken parties. She didn't like how Brad couldn't seem to stick to one task. She left when their son was around eighteen months old, taking the boy and that punch with her. The boy grew up never knowing his dad. No maintenance was ever paid.

Dianne didn't know the date of her own wedding but the records can assist. It was 14 July. Exactly the same day, seventeen years later, that Murdoch went looking to steal himself a woman off a Northern Territory highway. He ended up losing her, too.

# 1 GUNPLAY AT FITZROY

Aboriginal man Joe Ross passed the rifle and said, 'Here, take a look. You'll see what I mean.' We were standing high on the east side of the old low-level causeway at Fitzroy Crossing, in Kimberley country in upper, remote Western Australia, a land that is too far away even for many Australians. Those who do make the journey tend to do so on their last legs, as part of a duty to see their Australia before Australia sees to them. They do it in newly acquired four-wheel drives – Prados, X-Trails, Pathfinders and the lesser Jackaroos – bought with superannuation payouts or life savings. Age steals much from the elderly. It creaks up knees and elbows and weakens valves, meaning roadside stops are frequent and urgent. And it altogether wrecks good road sense, especially among those towing caravans, who invariably select the worst possible highway bottlenecks to park half out on the road while they wander back and kick the tyres on their 'rigs', as they call them. Still, their efforts are rewarded. The Kimberley always seems to try a little harder to impress visitors with its vivid Kodachrome depths.

Ross was right. Even though the night was a near-moonless one, the view through the rifle's telescopic sight proved a revelation. Forms in the riverbed below, dark and shapeless when viewed with the naked eye, focus sharply through the tunnel of the scope's circle of cold, grey–green light. If a target was making its way across the sandy bed, maybe a wallaby, maybe a human, no spotlight would be needed to assist a rifleman in taking a clean head shot.

It is 2002, December, at a time of year when the loaded Kimberley atmosphere threatens and enthralls. The sky is given to dividing neatly in two, between dark and light, with great black clouds occupying one half while, on the other, the sun or the moon shines bright and clear. But step back a few months from these schizophrenic end-of-year wet season days and nights to August, when there are no rain clouds. So it was when a drunken Brad Murdoch had taken this same vantage point on an August 1995 evening. With starlight above and bonfires lighting up the dry riverbed below, the view through his scope was stark as day.

Murdoch's was a clear view but not, to his eyes, a clean one. From his sniper's position, he could see hundreds of Aborigines partying in the riverbed. Dirty blacks drinking beer by fires, dirty blacks who never paid for anything, not the land the government gave them, not the cars they drove, not the beer they drank. Murdoch settled, for starters, on the sedan parked in the middle of the causeway. As it happened, Joe Ross's car. Murdoch opened fire. For twenty minutes he and his flame-barking bolt-action .308 – interspersed with some cartoon fire from his .22 lever-action rifle – taught Fitzroy Crossing's blacks a lesson they would not forget in a hurry.

See how they run.


The Roebuck Hotel is where Broome does its serious shorts and singlet drinking. At three o'clock on a Wednesday afternoon, the main bar was quiet, the after-work crowd yet to settle in to the strangely oppressive and inefficient barn. The room – long, dark and carpeted, with a low ceiling – was a perverse challenge to what Broome was supposed to be about, which is blue sky and white sand for the German, British and Japanese backpacker girls and boys on the final rutting cusp of adolescence. But now it was November. The real northern heat had set in and they'd all gone home. The tourist trade was in its annual hibernation. There was no one in the restaurants, no dread-headed foreign dropkicks with black tattoo armbands or bolts of metal through their eyebrows and girlfriends with nipple rings straining visibly against overflowing bikini cups, making a sun-bitten King Gee local working man grimace at the absurd untouchability of it all.

At least the strippers were still flying in from Perth for three-day weekends. Two were staying in the room above mine: a cheap, themeless motel. Strippers come in different forms. There are the friendly saloon-girl types who offer sex – or suggestions of the possibilities of sex – in the manner of war nurses tending to stricken soldiers. They lie back on floorboard stages, seeming coy and sincere. They're usually the younger ones. Then there are the efficient, distant, heavily made-up mid-thirties types, who are strictly business people. Stone-faced, they do tightly choreographed routines, all their movements sharp and perfunctory. Not the sort who make eye contact. Arrangements can be made to get to know the girls better, both kinds of girls, before and after the shows.

Two transparent g-strings hung suggestively from the railing outside their room. A steady stream of visitors, clean-scrubbed, cologne-doused working men, presumably attracted by a local newspaper ad, climbed their costly stairway. So nervous and beaming were they, it was like they were approaching first love rather than a quick one on the queen-sized. I half expected to see them concealing flowers behind their backs.

Between appointments, one of the girls – they must have been running some sort of shared-bed tag – stood smoking on her balcony. Looking at her, greyhound lean in her sarong, top-heavy with investment breasts, her pretty, seen-it-all face, it occurred to me that her clients may have been getting their money's worth.

'Nice day,' she said, talking aimlessly into the humidity.

'No, it's not,' I pointed out.

She looked at me for the first time, flicked her butt onto the gravel below and walked back inside.

The Broome locals had regrouped and were bunkered down for the hard months ahead. There was honour in being a wet-season stayer. They all knew who they were. Four white men were sitting at the Roebuck's long front bar, having nothing to do with each other and silent before their beers. A group of six Aborigines were writing themselves off fast in a darkened corner by a jukebox. In another dim corner two men played table tennis. The taller man had Caucasian features wrestling for space on what wanted to be an Aboriginal face. Neither side had won out. The man's skin was light enough so as not to render what appeared to be the prison-issue tattoo on his left shoulder a complete waste of the artist's time. Of the pair, he seemed to wear the pants.

'You fellas know where I can find Tahnu Sahanna?' I said.

The taller man looked across at me and his opponent slammed the ball past him and claimed the point. 'Who's asking?' he said, dropping his bat and stepping up to within 30 centimetres of my face.

A friend had told me Tahnu Sahanna was a 'great observer of activity on the land' around Broome. If anyone knew what was going on in these parts, it would be Sahanna. I wanted to know about any run-ins the Aboriginal boys of Broome might have had with Brad Murdoch, a former resident of the town who was said to have a pathological hatred of Aborigines.

'Who hates Aborigines?' said the tall man, whose name was Neville, computing nothing but key words.

'Brad Murdoch. On his inside forearm he's got a tattoo of a black man being lynched.'

'Wait, wait. You say Murdoch?'

'The bloke they want for the murder of Falconio. Peter Falconio, the British backpacker. Murdoch is the bloke who a few years ago shot into the crowd when a whole lot of people – Aboriginal people – were partying after the football grand final at Fitzroy Crossing. He went to jail for it. Remember?'

'Yeah, I remember. That name, Murdoch,' said Neville. 'That's not a very well-loved name in this town. You should be careful using it. Why do you want to meet Tahnu? How do I know you're not a cop?'

I told him I'd walk away now, no hard feelings.

''Cos you're talking about my bro,' said Neville. 'Tahnu Sahanna is my bro and in this town, he's *the man*.'

'Well, that's what I heard,' I said.

Neville relaxed. 'Why don't you go and buy us a jug. I'll make a call.'

The jugs in the Roebuck are plastic so no one can get brained or glassed. The beer is Emu. Neville returned from the wall phone. 'I can take you directly to Tahnu Sahanna, bro, but you better not be fucking with me.'

Something told me Neville hadn't actually got through to Sahanna.

'No, I didn't speak to him,' he confirmed. 'But I left him just a short while back. I can take you to him, bro. For the questions you're asking, Tahnu is the man to answer them. But you gotta show respect when we meet him.'

Tahnu Sahanna, having so far been ectoplasmic and formless, was beginning to take shape: he was huge, black and shiny, wore a heavy gold medallion, wraparound shades, was a disciple of dead rap gangsta Tupac Shakur and employed a brace of white bikini girls who wore librarian spectacles and got yelled at a lot.

Brad, Neville's table tennis opponent, was from Carnarvon, the banana town about 1400 kilometres to the south. 'Can you save me some of that cigarette?' he asked, pointing at the one I was smoking. 'You can just have one to yourself, Brad,' I said. Brad was kind of nervy, although not on my account. He just was. A shambler. He sucked the very guts out of the Stuyvesant Classic in fast gulps. But he was a gentle presence, unlike the white bloke in his late twenties fast approaching the table and pointing questioningly at me.

Neville introduced Alvin, who was wearing track pants, Adidas thongs and an athlete's singlet. Alvin's body was a tattooist's unfinished project, his torso covered in heavy blue outlines of Indian chiefs and bald eagles yet to be coloured in. He was probably pacing out the pain. Alvin had chosen to honour the dead tribalism of a faraway nation. It occurred to me that no white man ever seemed to turn himself into a full-body Aboriginal dot painting. Nor had I ever seen a white man paying tattoo homage to the spirit creatures found in the of rock art of Arnhem Land or the Kimberley country here. Maybe there's a cultural cringe among the tattooed about the world's oldest living culture. Maybe Aborigines would get annoyed.

Alvin appeared to be unable to talk properly. Judging by his half-formed speech, which came out in groans, he was a little slow, maybe. Brain damaged. My immediate impression was: motorbike accident. So it was curious that Neville and Brad deferred to him. Perhaps it was because Alvin was carrying a great deal of money. Fifties and hundreds spilled out of his pockets onto the ground. Alvin was out of it, on something. His fingers were rubbery and devoid of prehensile authority. Alvin reeked of jail. Either a jail he'd been in or one he'd be in soon. Neville, too, had a hint of the cell block about him and not just because of his homemade tatt. There was a slight glaze to his eyes, not the product of the drink in him, but somehow more permanent. He had a defiant way of holding out his chin as if daring someone to punch it. The friendly, shambling Brad didn't look like he'd last long in jail.

When Alvin heard Neville mention the word 'journalist', he became visibly upset and a tragic strangled groan exited his mouth: 'Aaarrgghhh.' He looked at me, unhappily, repeating: 'Aaaarrgghhh.' Alvin pulled Neville aside for a word.

'I vouch for him,' I heard Neville tell Alvin, before turning back to me. 'You hear that, bro? I'm vouching for you. I've just come out of a long stint in prison and I don't want to go back in yet. I'm going to take you to do what you've got to do, and you'll see and hear things. I'm vouching for you. You understand? Don't let me down. Don't be a cop.'

A middle-aged Aboriginal man from the hard-drinking group in the dark corner of the Roebuck staggered over. According to the health statistics, being a middle-aged Aboriginal drinker means you are, statistically, already dead. The man was introduced as an 'important lawman' from the area. One thing you invariably learn in the north: if someone is introduced as an important lawman, he isn't. On cue, the lawman started slurring about his supernatural powers. He said he could remove the kidney fat from his enemies without them even knowing it, and next thing they're dead.

The taking of a person's kidney fat remains the pre-eminent sorcery scare tactic used among Aborigines across northern Australia. It is not mythology. It is vicious and rudimentary surgery performed under non-sterile conditions. An ancient Catholic nun once told me of finding an Aboriginal woman sitting in the dust at Wadeye, in the west-coastal Northern Territory. The hysterical woman was pleading for help as she watched her own blood pool about herself. The nun saw that a wide, neat band of skin and fat running across the woman's back midriff had been flensed clean off. The woman was an adulterer, allegedly. For this, her kidney fat had been accessed by witchdoctors and taken. 'And probably eaten,' added the nun.

Those things still happened – less so these days, but the custom, or maybe the threat, was not extinct. Aborigines usually talked about it very carefully, and then only in whispers. No lawman would ever discuss it at the pub. If the real lawmen knew that serious tribal business was being sold for beer and cigarettes, they'd cut out this drunk's own kidney fat in a flash. I read this man as the equivalent of an ex-communicated priest, all knowledge and no influence. But my new friends were keen for me to be impressed.

The lawman wanted to give me a skin name, in order to place me as one of his brothers in life. Aborigines hand out skin names to white people as a compliment. It makes the outsider feel welcome and gives him a rating or a ranking. For some white people, the getting of a skin name completes their universe. They will insist on referring themselves to their white friends back home not as Wayne but as Barramundi. They will never forget the moment they were given their special name. But it is to be noticed that whites are often given insect names. Or worms.

I have been given about fourteen skin names so far and have never remembered one. I do not want to be a spotted moth or a mangrove maggot. Not that I'm ungrateful, it's just not my world. It's hard enough being human. Besides, in this instance I was not flattered at the prospect of being tribally assimilated by a man who wouldn't remember me in the morning. What he really wanted was a drink and a cigarette. I was more than happy to comply because it meant he would go away. I complied. Like magic, the lawman faded from view.

Alvin was talking like a post electric-shock therapy patient, his words not really making it into the open air. 'Black men are my brothers,' is what he seemed to be saying. I took this as a warning that he had protection, rather than any statement about people needing to get along in the great big melting pot of a world. He kept slapping Neville's back, calling him a 'black cunt'. Each time he heard this, Neville would stiffen and grimace. But then he would also laugh. It must have had something to do with the money in Alvin's pockets.

'People are starting to look at us. Let's get out of here,' said Neville.

I'm tall with short hair; they didn't want anyone to think they were hanging around with a cop. Neville wanted me to tag along. Alvin wanted to lose me. Unhelpfully, for Alvin, I didn't offer to disappear. As we exited the Roey looking for a taxi, Alvin ripped out $50 and handed it to Neville, who was just in time to catch the start of a dog race. A few minutes later, three shredded betting slips fell to the ground. Alvin had a high disposable income. We entered a minibus taxi, the driver asking everyone if they wouldn't mind not smoking in the vehicle. Neville, Alvin and Brad agreed. They smoked with their heads out the windows.

We pulled up in front of a house in Anne Street on the west side of Broome, Alvin fumbling fifties as he tried to pay the driver. A young Aboriginal man stepped out of the house holding a baby and gave the upturned, open-palmed hand signal which can mean various things to Aboriginal people, including, 'What's up?', 'Where are you going?' or, in this case, 'Have you got any?' Nods from Alvin and Neville in the minibus.

Neville spotted an open-top Toyota short-wheel-base cruising past, packed with young Aboriginal men. Neville shouted and made the hand signals but the Toyota didn't stop. 'Tahnu,' declared Neville. 'Don't worry – I know where he's going. We'll go and find him soon.'

Up a flight of stairs to Alvin's housing commission flat in the so-called Bronx of Broome, Alvin suddenly found his voice. On home terrain he transformed, jogging around his unit and actually flapping his arms like wings as words, recipes for marinating beef satays and how marijuana is solving the nation's problems streaming forth. Two pretty Aboriginal girls, one sullen and the other smiley, were lying on ripped vinyl couches, too hot to move. They looked to be about the same age but it turned out they were mother and daughter. One got up to wander past to the toilet and Alvin grabbed a great handful of her butt. She didn't seem to notice. 'My girlfriend's daughter,' Alvin explained.

Neville took a seat at the laminex table and declared his hand. 'You know what we do here?' He was a solemn bloke who talked quietly and buried his words so that sometimes you'd have to ask him to repeat himself. I told Neville that I was getting an idea. 'We're drug distributors,' he said. 'All right,' I said, wondering what this was really about. 'I said I'd take you to Tahnu Sahanna,' said Neville, 'and I will, but for the meantime I recommend you just sit here and watch. You're going to meet some interesting people.'

Two full plastic sandwich bags of tight marijuana heads arrived on the table. When the clip seals were opened the house became infested with that vile purple smell. Alvin ordered one of the girls to grab a pile of pre-cut sections of foil from beneath a bookshelf which was not home to a single book. Into the foils Alvin began shaping $30 deals. Good deals.

I was offered a pipe but declined. This was possibly diplomatically unwise, but I was not a marijuana enthusiast. As it turned out, no one was offended. It wasn't like refusing horse-milk alcohol in a Mongol's tent. Only two people in the room actually smoked – Neville and the sullen young girl. The dope looked like strong skunk. Alvin continued to foil up, but he was becoming increasingly unhappy with my presence. He wanted to see my ID, my 'press card'. I told him I had nothing apart from a driver's licence – besides, if I was a cop, I'd already have hit the buzzer. Then wanted to see the driver's licence. I showed him. He pretended he could read it, like it had a hidden barcode.

'I told you I vouch for him, man,' Neville told Alvin. He was clearly group bodyguard. 'Don't let me down, eh?' he said to me. I explained to

Neville that I didn't actually ask to see any of this. 'You gotta see this,' he said.

An Aboriginal woman turned up to drop off two skinny kids to be babysat in the drug flat. They were placed on a sofa-bed in front of the video player. Alvin kept on foiling up on the table, but every few minutes he'd suddenly jump up and jog around the room. On one such sortie he noticed the kids were watching two actors in a deep tongue-kissing session which was rapidly turning into a crotch-grabbing sex scene. The characters were tearing at each other's clothes. 'What the hell is going on here, kids?' he yelled, standing with a cushion over the screen, peeking behind it now and then and giving the all-clear once the scene had ended. Alvin jogged back to the table with his arms straight down by his sides, his hands making little birdie flaps.

'Man, I am out of it,' he said. 'The cops have been watching this place all day. A couple of hours ago I thought they were coming in to bust me so I dropped ten eccies rather than flushing them.'

'Ten ecstasies?' I queried, betraying my doubts about the feasibility of such immense drug ingestion.

'One day I had thirty,' he said, daring me to contradict him.

I was tiring of Alvin and wanted to find Sahanna. I didn't have long in Broome. Brad Murdoch was, at that moment, standing trial for the rape of a mother and daughter in South Australia. The trial was fast drawing to a close. If he was acquitted, he was to be extradited directly to Darwin to face committal for the murder of Peter Falconio. The chances of him being acquitted of the rapes seemed remote given the facts, which pointed to Murdoch as an unusually organised and cruel predator. But juries are strange creatures. If Murdoch did get off, word was already out that he was to be paraded through Darwin airport in handcuffs, for the media's benefit, before being taken to the remand section of Berrimah prison. I wanted to be there for it.

'Relax, man,' counselled Neville. 'Before this night is through, you will begin to know about Brad Murdoch.'

'Who's Brad Murdoch?' The sullen girl was staring at me over a pipe.

'Murdoch,' I told her, 'is the guy that Northern Territory police have fingered for the murder of Peter Falconio.'

'Who's Peter Falconio?' she said.

'Where have you been?' I asked.

'Here,' she said.

Falconio, I told her, was the British backpacker who was shot on the Stuart Highway near Barrow Creek in the Northern Territory, in July 2001.

Her face registered nothing.

'Falconio, whose body has never been found. Police think this Murdoch, who used to live in Broome – in fact, for a while, in this very street – did it.'

'So?' she says.

'So, Murdoch is also on trial in South Australia for a double rape. Of a mother and her twelve-year-old daughter.'

'Did he do it?' she asked.

'Which one?'

'All of them.'

'Police seem to think so.'

'What do you think?'

'I don't think anything. All I know is they have some of Murdoch's DNA on Joanne Lees' t-shirt. And it looks like he was in the area at the time.'

'Who's she?'

I couldn't believe she had never heard of Joanne Lees or Peter Falconio. 'Have you ever read a newspaper?' I asked. What really gets to a journalist when people display total ignorance of stories they have worked on is: this person has never heard of *me*. Journalists are the vainest of creatures, second only to lawyers. Still, you'd think she'd have heard of the case. And what had happened to that supposedly all-seeing rag which bears no journalist's by-line, the famous all-seeing Bush Telegraph?

She shrugged. Get on with it.

'Joanne Lees was Falconio's girlfriend,' I told her. 'They were hijacked on the highway in the Northern Territory. On 14 July 2001. Falconio was executed. She was tied up by the attacker, who they think is this Murdoch guy, but she managed to escape. Murdoch – well, they *think* it's him – was photographed refuelling at the Shell Truck Stop in Alice Springs a few hours after Falconio went missing. You remember how there was a picture released of a bloke going into the shop?'

No response.

'Anyway, he was one of your neighbours. As for the rape, we'll know soon. Whatever happens, the Northern Territory police will extradite him to Darwin to stand trial for the murder of Falconio. You know what a trial is?'

'Yeah, it's where cops make up a whole lot of bullshit to put blackfellas in jail,' she said. I looked around at the mostly black faces gathered around the laminex table. No one was laughing.

'That woman is suss, man,' said Neville. He'd heard of Lees. At that time, in Australia, it didn't matter whose table you sat at no one much liked Joanne Lees. Not her and certainly not her story. Lees, who made an extraordinary escape from what would have undoubtedly quickly transformed into a horrific sexual assault ending, almost without question, in her death, was regarded as suspicious.

It wasn't suspicious. It was miraculous. But it was hard to call to mind too many stories of famous women survivors. No one talks about women who've survived domestic violence. Perhaps men are not comfortable with stories of women making it themselves. The North Americans had a shot at it by carefully producing the story of Private Jessica Lynch, a US supply clerk who sat cowering in a Humvee after running into an Iraqi ambush in Nassiriya in 2002. It worked, for a while. The story of Lynch, who had been unable to lift a finger to help herself, became arguably the single most reported incident in the Iraq war prior to the capture of Saddam Hussein.

Lynch was with the US's army's 507th maintenance group, which took a wrong turn and fell to an ambush. Nine of Lynch's comrades were killed but

Lynch did not die and was taken to a local Iraqi-run hospital. The Pentagon would later claim she had a bullet and stab wounds. She had no such injuries – just run-of-the-mill road smash pummelling. Iraqi doctors attended to Lynch for eight days and then tried to deliver her, in an ambulance, to a US roadblock. The mercy vehicle was fired upon by the Americans and the ambulance had to retreat back to the hospital. Even though it became known to the US authorities that doctors wanted to hand Lynch back, it was decided the US Marines would raid the unguarded hospital and 'rescue' Lynch. Private Lynch had shown all the self-preservation instincts of a road bollard, yet she came to represent triumph and survival to the American people at a time when things weren't going well. Perhaps they needed Lynch. But Australia did not need a Lees. Nor did the British.

The Australian public seemed to have made up its own mind about Lees without the assistance of the press, who had played the early reportage with little comment or innuendo. The British public were force-fed a weak but sufficiently cloudy stream of urine about Lees, including the notion that Lees was insane and had 'lost', in similar fashion, a previous boyfriend. Some British reporters seemed to like the idea that Falconio wasn't dead at all but had pulled some insurance scam and was hiding out in a tropical island hellhole – New Guinea, perhaps – where Jo Lees would later hook up with him and they'd live gloriously ever after on a nonexistent insurance payout. Australian reporters liked it, too, but were by nature more circumspect than the ruthless British press. Still, we were prepared to learn. Yet there was always Lindy Chamberlain to remember. She sat there on our shoulders, wagging her finger.

Lees, unlike Jessica Lynch, had never been trained to expect the worst, and had suddenly found herself alone and in the most dangerous kind of peril an individual could ever face. Her boyfriend had been shot dead – or, at least, she had good reason to believe he had been. She was sure she was about to be raped. She was not in a war zone, nor had she turned the wrong corner into a dangerous neighbourhood. She was on a friendly open highway in a supposedly welcoming land. She'd been bound and gagged and set to one side while the killer scuffed red dirt over the bitumen in a half-hearted attempt to conceal the pooling bright-red brain blood of her dead boyfriend. Lees had not only lived to tell the story but would soon point the finger at Brad Murdoch, the man she believed was her attacker.

Hero is a word easily pinned to any survivor, and space was quickly made on the uniform of the clueless Private Lynch. They would not cast that medal for Joanne Lees. Surviving was not a sufficient gesture on her part. Being raped and thrown to the dingoes might have done it.

'That Lindy Chamberlain, she did it,' said the sullen girl.

'A lot of people still think that,' I said.

'She just did it,' she challenged, big eyes sharpening.

I considered telling her how it was curious to me that people who have themselves experienced prejudice – as she may well have, being a person of Aboriginal descent – were often the first to employ its insidious broad-sweep vagaries upon others. You'd think, I didn't tell her, that a person in your position might cut an outnumbered person some slack.

Instead of being a white man lecturing a black girl on prejudice, I outlined a pro-Lindy case. I did this not to dissuade the girl of her views, only to show I had the sort of knowledge of the Chamberlain case which they – particularly Alvin, who was breathing down my neck, still wanting to see that press pass – might ascribe to someone more like a journalist than a cop. However, listening to myself, it began to occur to me that I did sound like a cop. So I drummed home the point that the cops thought Lindy did it, whereas I had always thought Lindy was innocent. Or, at least, not guilty. If they could get the distinction. Which they didn't.

They were all looking at me. Alvin's jaw had dropped, partly because he was entering an explosively warm and love-festooned paradise, but mostly because he was not used to anyone besides him dominating a conversation for so long. He slammed a small white pill on the table. Take it, he challenged. Prove you're not a cop. I took it and continued, outlining the famous ten minutes in which Lindy's movements were not accounted for at the camping area. It was in that ten minutes Lindy was supposed to have killed her baby daughter, Azaria.

In that short time after Lindy left the Ayer's Rock barbecue area, making sure her little son Aidan didn't follow her, as a child sometimes does with their mother, she would have had to change into fresh clothes, go to the car with her baby taking a pair of scissors, sever the baby's throat, wait for the baby to die, hide the body, clean up the front of the car where the baby would have bled a warm jugular spray, change out of her clothes which were most likely bloody and back into what she had been wearing before, hide her stained clothes, go into the family tent and drip her daughter's blood around the place to make it look like a dingo had taken her, go back and sit down happily, pretending nothing at all had happened. In ten minutes.

Still, being Australian meant you had inherited that horrible unblinking shark's eye. You circled, studying the subject with all sorts of doubts and wonder. You were DNA-obliged to look for any weakness. It was only sporting to consider ways in which Lindy *might* have killed her baby. If not with her own hands, how then? A contract killer? Certainly not. There were no suited Mediterranean types in that camp site. But it was well known at the time that dingoes were becoming brazen and cheeky and sneaking around in tents. There were indeed signs warning tourists not to feed them.

'So how did she do it?' said the sullen girl, insistent.

'I didn't say she did. But what if Lindy had lured one of the dingoes into the tent with a trail of fresh meat – sausages, let's say – so that the dog would snaffle the baby, the baby *she didn't want?!?*'

'That's the perfect crime!' cried Neville.

'It was before I told you about it,' I told him.

The sullen girl leaned forward. 'So you think –?'

'I don't think anything. It's just an angle.'

The Crown never offered a motive in the case. It only gave up an absurd explanation of how Lindy might have done it. And the stupid jury bought it. Lindy should never have gone to jail on the evidence, but that old Darwin jury reached deep into its heart and pulled out a lot of small-town hate. The press is still blamed for Lindy's conviction. That's too convenient. The jury did not do the bidding of the press. It did the bidding of the nation.

Lindy Chamberlain was not an argument that could be won. No one ever made him- or herself available to be persuaded to the other's point of view. Minds were made up and most were anti-Lindy. 'Lindy' became such a personal issue it was as though everyone's own child had been killed. Parents wondered, 'How could she?' Non-parents did too. And missing from every conversation, just as it would prove absent in the Falconio case, were a few spared words for the victim. No one said, 'That poor Azaria.' Instead they said: 'That woman…' The matter, to this day, was beyond mediation. And I'd never heard anyone say, 'Poor Pete.' Except for Lees. And Pete's family. And the cops. Well, maybe a few more than that.

Anyway, I told them, Lindy was exonerated after a royal commission. Word was she didn't do it. I'd left them totally confused.

'Do you think she did it or didn't do it?' demanded the sullen girl through big stoned roadmap eyes.

'All I'm saying is we can't just go around solving all our national mysteries. That would be a disaster.'

'Why?'

'What would we have to talk about?'

'And the trail of sausages?' asked Neville.

'Is just a trail of sausages. Regard it as such.'

Neville was impressed. The marijuana had made him susceptible to strange logic. 'Listen to *the man*,' he said, showing me off around the room. 'The man *knows* stuff. He *knows* what's going on.'

Alvin was studying me through a violent ecstasy shudder: 'He knows too much.'

Customers had started to arrive. Word was out that dope central in Broome was here, tonight, in the Anne Street flats. It was an appallingly indiscreet affair and Alvin couldn't give a shit. There was no one on lookout, no one surveying for cops among the steady stream of Aboriginal homeboys, mothers dragging kids, kids running upstairs to score as parents waited below in cars – Malays, Chinese, Japanese, white folks, famous multicultural Broome all after their $30 worth of the calming raft. It wasn't that way for me. Not a riverboat ride but a haunted still-water canoe paddle with demons, stagnant leaves and detritus floating at the dead-end of the creek. Crocodiles.

I'd once found a hydro-grower friend crushing up contraceptive pills to spray on his baby plants. Maybe his science was good, but his corporate goodwill program – as growers and dealers liked to speak of it – was suspect. Marijuana was different now.

Alvin explained that, thanks to him, thanks to his work, no one was drinking alcohol in Broome tonight. He ought to be *thanked by the fucking police* for keeping crime and domestic violence levels down. I was introduced to everyone who stuck their head in the door: 'This is Paul. He's a journalist. He wants to know about Brad Murdoch.' Everyone had heard of Murdoch and could put a face to him, but no one really knew him except to say that he was a person about whom there was a general alert, an alert that radiated from within Murdoch himself. It said: stay clear.

A young Aboriginal man brought in a conical plastic vial, popped the cap and let a misshapen pearl roll around on the table. 'What'll you give me for this?' he asked Alvin.

Broome is a pearl town. This small and slightly off-centred orb had journeyed from the pearl beds from where it was grown and stolen – in all likelihood hidden in an employee's arse in order to pass inspection at knock-off. Neville stepped in, claiming to be able to discern whether or not a pearl was the genuine article. He put it in his mouth, rolled it around and declared it to be real. The pearl seller hoped to get two foils for the pearl. Alvin, aghast, explained that he wasn't running a charity or a pawnshop. He threw one foil at the kid, who walked away happy. Once the kid was out of range, Neville suggested the value of the pearl was $150 or more.

Standing in the doorway looking at us all was a beautiful, flashing-eyed Aboriginal woman in her early to mid thirties, upstanding breasts jostling for space within a see-through yellow singlet. Long straight hair and an easy smile. And a tiny skirt. She was, in fact, a complete knockout.

'That chick,' Neville told me in a confidential aside, 'wants to fuck you.'

Alert, I asked: 'How do you know that?'

'Because if I *ask* her to fuck you, she will. I told you, bro, I'm going to look after you.' I thanked him. And told him, with sincere regret, that I must decline.

'Don't you like black chicks?' he asked. It wasn't that. 'Then what?' He was all curiosity.

It wasn't the notion of being assigned a partner that bothered me. It happens, in adolescence, when your best mate's girlfriend tries to flog off her best friend in order to get her, and you, out of the way. Maybe, in this case, it had something to do with the fact that she hadn't been consulted. There were other considerations as well. But I didn't reveal any of that to Neville. What I told him was: 'I'm working.' Neville looked at me weirdly. I appreciated his mystification more than he'd ever know.

A fey, homey-type black kid walked in with a $30 stick he wanted to sell to Alvin. 'Man, I don't buy dope – I *sell* it,' said Alvin, looking to the heavens for back-up. 'You think I need dope? I've got tonnes of the shit! What the hell *is* this?'

'Please, man, just buy it from me,' pleaded the young man.

'Yeah, so you can go and whack up that heavy shit you're on,' said Alvin. The man did not protest, just looked sheepish. 'I can't believe this,' said Alvin, examining the low-grade leaf and handing over $30. He wrote off the loss and filed it under: 'Philanthropy'.

This, the public relations end of the drug trade, is the side that Brad Murdoch never concerned himself with. He ran drugs across the inland back roads of Australia, amphetamines, but mostly marijuana. Guns as well. He was the conduit, the delivery man. He didn't sit in flats dealing foils. He didn't have the personality for it. He'd had a go at it but people got the creeps. And he would have regarded these people, black customers especially, as vermin. Big Brad was no salesman. He just made sure the mail got through.

'This Murdoch,' said Neville. 'I didn't know the dude personally, but I seen him around. And I can tell you one thing. He regarded Aboriginal men as moving targets. But at the same time he liked to fuck black chicks.' That's what I'd heard too.

There was a time when Aboriginal women were borrowed for a side of beef, or just plain thieved away from their husbands and children by the early miners and cattlemen. White men set aside their distaste for the Aboriginal race so long as a pair of compliant black thighs softened the thud when the men hit the swag of a night. There was love, too, through the history of black and white Australia, and the people in this room could just as well have been the descendants of love as of necessity. But up until the 1960s it was illegal for the races to marry without permission.

The price of a woman had moved on to reflect the times: it was no longer a side of beef. Usually a carton of beer or a four-litre cask of white wine, Coolibah or Fruity Gordo, and a packet of cigarettes would do it. It was consensual, more or less, and girls were never hard to find. I still see it some days outside my own door on a busy Darwin avenue: an Aboriginal woman walks alone on the footpath; a car driven by a white man pulls alongside; she gets in. It's directly off to the drive-through bottle shop then into the bushes.

When first observing such perfunctory contracts my instinct was to view it with disgust. I had to pull my head in from such assessments. It was only the matter-of-factness of the exchanges that could be unsettling. A lot of the women were beaten-up ugly, filthy, alcohol-deranged, staggering, homeless and desperate. I wondered how anyone could possibly want to fuck them. It raised more questions about the white men who prowled for them. They tended to present slightly better than their targets, being in a position to shower, shave and clean their clothes in a washing machine rather than in sea water on high tide at the closest beach. In the north these men are called gin-jockeys or gin-burglars. If not for the availability of Aboriginal women, who would they target? White women. And then they would be known not as gin-jockeys but as predators and sex monsters.

A customer of Alvin's called me off to one side for a word. 'You know that Murdoch? Well, everyone's always talking about this Joanne Lees.

That's because she's a pretty white girl. But you know, we got two Aboriginal girls who disappeared from here. That's Sara Davey and Petronella Albert. They were from One-Arm Point, north of here. And they just disappeared, never to be seen again. That was just a couple of years ago. They're our people, know what I'm saying? Cops never found nothing, of course. Maybe 'cos they were Aboriginal chicks. And you know what? That Murdoch cunt used to drive trucks up to One-Arm Point, making deliveries. So I'm just telling you, bro, to check it out. People want to know.'

I told him I'd do that.

'Come with me, man,' said Neville. 'There's a bloke who you should meet.' We wandered a few streets over to a clapped-out housing commission home where angry voices rumbled from within the grey brick walls. A group of Aboriginal men, all trashed and standing around a heap of dead VB cans, were shoving each other.

They staggered towards me, trying to focus. The eyes of Stumpy Williams seemed to have left their sockets and were dangling free. Neville attempted formal introductions, which made no impression. They thought I'd come for a fight. Neville cooled the situation and explained. Something registered in Stumpy's brain. 'Come and see me in the morning,' said Stumpy. 'I was in jail with that Murdoch prick.'

Back in the Anne Street flat a very stoned Chinese man strummed soothing Broome folk music, island sounds on the mainland. Alvin had disappeared. Neville dropped off in his chair. The desire for drugs had been sated for the night. Customers were no more. Tahnu Sahanna? Who knows? That beautiful Aboriginal girl? Long lost. I called a cab to take me to my themeless motel. The transparent g-strings were no longer hanging from the railing above my room.

## 2 BONES FROM THE CAVES

'You have to understand the Aboriginal way,' Neville was explaining as I put up a fight I'd already lost. 'Man, I've helped you out here. They wanted three cartons. I've already talked them down to two.'

It was the morning after and Stumpy and his mates were refusing to discuss Brad Murdoch without payment in beer. The thing I had to weigh up was whether it was ethical to pay for information in beer. I suspected it probably wasn't. But more important was whether the information, on the back of the beer, would be reliable.

A conscience can be a selective companion. I'd never paid for information in my trade as a journalist but, then again, I had. I'd taken a lawyer out to dinner and bought three bottles of good red wine on company expenses, all in the name of a story. No one ever questioned that. *I* didn't question it, apart from hoping that some wretched company accountant stranded in some faraway high city tower didn't want to make an issue of me being forced to drink in order to get the job done. I was questioning it now because I was dealing with alcoholic Aborigines. It was a tangle constructed on what I realised were my own monumental double standards.

Neville, who I was beginning to like, solved it for me: 'Bro, I know you've got shit you've got to deal with it. I understand – I do. But these guys are *drinkers*. Let me tell you something, just so you know I *do* understand.

You know Aborigines play cards, right? You know we gamble, heavily, on cards, right?'

I wasn't sulking about my predicament, just fascinated by it. Also by Neville's motives. As my imposed guide in Broome, he knew if I bought beer then he would drink beer as well. But he wanted something more. And it was not beer or money. And, yes, Aborigines – women, mostly – do like to play cards. They'll sit around on blankets, throwing their welfare money into the middle while their kids go hungry. A friend who regularly visited Cape York in northern Queensland told me some women would piss their knickers before leaving the gambling blanket. I believed it.

'And you know what our people do when they play cards, to make luck come their way?' asked Neville. 'They go to the caves of their ancestors, and by that I mean the caves where grandmother and grandfather are stored, in the hillside, and they take a bone – just one bone – and they put it in their back pocket. Then they go down and sit on that blanket and play cards. Play all day. They believe that bone will bring them luck. I've seen them do it. Ethics? I know, for a fact, that some of them lose those bones between the card game and the pub afterwards. And those bones never go back to that cave. See what I mean? Yes, they panic and worry when they lose those bones and they *will* feel cursed by what they've done. Until they want to get lucky next time. I can tell you for a fact: there is no such thing as ethics.'

I bought two cartons of Emu Bitter and we found Stumpy. These would be the first beers of the day. So even if it was still morning, at least I'd got them – the interviewees – cold. Stumpy was clear-headed and thirsty. One carton of Emu Bitter cans stood by the table, with many hands ripping at it. The other carton was stored in an unenthusiastic fridge. Whose house we were in, I didn't know. Everyone seemed to live in everyone else's house around here.

'I met him in jail. Would've been '95,' said Stumpy, a very dark man with a messy face that looked as though it had been made by a clay sculptor in his first freeform art class. 'We all knew about what Murdoch had done in Fitzroy, see, shooting up our brothers at the Old Crossing. Every day the screws were telling us, "That man coming in to Broome." The whole prison knew. We just wanted to do the same thing to him. He killed our people, so we kill him.'

But Murdoch didn't actually kill anyone during his Fitzroy Crossing sniper hunt.

'Kill, not kill, make threat to kill – same thing,' said Stumpy. 'All the mob from Balgo and Fitzroy and Halls Creek and all that, we're all there in prison. When he came in, with the police escorting him, we were walking straight up to him, going like this.' Stumpy drew his finger across his throat. 'We came at him straight away. Everyone singing out, everyone saying, "We're going to get you and kill you." All that shit. But no one touched him.'

Aborigines run Western Australia's prisons. They make up the majority of prison populations from the deep south to the far north of the state. Despite the numbers they couldn't get to Murdoch. He got protective treatment – he was put in the women's section. There were no female prisoners in Broome jail at the time.

'I was working in the laundromat, right next to the women's prison,' said Stumpy. 'But we couldn't get into the women's side. I could only peep through the doorway. I looked at him, went like this.' Finger across the throat. 'He just went to his bed and laid down. He couldn't go out. We're all a lot more Aboriginal people what's in prison than whites, see, and we wanted to smash him up, do the same thing what he done to us, our Aboriginal people. We was watching him all day but there was a big mob of screws there watching us.'

It was hot. It was thirsty work watching Stumpy's people guzzle Emu Bitter. I asked if they'd mind if I had one of the beers. Stumpy launched himself from his chair and screamed. 'You crazy? Have a fucking beer, my friend! Now you're making sense!' I took a beer and the mood in the room noticeably softened. I felt a welcoming clap on the back.

Because Murdoch was a remand prisoner in the pre-trial stage, they couldn't put him in the maximum security wing. 'Maximum? He'd get killed!' cried Stumpy. 'You're locked up with a big mob of blackies! He was there two weeks, that's all, before they took him away to jail in Perth. See, the boys always come up to me in the laundromat, asking about him, wanting to get to him. You can always get a knife or a fork, cut his throat. But he was always there in the women's shelter, women's side. He couldn't come out for lunch or cup of tea or anything. No women in there.'

Asked whether Murdoch ever seemed worried, whether a flash of fear ever crossed his face knowing a large crowd of Aborigines wanted his very gizzards, Stumpy Williams told a reluctant truth. 'Nah, nothing. Not a thing.' Stumpy was in for belting his wife and was doing easy time with a mountain of relatives. Prison, for Stumpy, was something Aboriginal men had to do now and then. Murdoch would not have had the same attitude but may have taken some satisfaction from the fact that, after committing a race-hate crime, he'd been fully segregated.

'He was happy-go-lucky,' said Stumpy. 'He was giving us the up-sign and everything. He was a fruit fuck. That's what we call people like him. Fruit fuck. And when he got transferred out of Broome prison, the police came and escorted him out. I don't know what happened when he went to Perth. Maybe they belted him up there.'

Attempts to draw out the semantic provenance of 'fruit fuck' went nowhere. I wondered whether it was because 'fruit' was dated language for 'queer'. They were politely bored by this line of inquiry. 'Anyway, maybe it is, but who gives a fuck, 'cos he was a fruit fuck,' said Stumpy.

Murdoch was sent on to Perth where he did the remainder of his time – some nine months. He came back north and continued doing what he knew best, working on diesel engines and truck driving, trying to sell pot on the side. His debt had been paid in the eyes of society. Perhaps he reasoned the local Aboriginal population would see it that way as well.

One night Murdoch was drinking at the Nippon Inn, a late-night joint that attracted much attention from the police and licensing authorities for its high number of victim-reported assaults. And that, said Nicholas Williams, Stumpy's nephew, was when the Broome boys put Murdoch 'in the middle' to make him pay for Fitzroy Crossing. Not that they really knew the fine detail of what had happened up at Fitzroy. But they knew that Murdoch had not singled out any one person: he had taken a stand against all Aboriginal people. In this part of the world it didn't matter whose name was on the title deed. In Aboriginal eyes it was all Aboriginal land.

The younger Aboriginal men about Broome were in no rush to repay Murdoch for Fitzroy Crossing. Instead, they acted in the manner of their forefathers, at times marathon-ranging hunters yet who always – if they had the choice – were opportunistic, preferring if game simply crossed their path. It was inevitable that Murdoch, with his attitude to Aborigines, would find them.

'Then it happened,' said Nicholas. 'A young Aboriginal man walked into Nippon Inn – and he *was* real pissed, this boy. Murdoch grabbed him by the throat and chucked him, threw him out the door. But by the throat? You don't need to do that. You should just turn him around and walk him out the door. The boys were all watching and the boys didn't like it one bit. So they went for his left leg first, bringing him down. Then starting hitting him on all sides. They put him in the middle.'

'You gotta be a good man to get out of the middle,' said Stumpy, who reckoned some eighteen men descended on Murdoch.

He needed an ambulance?

'Shit, yeah,' said Nicholas. 'They didn't put him in the middle for nothing. When someone goes in the middle, that's it. They carried him away, he was pretty messed up. You couldn't recognise his face. Even his own mother wouldn't have recognised him. When things happen like that, when you hit the ground, you don't get up. It's like, see if he can talk turkey now.'

'That's when he lost all his front teeth,' said Stumpy. 'He had his front teeth when he was in Broome jail. He lost them at the nightclub that night.' The other bouncers who came to Murdoch's aid copped it too; the Nippon Inn closed early that night.

But why was Murdoch allowed to live after his Fitzroy Crossing gunplay? No one could get at Murdoch in jail, that is understood, but they could have killed him when he came back to Broome. They could have killed him at the Nippon Inn.

'I think they did try to kill him that night,' said Nicholas, quietly.

Brad Murdoch is a great, blundering brute of a man. He'd be 120 kilograms. Not all muscle, but not all fat either. Just twisted, dried-out meat. Hard to put down and hard to kill. Some years on from the events of the Nippon Inn that Nicholas was describing, in 2005, Murdoch sat in the dock, in Darwin, during the committal hearing for the murder of Peter Falconio. One of the witnesses said something Murdoch didn't agree with. He gave her a weary sneer, as if to say, 'Listen to this dickhead. You've got to be joking,' and in doing so provided a rare glimpse of his front teeth, of which there were none. Just a nasty black hole.

'We'll kill him slow,' said Stumpy. 'Take a hair from his head – that's all that's needed.' He's talking black magic, but white men are not susceptible to black magic, are they? 'Oh yes they are,' said Stumpy. 'Doesn't matter whether he's in America, doesn't matter where he is. They'll still get him. They'll do that. They'll get a hair from him, doesn't matter if he's a whitefella.'

I've got my doubts about whites being vulnerable to Aboriginal magic but it's best not to question it, lest you throw down the challenge. Besides, Aboriginal magic is not all bad; there is good magic, healing and love magic, which is sometimes used on white boys and girls who go to work in Aboriginal communities. The sweat or a hair from the desired one is surreptitiously stolen by the desirous one. Next thing, they're lovers. The magic is helped to reach its mark by a simultaneous whispering campaign, of which the target invariably becomes aware.

With all Stumpy's talk about 'killing' Murdoch, they did not kill him. My persistent questioning of Stumpy on this point went nowhere. 'Look, bro,' said Neville, pulling me to one side, realising his friends were finding it difficult to respond without losing face. 'It's because they know he's a *shooter*. His friends are shooters, too. We might talk magic, we might talk revenge, but people like that are dangerous.'

Late that afternoon we finally located Tahnu Sahanna. He was at a housing-commission joint on the south side. I was right about him – except for the bikini babes. He was big, more LA than Broome, with wraparound shades failing to conceal a whole lot of attitude. The bikini babes turned out to be six or seven men, of similar size to Sahanna, back-up drawn on his charismatic tide.

'Murdoch?' said Sahanna. 'Don't know the man.'

Next morning, after an early check-out at 6 am, I was Fitzroy Crossing bound. Neville was lying wounded on the ground outside my motel door. He'd copped a serious flogging. 'I've got to come with you to Fitzroy,' he said. 'I've got to go see my witchdoctor to get some curing.'

Neville cut a miserable figure in the front passenger seat. We had to stop now and then so he could smoke his painkillers. His bottom lip was twice its already considerable size and he was sitting in an awkward, twisted position due to the kicking he'd received the night before. Neville told how he'd been drinking with some mates in a flat. He had finally gone into a bedroom to fall asleep when this girl – she was gorgeous, a spunk, stunning, but only sixteen – had come into the room and 'tried to crack onto me'. Neville resisted. He swore he was trying to get her to leave when the bedroom door was bashed open. There was a mob of them: the girl's brothers, uncles and cousins – all Stumpy's crowd. They began stomping the bejesus out of Neville. The damage bore the hallmarks of a distinctively Aboriginal assault: a frenzied kicking attack on the calf muscles to really stuff someone up for walking. Neville was put in the middle, but not the full middle. His teeth were intact and his eyes weren't bruised. It was the backs of his legs that were kicked black and blue. Now he needed to get out of Broome to regroup with his extended family in Fitzroy Crossing, to plot his revenge and, he said, to seek traditional healing.

During the 400-kilometre drive east to Fitzroy, Neville recounted, through that great hanging precipice of a lip, growing up in the south of

Western Australia, using his fists as his spokesmen. In 1999 he went to jail for three years after he was charged with indecently dealing with a minor. She was thirteen. 'I didn't do it,' he said, claiming he'd been press-ganged into pleading guilty. I passed no comment on the apparent consistencies with events of the previous night.

Whenever Neville became too influential in a prison block – according to Neville – the authorities shifted him on. He knew the layout of the Albany, Casuarina, Geraldton and Broome prisons. He drew aerial maps of the prisons to prove it. It was in the West Australian prison system that he earned a reputation as a fixer of problems, mainly acting as a mediator-enforcer between the dominant Aboriginal populations and the white men who felt they needed protection from them.

I grabbed a tape from the console, imagining it was probably some country music compilation I'd been too lazy to label. It turned out to be interviews I'd recorded on the day the stolen generation case was lost in the Federal Court in Darwin in 2000. Lorna Cubillo and Peter Gunner, the two Aboriginal applicants in the case, had – like thousands of others – been taken from their families by white welfare patrol officers when they were small children because they were, in the language of the day, half-castes. Fraternising between races at any place other than a stock camp, racing track, football game or boxing ring was frowned upon. Those half-caste children were, to the government of the day, an embarrassment.

Lonely white men, sent to the north by their companies or their inability to connect with their own kind, ended up pairing off with black women. The relationships were not designed to last: not only were they unlawful, how could you ever bring a full-blooded, black, bush woman home to mother? Some tried to live with their women and children in bush camps, but would soon find themselves not only outcast from white society but never quite accepted in black company either. One way to keep their women from wandering off with other black men or whites who were sniffing around was to keep them on a short leash by feeding them alcohol, and sometimes the nastiest, cheapest alcohol around: methylated spirits, which turned the drinker's tongue an incriminating purple and identified them as surely as a ringer's burning brand labelled a cow. But in most cases, once a white man had satisfied his immediate needs, he fled the scene, leaving mixed-race children with their black mothers. Who, being mothers, loved them.

These kids were different to their full-black siblings, but only in skin colour. They spoke the same language and lived the same way. The government took the view that the white part of these children needed saving. Patrol officers on horseback – later they would come in Land Rovers and light planes – scoured the bush camps looking for such children, who were taken away as grief-stricken Aboriginal mothers bashed their own heads with rocks and bled. There was no such thing as a lawyer to advise the mothers of their rights. Even if there had been, it would have done them no good. Aborigines were not recognised as Australian citizens.

The children were sent far, and sometimes not so far, to mission homes. They were counselled to forget their language and their family. Some did forget and grew up without any animosity to either the Commonwealth or the Christian-run orphanages which had raised them. Others did not forget. Those who later developed alcohol problems, had broken marriages or difficulty relating to their own children believed their broken childhoods explained much about their adult lives. They wanted formal acknowledgment.

The Commonwealth responded that it had done the kids a favour by removing them from their families and contended that in some cases intervention had saved lives. They argued that full-blood Aborigines did not like white blood infiltrating their tribes and were known to treat half-caste children cruelly. Peter Gunner was said to have been buried and left to die beneath an anthill by his own people before the Commonwealth's patrol officers rescued him.

In this court case, Australia's historical prejudice against its first people was neatly shoved back in Aboriginal faces. Never mind that Aboriginal mothers coloured their half-caste children charcoal-black in order to trick the patrol officers, no matter the terrible displays of anguish when children were taken, nor even how desert-based families would wander to Alice

Springs or Darwin looking for their children, and would camp outside the perimeter of orphanages only to be shooed away by their children's new guardians. The implicit suggestion was that Aborigines, after tens of thousands of years of hard-fought survival, were incapable of raising their own children. Or worse, that being Aborigines, they were not sufficiently blessed with the humanity to care for children.

Most Australians could accept that the policy had seen these children badly done by. But, like the government, they didn't want to pay for it. Many southern Australians knew, or knew of, some part-Aboriginal person who had been raised in the white world and didn't seem the worse for it. On closer examination, a lot of those Aborigines turned out to be boxers, footballers or track stars. In the Northern Territory and Western Australia, where white people grew up alongside Aborigines, there was simmering resentment about the stolen generation court action. The argument often went: 'I went to school with her/him. She/he never talked about being an Aborigine then.'

The Cubillo-Gunner court case was an important one, watched all around Australia. If Gunner and Cubillo won, thousands of other stolen generation children – now adults – might have to be compensated. The Commonwealth was understandably horrified at the prospect of having to fork out millions for the actions of an ancestral government. It sent a tough team of lawyers to Darwin to fight the case.

Cubillo, taken as a small child from the Tennant Creek region in the central Northern Territory, had been farmed into a Darwin orphanage. She left it in her teenage years to become a white man's maid. She found her freedom but became a Darwin woman who found it hard to love her children or her husband.

Peter Gunner, taken from central Australia, had been sent to Alice Springs and always lived in his own part of the world. His story was possibly more painful, because once released into adult life he wanted tribal acceptance but struggled to get it. It was a hard road. Like Cubillo, Gunner always opted for his Aboriginal half. Cynics said: why not acknowledge your white half?

Gunner and Cubillo knew they were Aborigines because they had always been treated as such. They weren't abused for being white: they were called coons. But it was the children of these stolen generation people, most of all, who were pushing this court case. They needed to see their parents vindicated because they, too, wanted to take their rightful place in the community. They didn't want to be nowhere, in-between people.

The claimants were enveloped by supporters in Darwin and the mood was positively giant. Their full-tribal brothers and sisters in the Northern Territory had long since won full land rights, giving them total control of half of the land in the Territory. This case, thought the stolen generation people, was the next step on the justice trail. The fact that the Federal Court had even decided to hear the case meant a great deal in itself. Now, all the stories about how the children were stolen, and how they were then treated, would come out. Deliverance was imminent.

Much was said about Gunner, that his own people had rejected him because he carried white blood. It was said as an accusation: that Gunner's own family had willingly allowed him to be sent away to a Christian boarding school. The proof of this was there for all to see. It was a signature on a document, which showed that the welfare officers had taken Gunner away with full consent. The signature was a shaky, illiterate cross.

When Lorna Cubillo undid her top in court and showed the judge how her nipple had been whipped off by a missionary's belt, it was easy to get caught up in the emotional view that, surely, this was the case sealer, final proof of the malicious mindset that saw children put in the care of white monsters. Level-headed legal cynicism saw it differently. The stolen generation could say what it liked about the Christian orphanage cruelty, but the case was against the Commonwealth, not the orphanages. Got a problem with the Catholics and the Anglicans? Sue *them*. The only question to be answered was whether the Commonwealth had broken its own laws by removing the children. The judge said it had not. Cubillo and Gunner had no case.

By the time he died in 2004, Gunner mercifully knew who he was. Supporters, black and white, made sure he understood he was a man fully of two worlds who could choose to be of whichever world he wanted. That was his indelible right. In the few short conversations I had with him, he seemed a wounded, scattered man. But he was buried as a black man, shown full respect by central Australians, black and white.

The tape Neville and I were listening to was not the usual road-journey soundtrack. It was a heartbreaking series of post-judgment interviews with bitter lawyers, with sad, defiant Lorna, confused Peter and all their distressed supporters. I looked over and saw that Neville, by birth a southern Aboriginal man only vaguely connected with these powerful northern politics but nonetheless seamlessly joined to it by experience, had his chin on his chest, crying.

This was Brad Murdoch's world, too. He had grown up amongst such people in Northampton, Western Australia, some 600 kilometres north of Perth – not far from where Neville did his growing up. Murdoch couldn't see what had happened to the Aboriginal people. And it wasn't his fault. Then, no one could.

Neville said that, like Murdoch, his job was dealing drugs, running back and forth across the country, shifting kilos of marijuana. If so, he wasn't too good at his craft. He had nothing to show for it – not, it seemed, a single possession. There was talk of his Ford GTHO Cobra, garaged somewhere in the north, a beautiful drug-money-bought machine he was waiting to collect when he next had some money. It all sounded a little hopeful.

I still didn't understand why he had taken me under his wing in Broome, what it was Neville wanted me to see. 'I've just never met a journalist before,' he now said. 'You write stories. I want to tell my life story. I want people to know about me, how I'm a drug dealer, how I've been to jail, to understand the things I do. Have I got a story?'

I told Neville his story was not ready to be told. He was between places, between jobs, and somewhere between Aboriginal society and white society and not quite sure where to put his foot. I reminded him how he had let Alvin call him a 'black cunt'. I could understand why: Alvin had money and drugs and Neville was in need of both. Yet there were two types of conviction. So far, Neville only knew about one of them.

It can't be easy to be a man of different parts, as he was. I'm just monoculture man, no in-betweens. Besides, I was supposed to be looking into a killer and rapist who shuffled serious amounts of dope across the country, not the occasional kilo.

'I'm an Aborigine,' says Neville, 'and I want to change my life.'

'That's fine. But I'm not your priest.'

Neville nodded grimly then smiled. I dropped him at a town camp in Fitzroy Crossing, hobbling miserably into a decrepit house. He came limping back out with a road tape for my journey – Fitzroy Express, the local Aboriginal band made good. The usual unkeepable promises to see each other somewhere down the track were made.

# 3 SHADOWS ON THE LAND

Brad Murdoch is not just Brad Murdoch. He's a breed, a kind. There are Murdochs all across northern Australia and they run to type: fastidious men with pissed-off, resentful minds, white or beige Toyota Land Cruiser HZJ75 utility, non-standard, all-terrain oversize 16-inch tyres on wide, non-standard white Sunraysia rims, amphetamines, dope, full survival tool-kit in the back, maybe a winch, definitely a kangaroo jack, compressor for pumping tyres, three kinds of heavy rope, towing chains, long-range tank, don't mind a cup of tea, prefer a beer, whack your nose over this, Jim Beam on ordinary nights but Jack Daniels to celebrate. Love their mates but always disappointed by women.

Canvas canopy off the back with built-in flyscreen mesh to keep out the mozzies and sandflies when sleeping in hiding holes; portable gas ring for tea and coffee, lightweight steel barbecue plate as back-up or when they feel like cooking, civilised, on a fire. Six-pack foam esky for up the front of the cab on long drives and a serious full-grown Rubbermaid esky for the back of the vehicle, to be accessed on piss-stops. Engel electric car fridge, naturally. Cop-type swivel camping spotlight at the rear.

Weapons of various types – revolvers, pistols, rifles, bludgeons. Wood-handled Green River knives, cheap-bladed perhaps, but nevertheless quick to sharpen and easy on the hand; and for special occasions, which tend not to arise, quality German-made knives, the sharpening of which to a state of unnecessary quickness helps pass the time, on a high-quality two-grade fine-and-coarse rectangular stone, oiled with diesel or CRC and stored away in a purpose-built wooden box. For unexpected trouble a lovingly fashioned mulga round-handled stick, stored for easy access under the feet in the cabin.

The barramundi, handsome perch-like creature and preferred river-system and close-to-shore fish of the north, is poorly prepared to deal with the tackle box he carries, loaded as it is with old-fashioned Finnish Nils Master lures and the Australian-made copies (which work), and the more recently fashionable treble-hooked squidgies, the rubbery and lifelike little fish with motion-vibrating tails. But crabs are what he really likes. Crab pots required. Sheep necks for bait. Or bits of shot bush pig. Big green mudcrabs. Muddies. Real big cunts. Check out this claw. He knows the spots to get them. Tourists don't.

A feed of crabs, that's what it's all about. That's why they've got a dinghy with a 20-horsepower Mariner. Just for taking it quiet, maybe hammer it a bit to clear out the cobwebs, a carton or two on ice, a mate or two, put the canopy up and go somewhere there's no tourists. Or blackfellas. Mate, you should try my chilli crab sauce. Bit of Worcestershire, bit of Tabasco, bit of Rosella Big Red – hang on. *Too much information there.* The recipe is confidential. Good, but. You should come out crabbing with me one time …

They are tattooed, white, like to appear as if they work and, indeed, take on the appearance of working men but may only very occasionally lift a spanner or sledgehammer. The overall mission is fishing, shooting or sticking pigs, being a citizen of the north, checking in on old friends in small towns, never disclosing more than is necessary because the mission is, really, yet to be determined. It is not even possible to articulate it. It is simply life, the way of the track. The government sometimes sponsors these decades-long, self-indulgent journeys, but not by providing unemployment benefits. They usually rely on sickness benefits. They get themselves pensioned off in their forties, with some concocted or grossly exaggerated illness.

Not, of course, that it's a matter ever discussed among friends, because it tends to hint at frailty or, even worse, the truth: that they are malingerers and bludgers. And we can't have that. Only blackfellas are bludgers. Some make fewer demands on society than others. They do it by running drugs or being part of the chain.

They occupy little outposts in small outback towns. They are the associates of outlaw gangs and provide resting points for colleagues moving amphetamines and cannabis around the ever-enthusiastic drug-fuelled nation. Or locations to temporarily stash shipments or cash when drivers take shift changes or while waiting for police interest to wane. They are the junction men, giving succour to the drug resistance, flagging the couriers through. Sometimes, although this is a harder act to disguise in a small town and carries a greater risk of prison, they are the amphetamine cooks.

They'll drink light or mid-strength beer. Don't suggest to their faces that it's less manly than drinking full-strength. The reason they drink light cans – always cans, because stubbies can get busted on a rough track, and losing a stubby is like losing a son – is that they can drink them all day. It allows the drinker to maintain a semblance of sanity. The cones – they always smoke cones, sucked from harsh, waterless pipes or bongs, because joints are wasteful and marijuana is a carefully regarded resource – take the edge off the beer. The speed in turn helps to cut out the mental slovenliness the dope creates, but doesn't entirely destroy the dope's effect. The dope also helps mitigate the jumpy anger that straight speed-beer intake can sometimes promote. It's a balanced medication regimen. With twelve light cans, four cones and two lines under a man's belt, any variables a day might throw up become just about manageable.

They have dogs. Like Murdoch had his dog, Jack, a half-Dalmatian, half-pitbull. Some have heelers and some have real pig dogs – preferably with a bit of wolfhound. They love their dogs and sometimes beat the shit out of them. They feed them less than the dogs might like to be fed, usually every second day. Keeps them edgy. The dog will be a point of much discussion and admiration. It has invariably descended from a noble

Queensland sire that won many blue ribbons but was killed in a snake fight. Got a bit of dingo in it, but.

They are meticulous with their self-contained vehicles, totally mobile, just a bit too young to have been in Vietnam and therefore with no legitimate excuse for their general unpleasant disposition. They have learned that these days it is acceptable, in certain male company, to weep. The real reason for heading outback is never discussed. She was going to become his wife. That was the plan. But that was twenty years ago, when she issued marching orders. She paired off with some wimp and she's bullshit and she's history. Except when, all alone, they unroll that swag and the shoulders slump and the mouth turns down sour.

Women are never credited as the reason for choosing the outcast bush life. That cannot be. That would be to bestow on women a power that they would prefer was never given. Like Brad Murdoch. He told people he left his wife because she turned religious. He didn't say how she'd turned religious because he'd turned animal.

Your mates, those who are married, are always the first to leave the pub at night, poor bastards. They have kids, two or three of them, and all of a sudden the oldest boy is six or seven and his dad – your old mate – would love to take him fishing. But not with you. Because you're always talking about cunts and bitches and dogs and giant fucking-cunt crabs. Rather than learning some manners, you interpret it the only way you can: your mate is pussy-whipped. He's lost to 6.30 pm dinners and dishes, and Saturday mornings driving kids to their footy games, and perfunctory sex. If she ever puts out. All you know is that you are as lonely as hell and you're not really sure why.

All is not lost. There is still a woman who is attracted to – or forced into close quarters with – your condition. She smokes fifty-pack cigarettes, those giant boxes of stick-thin, rasping fags like Holiday or Horizon, drinks vodka cruisers or chardies and waits at the bar. For someone. It doesn't matter if he's the devil's personal envoy. Everyone has their reasons. So long as he's a gentleman. A regular drug supply also helps. She's not after a man who'll open the car door for her. Just the type who doesn't hit, preferably.

Or inquire as to the precise details of the lousy journey you took to get to this plastic barstool in far north Western Australia.

She doesn't eat from the bar menu, with its oysters Kilpatrick and schnitzel and t-bone with the grim over-boiled pea, carrot and potato trinity. Food interferes with drinking and makes a soul sleepy. Her main meal is in the morning. She's an alco. Alcos need a good start to the day. She hates the rich and the unemployed with equal venom, uses the words 'snooty' and 'darl' a lot and is praying for deliverance or death. She knows it won't be the former. The prettiness is hard to see, mostly washed and stripped away by the acid effect of alcohol and nicotine and the long-abandoned man whose name is never spoken. But you can see it, just.

She's actually a doll, in her way. She tells the pretty young Dutch and German girls who come through with backpacks and boyfriends: 'I was like you once.' It frightens the hell out of these children. City life doesn't work for her because in the city you can wear out your local bar in no time. The unspoken social etiquette of the Australian bar is that if you should pair off with one of the local blokes and it doesn't work out, the woman must take herself into exile and let the drinker quietly return to his circle of mates, who'll give him a nudge but that's all. They'll turn back to the trotting guide with little more than a welcoming sigh. Knew it wouldn't last. Never spoken of again. They understand. Nothing lasts, not when it comes to women. It's hard enough to depend on anything around here. Friends are always getting out, leaving town.

He's sympathetic, if not aligned, to the outlaw motorcycle gang road-warrior mindset but ultimately he's causeless and alone, a bush-bitumen man, just turn the freewheeling hubs onto lock, engage low and head inland. Oil changes – not just the engine, but front and back diffs – more important than visits to the doc. No one will ever find him or his campfire. This countryside he loves. Although it is never assessed by its backdrop of human history. Far from it, it is terra nullius and barra fullius. Blackfellas? They invented the boomerang and nothing since. Apart from grotesque liquor consumption.

Geography is given a passing nod. Igneous, sedimentary, metamorphic, the three basic rock strata can be seen – if you have the eyes for it – in the time-beaten hills of the north. The free-floating elements combine and form minerals. And minerals, one way or another, are what the north's all about. Iron-ore most important of all. It defines the north of Western Australia. It makes steel. Trucks, cars, trains, guns. And there's bauxite, which brings aluminium which brings house and window frames and beer cans. The mines create towns and all that goes with them, including outlaws.

Shifting, shadow-like, around the land on which the northern towns are built, are the ever-present blacks. Aborigines. A hard word to say. It means indigenous, nothing more. A common noun. But in Australia they decided to formalise them by giving them a capital A. Not even allowed to shoot them, they say. We'll see about that. Black women a necessary evil when the testicles start to hang heavy and the women in the *High Society* porn mag under the seat begin to look a bit static and bored. Black men? A fucking abomination, the lowest form of biology God ever spat forth upon the earth.

This man. There's a heap of them here in the north. He knows exactly where he is at any time, and doesn't need a GPS to remind him. So why is he lost? Wilderness, with all its open air, can be a funny thing. It can bottle a fellow up. Sometimes his feelings will need to find expression.


I made an executive decision: Brad Murdoch *would* be found guilty of the South Australian rapes. This would lead to much discussion between authorities in the Northern Territory and South Australia on precise arrangements as to how Murdoch – serving a sentence of, say, twelve years in South Australia – would be transferred to Darwin to answer for the Falconio case. Finessing the details, I reasoned, would take weeks, which meant I'd have plenty of time to get to Darwin. I was on a break between jobs so I decided to relax for a day or two in Fitzroy.


There are two views as to what really happened at the Old Crossing at Fitzroy in 1995. They are white and black. In a mostly Aboriginal-run town,

Dave Fielder represented the minority white view. I'd been warned, by the black side, to be careful with Fielder.

In the back of Fielder's standard-issue white Toyota Land Cruiser ute were two dogs the likes of which I'd never seen before. They were a Sicilian breed, blue-grey, dripping-browed animals which managed to look both dim-witted and alert at the same time. Great dangling folds of fur hid their teeth but Fielder assured me they wouldn't bite. 'They'll maul you to death,' he explained with a menacing laugh. 'So, you want to talk about Big Brad? All right. You can come in. First you have to walk past the dogs. They've got very good noses for a narc.'

Fielder said he'd chased a snooping journalist fair out of Fitzroy Crossing one time. He was asking about Big Brad too. 'Cunt shit himself,' Fielder explained. But Fielder said he liked the cut of my jib. So far. I entered what appeared to be a diesel workshop, even though it was not signposted as such. One of the dogs gave a short, profound growl but it stayed onboard Fielder's HZJ75 ute.

Fielder was one of Big Brad's Fitzroy Crossing mates at the time of the Old Crossing shoot-up. Fielder still counted himself as a mate. He said he was with Murdoch in the early part of the evening of 20 August 1995, just before Murdoch unleashed his attack on the riverbed crowd.

For a big man in tight stubbies, Fielder was a fast mover. A country and western tape was playing. When he liked a song, he'd roar over the ghetto-blaster to crank the volume and nimbly waltz with an imaginary girl. He was aggressive, thoughtful and not to be toyed with. Yet he clasped his hand on his heart and swooned when Dolly Parton's 'I Will Always Love You' came on. It was the version I happened to love as well. Those soft, rolling guitars and Dolly's way of sounding as though she really meant it.

When Dolly sang, every male divorcee from Houston to Derby recognised that she had delivered a hurtful truth disguised in Dolly-ness: women are stronger than men and will do what needs to be done. Whitney Houston never even got close to nailing it in her more famous version. She scared the pants off it.

Fielder took his seat and leaned back, studying me with hatred. 'Fucking journalist, eh? Which scum-hole paper do you work for?'

I'd already told him but said it again. 'I've just finished working for *The Australian* and I'm going over to *The Bulletin*.'

'Fine publications – the only publications worth reading in this entire country,' he said with genuine, heartfelt approval. I wondered if he read either but suspected he was not given to small-time bullshit.

'Tell me,' Fielder said, wriggling down into himself with a little smile, 'what's it like writing about stuff?' I told him I got to meet people. 'I'd like to kill most journalists,' he said, looking as though he really would. 'So far, you're safe. How are the kids? You got kids?' He really wanted to know about the kids. He was drinking stubbies of cider interspersed with enamel mugfuls of white wine. Not the standard tough-guy drinks but they seemed to be taking him – or maybe me – fast to a perilous place.

'Now,' he said, clamping a huge friendly arm around my shoulder, 'isn't it about time we gave these up?' He was talking about the cigarettes and was looking at me with the most earnest concern. 'I mean, really. They *will* kill you. Although I suppose it doesn't matter. Because something, or someone, is going to kill you anyway.'

The way he laced threats with shows of great human warmth made him impossible to read. This is what is must be like facing a very good leg spin bowler. But at least you can smash him to the boundary now and then. Or deliberately get out and walk back to the pavilion.

There were two other blokes sitting at the table drinking mid-strength beers. They were silent, watching. They didn't look like they'd be any help if Fielder turned wild. They did not say a single word except when Fielder headed off to the pub to get more white wine. Then they wouldn't shut up. They were interested in the fact that I lived in Darwin. Did I happen to know that in Darwin there was a pub where you could score a root for thirty bucks? I told them that it sounded awfully cheap. 'Fucken oath,' said one.

Fielder returned and the men lapsed back into their watchful silence. 'Now, if you're going to talk to me, you're going to drink with me,' said

Fielder. 'Got that?' He handed me a drink. I didn't drink cider, but I was drinking it now.

'You see, with Big Brad, some cunt's gone and stirred him up. That's what's happened,' declared Fielder.

Peter Falconio? That pussy English backpacker driving along the highway in a cheap, dying Kombi? He looked pretty harmless in the photos – a kind of smiling, prematurely balding, inoffensive type. Fielder nodded knowingly.

'The big fella doesn't get upset unless some cunt stirs him up. I don't know what the prick did, but he's gone and got the big fella all upset. Big Brad's a jovial bloke – he was back when I knew him. Don't know how happy he is now he's in jail. He was considerate. He'd look after you. He'd punch trucks up and down the highway all day and all night – and he'd fix things, too. He's a top man in that field. He always had his shit together. I like him. He's a good bloke. You're a good bloke, too, Paul. It's just that … you're a bit of a cunt, aren't you?'

'Look, Dave,' I told him, noting that the only exit route was guarded by the two huge medieval dogs, 'I'm just trying–'

'Hold on, mate, steady on!' he cried. 'Don't go and get pissed off on me! For chrissakes, we're all friends here! No, you're not a cunt. You're a journalist. *And you're all right.* If you were a cunt, you wouldn't be sitting here with me. Got that? Have another drink. Let's talk.'

I knew this person, I knew him well. But who was he? It dawned. He was the landlocked Long John Silver, the beautifully complicated pirate of Robert Louis Stevenson's *Treasure Island*, seemingly murderous one moment, only to turn on a piece-of-eight and reappear all tender and sincere.

'I was drinking with Big Brad the night that business happened down at the Old Crossing,' said Fielder. 'We were on the rum. We were having a good night. We were at the Fitzroy Lodge and the big fella drove home the back way to dodge the coppers.'

The Fitzroy Lodge is located over the river on the east of town, well away from Fitzroy Crossing's tiny CBD. It's about as exclusive a joint as

Fitzroy runs to. At the time, the lodge was considered the town's only 'dress-standard' joint. What it meant – although it was never stated as such – was that whitefellas didn't have to get dressed up but blackfellas did. It was the only place in Fitzroy where whites could drink relatively free from blackfella hassles. It's where Big Brad and his mates drank.

Murdoch was pissed and wanted to take the back way home from the Lodge. He was working as a diesel mechanic at Brooking Springs station at the time, the pastoral lease that borders Fitzroy to the west. All he had to do to get home to the station was take the river track down to the Old Crossing, idle quietly over the causeway, sneak past the Crossing Inn, which is the blackfella pub, hope to Christ there were no random breathalysers in place and use the back road to pass around the top of the town. And then he'd have a clear run home.

The quicker route was along Highway One, from the Lodge to town, but it was too risky. Murdoch had no issues about whether to drink-drive, only the best way to do it without getting caught. Such decisions were informed by intelligence that was constantly being received and updated at the pub. If police had set up a breathalyser, there was no chance the drinkers at the Lodge would not have got to hear about it. Other factors came into play, such as the chance of being pulled over by a lone patrol car.

But every move the cops made in a place like Fitzroy was subject to observation. It was possible to assess, or guess at, the current state of mind of the small troupe of cops, how tired or busy they had been in recent nights. There were also important seasonal considerations, such as the national Australian Football League which, at this time of year, August, was approaching finals' crescendo. If the handful of Fitzroy cops wanted a quiet night by the television watching the Saturday night game, as any sensible person would, they would be unlikely to want to spend the night processing and jailing drink drivers. None of it perfect science, but all of it to be weighed in the balance.

Murdoch took the quieter less-travelled back road. But on this night the Old Crossing was the scene of a big post–grand final shindig for the local Aboriginal team. Two cars were parked on the causeway, blocking it, and a band was playing on a jerry-rigged stage in the riverbed off to one side. Murdoch demanded they move their vehicles so he could cross.

'They were all having a party,' said Fielder. 'They were all over the crossing. They told him, "Fuck off, back up, you cunt". Joe Ross – one of them on the crossing – he said that. The big fella backed up.' Murdoch, according to this account, decided to cross anyway. He drove off the edge of the concrete causeway into the sand, thinking he could just bypass the party and get to the other side. Humiliatingly, his four-wheel drive started chewing up sand and sinking.

'He got bogged, he got bogged and he got bogged again,' said Fielder. 'He finally got across. So he went out to where he was staying at Brooking and got a .308 and a .22. He said, "Fuck you, cunts, you can't do that to me". Black cunts thought they owned the joint. You got that? Write it down. He came back and opened fire. Joe Ross got one lodged in the dashboard. Second shot blew one of the tyres out. And he had Dickie Bedford' – another local Aboriginal leader – 'in line. Oh, he had 'em going!

'He had this green Nissan short-wheel base, rolled the cunt twice trying to get out of there,' said Fielder. And then it was Murdoch's turn to run. 'Big heaps of blacks were looking for him. He hid out at the two-mile bridge for two, three days. I gave him food out there. Bully beef. They came around hunting him. Damian Kelleher' – who ran a diesel business in Fitzroy Crossing and was a friend of Murdoch's – 'left town through that. Wouldn't stand his ground. But you know? The whole town benefited from that. There were no B and Es [break and enters]. Old people on the streets were saying, "Jeez, it's quiet around here!" There was fuck-all going on here for twelve months after that. It tidied up this town. Better than the police could. They were all going, "Thank fuck for Bradley!"'

Fielder agreed Murdoch didn't like Aborigines. 'He said to me one day, "They're worse than heroin addicts the way they lie around the streets and do nothing. Always smoking pot".' It seemed there might have been an element of hypocrisy in Big Brad's views, given he was a drug runner. I let it pass.

So, what was he like, Murdoch? Fielder paused, looked down. 'A lonely man. He couldn't get a fuck. He's fully covered in KKK tatts. No woman's gonna go for that. They'd just go, "Whoa". He's a top bloke. He used to run guns and dope and speed. That's what he did.'

It is not thought that motor vehicles, rifles and a belly full of piss make for good companions. But this would be one of the rare occasions when alcohol put angels' wings on a rifle. It made Murdoch miss. He wouldn't say that, later in court. He'd say he was an expert marksman who aimed to miss.

I asked Fielder why he stayed on in Fitzroy, outnumbered by Aborigines, increasingly pushed into his corner. 'Why? Friends, good times, happy times. I know thousands of cunts who come back here, just for that. You got to create the magic otherwise it's pretty fucked out.'

Fielder was engaging, sharp, stubborn and scary. Perhaps not so unlike Murdoch in his ways and views, but Fielder knew when to stop. Murdoch's personal kill switch – the kind that makes a person stop doing bad things – was not in working order. Both seemed to be outback militia dressed up as the last white settlers. No political party could ever properly represent their politics because it was too extreme to warrant representation. Government, councils, cops, public servants and lawyers especially should just leave the north to attend to itself. Leave the nurses and take the blackfellas with you. The country was fucked.

Asked how he thought Murdoch would handle time in prison, Fielder seemed certain. 'Bradley'll handle it. He didn't use no bikie code of silence. He used his own code of silence. He's a hard man. He'll never get out. Never.'

I felt a small electric hammer at the lower back of my brain, telling me that Dave Fielder had for a moment foreseen and described an absolute, unquestionable truth. His mood was turning to gloom. He considered me with great intent and said: 'Go. Go while you still can, Paul.'

I thanked him and took him up on his offer.

# 4  BLAME IT ON A NISSAN

There wouldn't be much that Joe Ross and Dave Fielder agreed on. Fate might have dealt them the same Australian Rules football team, the same way that fate, along with geography, saw them both liking country music. It was part of the north. They lived close to each other but were deserts apart. Ross was one of Fitzroy's smarter Aboriginal entrepreneurs, who had been heavily involved in the push to get most of the town's businesses in Aboriginal hands.

Almost everything – the pub, the roadhouses, the supermarket – was now controlled by local Aborigines. People passing through Fitzroy would not have noticed this, because white staff were not cast out of their jobs when Aborigines took control. Outwardly nothing looked different but things had changed. On my way through a few years earlier, I'd seen an Aboriginal child ask for the key to the toilet at one of the roadhouses. The white staffer flung the kid the key, which was attached to a Frisbee. It was flung with hate and skittered to a halt by the cheap sunglasses carousel. I picked it up for the kid and told the man he was living in the wrong part of Australia. 'You try cleaning these toilets,' he said.

The day after my encounter with Dave Fielder, I went into the national park to a waterhole, with Ross's family, Dickie Bedford's family and an esky full of beers. There was an Aboriginal man wallowing in the distant sandy shallows. Fifty or so metres from him, in the deeper part of the gorge, twelve freshwater crocodiles floated on the surface, sunning themselves.

A German couple admiring the gorge from a high bank saw the crowd of approaching Aborigines and looked nervous. Ross and the other adults settled them down with friendly hellos. Clearly relieved they were not about to be speared or put in a cauldron, they gabbled questions about the crocs in the pool and the two biggish barramundi lying on the bank. An Aboriginal woman had caught them on a homemade lure. Ross gave them a short, gracious spiel on the gorge's spiritual and geographical creators.

The German couple's delight in this basic encounter with Aborigines was evident. They gratefully searched through their bags for something to give the kids and came up with biscuits. They also managed to find a camera in there. The husband and wife took photos of each other with the friendly natives. The warnings about blackfellas that had been fed to them along their northern journey suddenly dissolved. They walked away, stumbling happily into trees as they waved bye-bye. When they were just out of earshot, someone mentioned The War.

I swam over to the shallows and shook hands with Kevin Oscar. I'd met him before, on the phone. Oscar was managing an Aboriginal-owned property when his neighbour rustled cattle off him. The matter took years for the West Australian police stock squad to investigate. The police case kept getting slowly beaten down, even before it reached court. Then word leaked from the Broome courthouse that two white jurors were being difficult, insisting the rustler ought not to face serious sanction for 'stealing from niggers'. He got a minor conviction.

Aboriginal towns like Fitzroy, home to only a thousand or so people, are mostly unvisited and unseen by Australians. Still, sometimes small outback places have had the power to awaken the national consciousness. Just near here in 1980, on the Aboriginal-controlled Noonkanbah pastoral lease, Aborigines fought an oil company which was seeking to enter and drill land near a site they held as sacred. Aborigines wrongly believed that owning the pastoral lease gave them the power to prevent mining. Police were sent in to remove the blockades and part the way for the miners. In the end, no one really won the battle but it further confirmed that Aborigines were deadly serious about their land.

For those peering into the outback from the nation's coastal perimeter cities, Aboriginal politics were of little interest and even less consequence. What mattered more was an alleged conduit connecting the outback to the white urban national psyche. Academics, commentators and bored authors were forever trying to unearth the thing but usually only ever hit the bedrock of bushrangers, balladeers and drought-thirsty rural types. They laid claim to a dubious contention that all white Australians had inherited vaguely roguish, stoic traits and were forever on the brink of bursting into trouser-hoisting jigs. Now, all that was dead. Instead they wrote about how we were a coastal people who took our latter-day dreaming from the great murmuring seas. Still, the mystery of the inland – and lesser-known parts of the perimeter – was real enough. Whenever someone went missing in the outback, was grabbed by a crocodile or murdered, editors rarely hesitated in pushing the story to the front of the morning's news pages.

The 1986 deaths of teenagers James Annetts and Simon Amos were such a case. The boys were working out bush for the first time when each was sent, separately and alone, to outposts on Flora Valley station where they were assigned jobs as bore runners. This meant each would head out alone, all day, refuelling the generators that pumped bore water to the cattle troughs, and making sure the floats on the troughs were working. The boys became overwhelmed by their isolation and intimidated by a bullying boss. They fled Flora Valley in a borrowed ute which broke down on a track in the Great Sandy Desert. They walked almost 20 kilometres in forty-degree heat before Simon shot himself and James died of thirst. Their bodies weren't found for four months.

Robert 'Kooky' Bogucki was an Alaskan firefighter whose weird 42-day religious pilgrimage through the Great Sandy Desert in 1999 set off a national circus. Bogucki had gone out to locate god, but the term 'godless' could well have been invented for the Sandy Desert. Bogucki found a ravenous thirst instead. The media crush in Broome, from where teams of journalists and cameramen were commandeering helicopters to undertake their own searches, suggested a desperate will to find the poor man. No such thing. No one cared at all about the wretched loon. Each just wanted to find him first so they could either stand tearful and near-speechless over his pathetic corpse or sign him to an exclusive contract. It was indeed a helicopter chartered by a television crew that located Bogucki's stumbling skeleton. He had survived by drinking from scummed-out waterholes.

Bradley Richards and his nephew, Mac Cody, perished in the Great Sandy Desert in 2005. Cody was doing a runner from a court appointment in Broome. The pair took an inland desert road they knew nothing about. They became lost, stuck and thirsty. They went looking for water but never found it. They died in the shade of Richards' old Land Rover.

In each case the victims had their reasons for taking the hardest back tracks imaginable. Funnily enough, it was only the crazy foreign man who survived. Get stuck off the main highway and the chances of being found alive are poor. Wander away from your vehicle and you may never be found at all. The scribbly bush grows just above head height and to unfamiliar eyes it all looks the same. It will cover a person over in no time. That is why Peter Falconio will never be found. Unless Brad Murdoch tells.

Only a few defiant whites remained in Fitzroy Crossing. They didn't much like blackfellas and could see the curtains closing on their small-town world. With the new Aboriginal ownership and, in the mid 1990s, emerging native title claims in the area, some people imagined they were losing all their rights. It made Damian Kelleher angry. He owned Kelleher Diesel on the east side of town, near the new bridge. Kelleher wanted to shift location to the west side and in 1994 he pegged out an industrial block and bought it off the state government.

By 1992, national native title legislation had come through. There was panic about. Pastoralists and landowners in the north wrongly thought they were going to have to abandon their holdings to the bludging blacks. Long before the white farmers of Zimbabwe were marched off their land at gunpoint, some West Australians had convinced themselves that it was only a matter of time before they would be evicted from northern Australia.

The West Australian government knew better: Aborigines would not in fact be able to claim back exclusive rights to any traditional lands, or take them from anyone. At best, Aborigines could make applications to gain access to their ancestral lands. The government did not seek to persuade anyone of the truth of this or attempt to calm fears. Instead, it did its best to thwart the native title process. It sought to clog up the system by making it difficult for Aborigines who were seeking information about land title. The government shut down its far north regional Department of Land Administration offices and sent all the files to Perth. That way, went the logic, Aborigines would be forced into a frustrating bureaucratic bottleneck. If things went to plan, Aborigines would lose interest, greedily sign away whatever rights they had for a quick buck, and life would return to normal.

At the same time, the West Australian government had begun awarding freehold leases to citizens, usually whites, on Crown land that was already subject to native title application. In places like Fitzroy Crossing, they ignored the native title process and told prospective buyers that the land was now available. People bought land believing it was unencumbered. Damian Kelleher was such a person. After finding the site to relocate his diesel business, he went to the bank, thinking he had a freehold block. Then he found out about the native title claim over Fitzroy Crossing.

Joe Ross's mother was one of the senior traditional owners who shared a nominal interest in the block Kelleher had bought. 'We said to Kelleher, we've got no objection to you having this block,' said Ross, 'but you have to go through the process. It's the law.' Which meant Kelleher had to lodge advertisements in newspapers notifying his intention to occupy the site.

'So he was humbugging my mother on the telephone, kept ringing her up, writing her letters – and Mum couldn't read very well,' said Ross. 'I went round and seen him and said, "Hey, you cut out that swearing at my mother on the phone. You just come to our meeting, we don't even care about that block". We had a meeting at the old post office. We said, "Look, it seems to us you've done what a lot of others have done. We'll give you support but you have to go through the sixty-day notice period".We were the only ones who could stand in his way. We said, "If we don't object then you've got your block". He must have thought we were obstructing him. At the same time, Murdoch was associating with Kelleher.' Murdoch, working at Brooking Springs station, took on Kelleher's problems as a personal crusade.

Murdoch's beef with Aborigines went back to his childhood in Northampton, north of Geraldton in the wheatbelt, where he'd copped hidings from Aboriginal kids and dealt out some of his own. What kids like Bradley didn't know was that they were defending the last, faltering vestiges of the White Australia Policy. It wasn't usually the parents or the politicians who threw punches. It was the kids. Country West Australian towns regarded the quiet, cat-footed blacks as trouble long before Aborigines became overtly political. I remember being in a country town north east of Perth as a twelve or thirteen year old, at a time when the town still had a high Aboriginal population. A procession of Aborigines – the ladies in floral dresses and hats, the men in black trousers, white shirts and black ties – were carrying a coffin through the town. My friend's father, a farmer, rolled down the window on his Ford LTD, spat and stated, in his heavy European accent: 'Look at da coons.' It was as if even burying their dead was somehow corrupt and worthless.

When I was about ten we lived for a year in Port Hedland, roughly 600 kilometres south of Broome. The Aboriginal kids I played with carried $20 notes. That was big money to a ten-year-old in 1972. Their mums gave them this money. The kids had access to instant junk I could only dream about. They bought sarsaparilla and creaming soda drinks, the likes of which I'd never seen, even in Perth. One kid had maggots in a sore on his big toe. They didn't have them in Perth either. They lived in concrete-floored tin shacks with no electricity.

At that time there was some sort of contagion rife in rural and outback Western Australia. It was not possible for me to know if this state was worse than any other. These black people lived apart and ate apart from whites but sometimes they worked together. Fringe-dwelling Aborigines had by then found the bottle. You'd see pissed whitefellas staggering down the main road on the white lines. You see Aborigines too, but they were always more pissed. Drama queens.

Murdoch was raised in the most uncertain period of Australia's race relations. The breakthroughs would come much later, like in 1993 when St Kilda footballer Nicky Winmar raised his jumper to show the Collingwood mongrels his black skin. This led to the creation of racial vilification laws in Australian Rules football and, most importantly, it also caused the ordinary punters to reconsider the easy way they dismissed Aboriginal people. But that was still years away. White parents in the 1940s and '50s honestly believed the Aboriginal race would simply die out, saving everyone the headache.

Instead, Aborigines were leaving their bush reserves and coming to the edges of town. The townsfolk used the same shops as the blacks, and might even have had to stand behind them in the queue. These unmeasured dark people – good with horses and footballs – paid for their Sunshine powdered milk and tinned meat with grimy notes pulled out of stained trouser pockets. The storekeeper might even hand those notes back to white people as change.

Aborigines were going from being placid pinafore and pressed shorts mission kids to entering the public school system and living in ratty, government-provided shacks on the edges of towns. These collective hovels would be located near some creek and named for their distance from town – Twelve-Mile, Six-Mile and Two-Mile. Aborigines had the right to drink and vote. They were getting some formal acknowledgment, finally, and Aboriginal kids weren't putting up with the crap anymore. White kids like Murdoch were hopelessly unprepared to deal with it. All they had been told was that something had gone wrong. The savages were circling. Western Australia remained unique for its pockets of stubborn resistance. To this day, it is the only state where you can still hear people openly talking about coons and boongs, with no caution for who might be listening.

West Australian country pubs were once homey places. Then it was decided in the early 1980s that drinking beer was impossible without a background of tits. Every bush pub suddenly needed to have them. They called them skimpies. The law said skimpies had to wear clothes, but the clothes could be fully see-through. Skimpies created a brief country-pub renaissance when they were first introduced. It didn't last. The skimpies stayed but most everyone else went home. They became the sorts of places where a truckdriver-mechanic like Brad Murdoch might feel himself entitled to wear a blue singlet which in no way hid his forearm tattoo of a black man hanging from a noose.

It had been well advertised around Fitzroy that there was to be a big party down at the Old Crossing on the night of 20 August 1995. The Fitzroy Crocs were playing in the local Aussie Rules grand final over in Derby, 260 kilometres to the west. Win or lose, Fitzroy was going to party. Most of the Fitzroy population was in Derby that day although some locals stayed behind to make ready for the bash. A generator and stage were set up so that Fitzroy Express, a sharp-rocking local all-Aboriginal outfit with its little hit song, 'S-S-S-Samantha (I love you so)', could play in the riverbed, which at that time was still months away from its seasonal transformation into a broad waterway. Firewood was gathered for bonfires and barbecues were dragged down into the sand.

The Crocs thumped the Derby Tigers in their first-ever grand final appearance, meaning this night would be special. The crowd didn't get back to Fitzroy from Derby until around 9 pm. Buses and cars were parked on top of the embankment on the western side of the river and people wandered down to party. No one parked on the high eastern embankment, because everyone lived on the west side. Murdoch was able to take up his position, unseen. Aborigines said Dave Fielder's account of Murdoch trying to get across the riverbed and getting bogged never happened. They said he just showed up and started shooting.

The Aboriginal-run backpacker hostel was also located up on the western embankment. Joe Ross remembers a young Russian man had come down to the riverbed in a worried state while people were setting up for the party. He was beside himself, desperately trying to convey a warning, saying some man had come into the hostel that day advising backpackers not to go down to the Old Crossing shindig that night. 'He could hardly speak English,' said Joe of the Russian. 'He came down and was trying to tell people. Everyone said, "Yeah, yeah, just sit down and have a drink".'

If Ross was right about the Russian, it confirmed Murdoch never tried to cross the riverbed that night. What happened was premeditated. Had anyone properly considered it, the chance of some sort of racial attack was not beyond comprehension. There had recently been a Ku Klux Klan party in town – not a meeting of actual members, but a fancy-dress party. It was held in a workshop and a sign was posted out the front: 'No blacks allowed'. There had been complaints to the Fitzroy police, who took no action. But no one treated the Russian boy's garbled story seriously. Who would attack a party of two or three hundred people, representing every Aboriginal family in Fitzroy Crossing?

Ross had a hire car for the drive to and from Derby. That night he parked it on the cement causeway, right in the middle of the river. Ross was staying close – it was the Crocs' grog car and there was an esky in the boot. People were hanging around the vehicle. Joe was in the driver's seat and his girlfriend of the time, Maria Malay, was in the front passenger seat. Both were leaning out their respective windows, talking to friends. Bradley Murdoch was behind them, sighting them in. There was another party vehicle parked on the causeway, facing east towards Murdoch.

'The first shots smashed the dash,' said Ross. 'The first couple of bullets come straight through the back window. One went whizzing by my head, the other grazed Maria on the shoulder. If you imagine the headrest on the seat, this girl was leaning her head back on it. It went straight through the side of her headrest. Mine went just by the side of the headrest. They were also shooting up high.'

'They?' I asked. Ross revealed that he and everyone else had always believed there to be more than one gunman. 'He, or they, were shooting down on an angle,' he said. 'It blew out my back window. But we still didn't know what was happening.'

One of Ross's mates was half leaning in the window talking to Ross. 'My friend said to me, "This smells like gunpowder". I said, "It does, doesn't it?" The whole back window was gone. The band was still playing. I went and told the band to stop playing. Danny Marr, my nephew, he's in the band and he's got this two or three thousand dollar Fender, and he's still playing. Danny's going, "Eh? Eh?". I said, "Somebody's shooting at us!" He's still playing away. Then he realised, grabbed his guitar and bolted.' Joe Ross roared with laughter at the memory of Danny Marr desperately trying to save the life of his beloved Fender.

'All hell broke loose,' said Ross. 'There was panic. How the hell nobody got hit, Christ knows. I reckon he fired a couple of dozen shots. Like, it was a .308. One bullet went straight through a bullbar and into the head of the motor. Just a clean shot. But by then you could see the flames from the .308.' Ross says some cool head trained the east-facing vehicle's spotlights on the gunman. 'Then the shooter was trying to have a go at the spotlights,' said Ross. 'He was being blinded through his scope.'

Murdoch's position on the road at the top of the embankment, looking down onto the causeway, did not give him great breadth to shoot. The track down to the river is heavily tree-lined – he couldn't shoot wide. All he could see was the crossing itself and perhaps twenty metres to either side of it. Those who fled either upriver or downriver were safely out of range.

'There's one real haunting thing people remember,' said Ross. 'People were scattered everywhere and every ten, twenty seconds there'd be a shot going off. Then all of a sudden one man, Foxy, is walking towards Murdoch. It's the weirdest thing I ever seen. You could see Foxy just walking quietly, straight up. I suppose Murdoch couldn't see him because the spotlights were in his eyes, or something. Foxy gets to the bottom of the hill and Murdoch bolted.'

The only way for Murdoch to get back home to Brooking Springs station was back on the road he'd come from, past Fitzroy Lodge and onto the highway. But falsely reasoning the police might soon be on to him, he tried to follow an overgrown goat track that ran along the top of the river. This, he hoped, would bring him out near the Fitzroy Lodge, after which he could hit the bitumen and head home.

Murdoch took a wrong turn in the vine-entangled riverside bush blocks. Confused, he stranded himself in a paddock close to where he'd been shooting. He roared about, crunching gears, reversing and lurching, searching for an exit. Then he realised his headlights were a giveaway, as was the noise of his engine. He had to kill them both. By now the party crowd was regrouping, moving towards the east side of the river, looking for the shooter. Others had gone to the police station. Murdoch was in a spot. His only choice was to abandon his Nissan, which everyone knew belonged to him. He scarpered on foot.

'Thing is,' said Ross, 'if we didn't find that vehicle we wouldn't know to this day who it was. When the shooting first started, someone went to see the sergeant. Sergeant told them to fuck off and come back tomorrow. The sergeant had no idea of working in the community – he was just after his retirement package. There were two or three attempts to get the cops to do something. Eventually there was a mass of people up there at the police station. They ended up ransacking the cop shop, demanding some action. The coppers turned their anger back on the community. The only investigation they were interested in was who smashed up the cop shop. The shooting was long over by the time the cops got there. By this time people were seething, wild at the coppers, wild at Murdoch.'

Despite being shown the abandoned car and being able to make an educated guess as to the identity of the assailant, police infuriated the Fitzroy crowd with their refusal to make an arrest – or even undertake a search – that night. They said it could wait till morning. The young Aboriginal men rapidly formed a vigilante party.

'There were about eighteen people in a Land Cruiser,' Ross said. 'They were hanging off the roof, with clubs and guns. They were serious business. Thank god for our boys they didn't find Murdoch, because they would've been up for murder.

'They were going around visiting all the known culprits. They pulled up at Kelleher's place and went through that gate. He had the most savage dogs going – ones that would fucking eat you. That night when those boys walked through those gates those dogs did nothing. It was like they just knew those boys were coming to kill someone. They confronted Kelleher. They said, "You got one week to get out of town". And he did. He moved tonnes of equipment out of town, dozers, all his gear, in one week, out of Fitzroy.

'That night they visited all the ratbags, even Dave Fielder, checking their motorcars. They wanted to see if engines were hot, asking everyone where they'd been that night.'

After three nights hiding under a bridge on the east of town and being fed Dave Fielder's bully beef, Murdoch gave himself up. He was taken from Fitzroy to Broome prison, where Stumpy Williams and his mates were hungrily awaiting his arrival. Murdoch was shifted on to Perth for his own safety.

When Dave Fielder said that Fitzroy Crossing quietened down for twelve months after the shooting, he was right, although Aborigines see it from another angle: all the rednecks had disappeared. Yet Fielder stayed. 'Yes, well, Dave's got a hide thicker than a rhinoceros,' said Ross. 'Anyway, he's trapped here. He owns a block and can't sell it.'

The then deputy commissioner for police in Western Australia, Les Aiton, flew to Fitzroy Crossing. His task was to look into claims by Aborigines that the police response had been lazy and racist. 'He huffed and puffed,' said Ross. But police couldn't be bothered taking the matter seriously. Murdoch was charged with the bare minimum: going armed in public. He served nine months. Fitzroy Crossing couldn't believe it. They'd wanted him charged with attempted murder. The shots through the headrests in Joe Ross's car seemed to confirm Murdoch's intention to kill.

Only one thing came of it. Bradley John Murdoch had formally introduced himself to northern Australia. As I pulled out of Fitzroy, I turned on the radio. Murdoch had been acquitted of the South Australian rapes and was to be immediately extradited to Darwin. I wouldn't make it in time for the airport party.

# 5  BLOOD ON THE TRACK

When Peter Falconio was gunned down on the roadside, I was, in outback terms – being only a thousand kilometres or so away – in the general vicinity. But I was unable to get anywhere near the crime scene. I was on the West Australian side of the desert working on a story about the Kiwirrkurra people who had been forced to abandon their township due to the heavy flooding of two years earlier. They were the very remote Pintupi people, the last Australians to come in from the desert to take up township life. When Kiwirrkurra flooded they had nowhere to go.

Ethnographically speaking, they were perhaps Australia's most unique and precious people but now they had dispersed throughout Western Australia and the Northern Territory, causing a small but intense humanitarian crisis: they were at large, with many on the drink or in prisons for small-time crimes. They would survive to rebuild Kiwirrkurra but in 2001 they were despairing. I had found some of the senior Pintupi people I had been seeking but had to cut the journey short: the rains were heavy and it was time to get out. The roads were becoming intolerably wet and the skinny-wheeled Land Cruiser station wagon wouldn't stay straight at any speed other than a crawl. To the sides of the dirt tracks the desert had sprung bright green, once again ridiculing those who would talk of Australia's dead heart.

Driving past some obscure mine site well out of mobile range, or so I'd thought, I was surprised to find my phone come with messages. There was an urgent one from Denise Hurley, who headed the Northern Territory's police media unit in Darwin. She related a rushed story of a British tourist who'd been abducted, possibly shot, on the roadside near Barrow Creek, 280 kilometres north of Alice Springs on the Stuart Highway. One thing I knew about police media: they'll never call you if it looks like another black-on-black crime. Or a white one, for that matter. In fact, they never call at all. This one was different – here was a woman survivor. Survivor, as Hurley knew, was a powerful word for the media. And police were going to need the media's help to send out alerts in relation to the killer or killers.

There was nothing I could do about it except listen to the radio telling of an armed and dangerous mustachioed man in a four-wheel drive with a green canopy. I must have seen him forty times that day. He was everywhere and anywhere. This was the kind of vehicle people drove around here. The southern part of Gibson Desert was flooding. All routes through to the Northern Territory had been cut or were about to be. I had to get to Kalgoorlie, fly to Perth and then back home to Darwin. It seemed like a good story but I wasn't too bothered. They'd have the guy by morning. They always did.

The Northern Territory cops must have been thinking the same way. Maybe they were too used to the usual Territory killings, whereby all they have to do is walk into an Aboriginal town camp, ask who did it and arrest the offender, who will invariably, in the sober morning after, be too remorseful and guileless to even try denying it.

Roadblocks went up in a few spots but there were no police watching the dirt roads on the WA–NT border. That's where Murdoch crossed on the morning of 15 July 2001, some 500 kilometres to my north. All the police had was the survivor, the quivering Joanne Lees. What she told the police was pretty straightforward. They – she and her boyfriend Pete – were in their orange Kombi van heading north from Alice Springs after dark when they were flagged down by a man coming alongside in a big four-wheel drive ute. Lees noted a dog in the passenger seat of the four-wheel drive cabin. Falconio pulled over. This was against Joanne's wishes. She was slightly stoned and a bit spooked. Peter went to the back of the van. He returned briefly to grab his smokes and mentioned that the bloke said he'd seen sparks coming out of the Kombi's exhaust. This roadside chat with the big friendly fella was a chance for Falconio to have a smoke. Peter asked Joanne to rev the motor. She heard a bang. And never saw her boyfriend again.

The man, whom she described as big and stoop-backed, wearing a black cap with a logo on it – she couldn't describe it any better than that – appeared at her window. He told her to turn off the engine, jumped in the driver's seat, pointed a silver revolver at her, secured her wrists behind her back using homemade cable-tie handcuffs, pushed her out the passenger side door where she hit the ground, knees first. The man had said nothing so far. He tried to bind her ankles but she resisted. He leaned down and punched her on the side of the head. She attempted to kick and grab the man in the balls, but missed. He wrestled her to her feet and tried to wrap tape around her head to gag her but it was tangling in her hair. He walked her to his car, pulled out a canvas sack and bagged her head. He pushed her into the front cabin with his dead-eyed dog. She remembered being pushed from the cabin through to the trayback section of the vehicle, through some sort of access passage.

She cried out: 'What do you want? Is it money? Is it the van? Just take it. Are you going to rape me?' The man came to the back of the vehicle and said: 'Shut up and you won't get shot.' She asked if he'd shot Pete, whether he was dead. He said no. She heard the dragging sounds – the attacker was shifting her boyfriend's body. She managed to crawl out the edge of the vehicle, hit the dirt, ran and didn't look back. At one point, shortly after she'd broken free, she heard the man pass close by her, on foot. So she waited, for five hours under a bush, until she was sure he had gone. She was able to move her cuffed hands under her body to the front. She found a tube of lip balm in her pocket, bit off the lid and tried, to no avail, to grease her wrists in order to slip free of the cuffs. When she was sure the man had gone, she approached the highway. She saw a truck coming and flagged it down. The two long-haul truckies onboard unhitched the trailers from the prime mover and took her for a cursory look around for her boyfriend. Amid her hysteria, Lees told them the bloke had a gun. They cut short the search and took her straight to Barrow Creek, where pub owner Les Pilton and his partner, Helen Jones, provided her sanctuary.

And that was it. Or it should have been. Had Joanne Lees come out of her hole and showed herself to Australia, and to Britain, in the days immediately following the crime, letting the swarming photographers take their shots, allowing the media to ask a few questions, she would have stopped in its tracks the suspicion, in the mind of some people at least, that will follow her to her grave. She was under no obligation to do the media's bidding. She was within her rights to tell the world to go away. But it wasn't just the press who wanted to see her speak publicly. The police knew her pig-headed silence was dangerous for two reasons: they wanted to find the killer and for Lees to come out and make a pitiful plea might well help bring information forward from someone who might know something about the killer. Secondly, they knew enough about the media and the public to know that her refusal to make a statement would only make things harder on her, and on them.

Lees refused to play along. She didn't see the need to make herself useful to the media and was not enjoying the long hours of police questioning. Lees was hiding something. The police would soon know it, but Lees' secret would not become public for another three years, when she took the stand to give evidence at Murdoch's committal hearing in Darwin.

Mark Wilton got a one-on-one interview with the survivor. It was to be the only time for a number of years that Lees would speak to a journalist without demanding payment. There was justice in Wilton getting the break. He worked for the *Centralian Advocate*, a small-town bi-weekly paper. The Sydney-based British press was in town in force, with orders to offer anything for an exclusive with Lees, who, coming from Huddersfield in West Yorkshire, they regarded as one of theirs. They felt certain she would want to get the message home that she was all right.

Helen Jones, who was working at Barrow Creek where Lees had been taken after the attack, and who used to sell ads for the *Advocate*, was nursing Lees in a flat in Alice Springs. Jones let Wilton know that she had Lees in her care. And Lees, as someone who had a hate for the media that seemed to predate her boyfriend's killing, was nonetheless monitoring every story she could get her hands on and quibbling with every detail.

Wilton spoke to Lees on the phone on Monday afternoon, less than forty-eight hours after the attack. Lees explained that out of respect for Peter and his family, who were still on their way to Alice Springs, she didn't want to do an interview. Wilton said, fair enough, but if you change your mind you know where to get me. Jones rang on Lees' behalf later that night, asking Wilton to drive them to another house. Lees was annoyed that a supposedly hour-long interview with the cops had dragged on for many hours. She had been staying with Helen at Les Pilton's parents' home in Alice Springs. She didn't like it, wanted to move somewhere else. She didn't think police had the right to come around and haul her off for interviews any time they felt like it. She gave the police her new phone number, but not her address. She didn't want them turning up without first making sure it suited her. She was tired of working on the soon-to-be-released Comfit image of the attacker. It would turn out to be a good likeness of Murdoch, but the impression she gave of her attacker's vehicle was so distorted it looked more like a Picasso than any known four-wheel drive.

Police were getting the idea that Lees was something of a control freak. It wasn't just the recent trauma, it was in her nature. She was a bossy, clunky little woman who liked things to go her way. It did not make her a murderer. The police had quickly split into two camps: those who thought she was involved and those who did not. Wiser heads prevailed and ruled her out of suspicion, but they still needed to clarify her position in long interview sessions. Lees asked Wilton whether he thought she should have a lawyer because of the way she was being questioned by police, which was leaning on the intrusive side. Wilton told her: 'Unless you are a suspect, I wouldn't have thought so.'

Prime Minister John Howard was in town to celebrate, along with the Northern Territory chief minister and the South Australian premier, the signing of a deal to build a railway line from Alice Springs to Darwin, which would finally see the nation linked by rail. The national press was having lunch at Bojangles, which is by day one of the saner Alice pubs. Meanwhile, the international and national crime media were trying to find Lees. She was sitting there, in Bojangles, with Helen Jones. It was from there that Jones rang Wilton, saying, 'Joanne wants to talk. She's upset at some of the stuff that is being written.'

Wilton said Lees was upset about 'factual points. It was just stuff about Falconio being dragged out of the Kombi with a gun held to his head. That never happened. She wanted a yarn to straighten all that out'. Lees had never given up, not even when she lost sight of her boyfriend and was certain she was to be raped. 'I was determined to escape,' she told Wilton. 'He would not have let me go. He must be captured. He will do it again.'

'I believed her from the absolute and very first moment,' Wilton told me.

Peter's father, Luciano, and one of his brothers, Paul, arrived in Alice Springs, desperate for news. Initially, Lees wouldn't see them. It must have been heartbreaking and frustrating for them that this woman, who they believed would one day marry Peter and who was the last person apart from the killer to have seen him alive, wouldn't give them the time of day. She might not have been able to tell them anything positive, but she could at least have provided some tangible connection to Peter's last moments. Embarrassed police had to pass on the inexplicable news to the Falconios.

Paul and Luciano Falconio had been told to brace themselves for the worst. If Lees had been the one abducted, and Falconio left alive, there might have been reason to hold out for the miserable hope that she was being kept alive and toyed with in some desert dungeon. There could be no such optimism when a bloke went missing. They felt certain Falconio hadn't taken a leg shot or been winged running away. Police were looking for a body. They were watching for the signals of the bush, looking to the sky to see where the wedge-tails and kite-hawks and falcons were assembling off the sides of the highway.

Paul Falconio tried hard to keep himself together but Luciano, a gentle man whose soft Crosby shoes and teddy-bear jumpers almost made you want to give him a big hug, broke down whenever he tried to say a few words. His strong Italian accent somehow rendered his sorrow even more heartbreaking. Lees was refusing to be photographed, approving only the release of a photo of her and Pete together in the front of the Kombi. It took her days to agree to see the Falconios, who had to accept her strange explanation that she had been too distressed to see them, or to appear in public.

Knowing nothing about Joanne's secret, trying their best to be supportive, Paul Falconio faced the press and dutifully read out a scrupulously prepared statement which Lees had agonised over, editing and re-editing it. Lees wasn't enjoying her predicament. She just seemed to have an innate sense of how to work her situation to its very worst advantage. She would not be counselled otherwise. When Paul Falconio faced the press, Lees was nowhere to be seen. And her message, released days after the attack, seemed primarily about her trying to preserve her dignity. 'I don't want to lessen the severity of what happened but I believe there has been speculation I was sexually assaulted. This did not occur,' said Paul, reading from Lees' statement. Would anyone have looked on her as a lesser person if she had been sexually assaulted? No, but Lees seemed to think so. While questions had been put to the police as to whether Lees had been groped or raped, the answer had been, firmly, no; and no journalist had reported that Lees had been sexually assaulted.

'I'd like to ask people to concentrate their efforts more on finding Pete than trying to speak to me,' went the Lees statement. 'And on finding this man. The police are doing 100 per cent, focused and devoted and trying to do their best.' She didn't believe it for a second, but in a rare moment of diplomatic clarity she had reasoned that it might be a good idea not to put them offside. They were, after all, probably trying to find the killer. She just wished they'd leave her alone. She didn't understand that her own selfish behaviour – 'I'm mad with them,' she had told Wilton of the incessant police questioning – was encouraging them to look at her in a more quizzical manner. Lees added, through Paul: 'I also want to say I am not prepared to sell my story to the media.' And then she went further to ground.

At a daily press conference with Northern Territory police commander, Max Pope, the dogs were finally set loose. Roger Maynard, Sydney-based correspondent with the London *Times*, asked Pope whether he was aware of Joanne Lees' history of mental illness. Pope's face nearly hit the ground. He said he was not. Much later Maynard admitted to me that his question was not based on any knowledge he had – he was just throwing it out there to see if it stuck. Such a question was, by Australian reporting standards, foul play. Maynard wasn't interested in the answer, just in floating the question. But in a strange way Maynard did everyone, except for Lees, a favour.

Lees' ongoing silence had led to all kinds of conspiracy theories. The Falconios were Mafia; Falconio had been dealing amphetamines in the local Todd Tavern; Lees had killed before. Now she was possibly a psychopath. And hadn't Yorkshire – where she was from – produced one of those before? The question broke the tension and put it all out in the open for discussion, forcing people to take sides. It was time to put something in writing, to somehow ventilate the fact that half the country was suss on her and the other half wasn't. There was no word for what was happening, so I made one up and wrote in *The Australian*:

> The Lindyfication of Joanne Lees has begun. For the first time yesterday, journalists began asking hard questions: whether police still believe her story and whether she has a history of mental problems.
>
> Northern Territory police commander Max Pope was firm on the first; they believe her. Ms Lees was 'free to go'. He could not comment on the question of mental illness.
>
> As the search for the gunman and Ms Lees' missing boyfriend, Peter Falconio, entered day 10, police did what they did not do

in the case of Lindy Chamberlain – they stood firm behind the woman in the middle.

The Lindyfication word, incredibly, stuck, so much so that people would even go on to misspell it. The shock jocks were on the phone that day wanting to talk, asking me if she was a killer or not. They seemed to have missed the point. Lees finally agreed, having been persuaded by the then Northern Territory police commissioner, Brian Bates, a bloodless-looking man who was always irritable and snappy with the press, to face the demonic media. Speak to them. Say something. He had flown down from Darwin especially to twist her arm. He badly needed her to do it. Police now almost believed her story, but she was such an obnoxious demanding prat that they had real cause to wonder, so they took out insurance by bugging her phone and observing her movements. As lunatics from every corner plagued them with 'information' about why she was the killer, they knew there needed to be a sharp refocus away from Lees and onto finding the killer.

Word came through that Lees was prepared to consider a list of questions from the press. We came up with thirteen of them. They were all pretty standard and non-confrontational. There was no 'Did you do it?' or 'What have you done with the body?'. They were returned to sender by Lees, who had excised ten of them with a red pen. Photographs and footage were to be pooled. And only one journalist would be allowed to ask the questions. No other reporters would even be allowed in the room. The 'interviewer' had to be a radio journalist because, in Lees' mind, they were the least toxic of the species. The following day, under the clever headline 'Lees open but still shuttered', my story appeared in *The Australian*:

She appeared only briefly, in the strangest of circumstances ... a press conference at which no journalists were allowed. Joanne Lees said she was feeling positive and strong, but she didn't sound it.

Ms Lees, 27, read a statement full of defiance for the media she said she loathed.

Until now, the woman who escaped from a gunman near Barrow Creek on July 14 after her boyfriend, Peter Falconio, was apparently shot and abducted, has denied the world any real glimpse into who she is and what she is going through. Yesterday, the world was not significantly enlightened.

'I am feeling positive and strong and believe it's only a matter of time now before the man responsible for what has happened to Pete and myself is caught,' she said at Alice Springs police station before a strictly controlled phalanx of photographers.

'I am confident everything that can be done is being done and I am hoping one of the leads police are following up will lead to Pete being found.'

The press were told to write a number of questions, which Ms Lees would examine before making her appearance. She whittled the 13 questions down and responded to three. When asked what her reaction was to those who expressed doubt about her story, Ms Lees was short. 'Anyone who's spoken to me or has been in contact with me, no one doubts me. It's only media that have questioned my story.'

Lees went on to say the media 'distort the truth' and 'make false accusations'. It was strange how badly Lees had used her moment. While some of those watching on television that night would have been delighted to see Lees bash the media about the head, questions only grew as to what all the defiance was about. The woman should have been counselled not just on her grief but on her attitude. She was supposed to be helping police find a killer. Instead, she was taking an opportunity to attack the media.

The next night, at the pub, I was confronted by the radio journalist who had asked Lees the questions. She was irate that I had described it as 'a press conference at which no journalists were allowed'. 'I am a journalist,' she seethed. 'Not yesterday you weren't,' I said. I tried to explain what had happened: Lees had just used the occasion to tell everyone to fuck off.

And that included her. *The Australian*'s headline had said it all. The journalist demanded an apology. I told her to ring the boss. She was also disgusted that Lees had chosen to wear a tight-fitting t-shirt with the 'Cheeky Monkey' logo emblazoned across her chest. It just wasn't appropriate, the reporter told me.

It turned out the woman reporter was not complaining about the logo but the tightness of her t-shirt. As all the boys had been quick to note, Lees had large breasts on a skinny frame. She had a rack. The police media had tried to talk her out of wearing that t-shirt. They wanted sackcloth. After all, a TV camera is not going to concentrate solely on your *face*, Joanne. The pool cameraman, who had a tripod, managed to keep himself together and did not waver inexplicably around the Lees bosom. Reporters drank heavily that night. All the waiting and indolence had come to this. The foreign press didn't know what to do. Should they leave town or wait for more of nothing? Mostly, they left.

Killing time, I drove up to Barrow Creek, north of Alice. Cath Curley, barmaid, was out on the verandah, sharpening knives with a deft hand. She was a tough unit, Curley, who liked to think of herself as a regular bush girl, flannelette shirts and Blundstone boots. She'd offered some assistance to Lees the night she was brought in. She remembered Lees saying something about a silver gun, and 'acting all shook up'. Acting? 'Yeah, acting,' Curley told me. 'She's so full of shit, little dainty English thing. She's behind this whole thing. You'll see.'

Curley seemed pretty sure of herself but didn't have too much evidence. Except she said there was some rugby game on TV at the time and two young English boys were watching it before they disappeared for an hour or so – round about the time Lees reckoned she'd been attacked. Curley said if you found those two English boys, you'd find the killers. Several years later, when Curley took the stand in Murdoch's committal hearing, I was expecting her to stick it up all the soft-handed city lawyers and give the court a bit of no-crap bush wisdom. Instead, she instantly broke down into a blubbering heap and needed urgent tissue intervention.

Les Pilton, owner of the Barrow Creek pub, was articulating something that I had always known but had never put into coherent words. I had studiously avoided describing the stretch of highway on which Falconio was killed as 'lonely', partly to avoid cliché but mainly because the highway was not lonely. The remaining reporters had by then descended to interviewing each other to get stories. A Sydney-based journalist told some English reporters that you'd have to be insane to travel the highway without a firearm. He reckoned everyone did it. Personal protection from maniacs. It was bullshit. The Stuart Highway was never seen as lonely or dangerous. It had had its moments – in 1999, when speed-overloaded psychopath Rodney Ansell shot dead police sergeant Glen Huitson at a roadblock near Darwin; and in 1957, also on the Stuart Highway but in northern South Australia, when Raymond Bailey committed the Sundown Murders, shooting dead and robbing Sally Bowman, her daughter Wendy and friend Thomas Whelan as they camped by the roadside on Sundown station. But, as Pilton told me: 'Two hundred thousand people drive past here every year. There is forced communication out here.' Pilton said you could live next door to someone in Sydney for twenty years and never speak a word to them. But if you were both filling up at a petrol station in Barrow Creek, you'd probably say hello.

Pilton operated his bowsers according to the laws of highway karma. They were not connected to the cash register inside. 'We ask people how much they put in the tank,' said Les. 'We don't double-check. If people aren't honest, it's not us with the problem, it's them.' He said if people lied about how much fuel they put in, the road would deal with them somewhere later on.

Les Pilton spent the first long, pre-dawn hours talking and listening to Joanne Lees as she slowly crawled out of herself. He told me of his first words to Lees: 'I hear you've been through a real bad experience. We'll look after you here. This is a safe place.'

For the next few days Pilton's partner, Helen, stayed with Lees in Alice Springs as family and friends arrived. 'When people are in shock and need someone to hang on to, it can be anybody – they cling to anybody who's showing kindness,' Jones told me. 'She was concerned about going to town and leaving everything here – Peter, her car, her things. She had nothing. You treat such a person just like one of your kids, I suppose. You just comfort them and try and steer away from the negatives. You say, "He is all right. He's going to be all right. We will hear news". Talk about her dog in England, her mum and dad.'

Jones, aged fifty in 2001, seemed a little out of place in Barrow Creek. She wore cashmere jumpers, stockings and nice-fitting skirts and spoke in a gentle accent all the way from Dublin. She was no reptile-skinned bush-pub matriarch who couldn't explain the missing Bundaberg Rum because she'd forgotten she'd drunk it all. And Jones knew Falconio was not all right. 'You're thinking the worst. It never got to the point where I told her that was how I felt. But I still walk outside here and think, Poor bugger, is he lying out there somewhere?'

Pilton wasn't hopeful either. 'This is where life is real,' he said. 'It confronts people, makes them see themselves. Death is real, as well.' In his quaint yin-and-yang way of seeing things, Pilton was trying to locate something positive for Lees to take away from all of this. 'She was given an opportunity to survive and she took that opportunity,' he said. 'I told her, don't throw your life away now, don't make it meaningless. And she won't. She's a very special person – she's blessed and she must reward that back.' Blessed, Les? Her boyfriend's been executed and fed to the dingoes. 'For me, she was such a wonderful example of someone drawing on a great inner strength, when she really could have gone over the edge,' he said. 'She is now in the position where she can help other people.'

The monk publican didn't explicitly mention god, but seemed to acknowledge the presence of powerful forces in his outback world. It wasn't just the two bottles of red we'd drunk by the Barrow Creek fireplace. 'I don't know why Peter had to disappear as quickly as he did. I don't believe

Peter will be found alive. I believe the gunman knew what he was doing. His intention wasn't for Peter, it wasn't for robbery. His intention was for Joanne.'

Despite the kindness they had shown her, Lees was to savage Helen Jones, in particular, in a paid interview with a British television program some eight months later. 'I'm quite disgusted she can get off on someone's tragedy,' Lees would say. In fact Jones had not discussed her time with Lees in any detail, with any reporter, just spoken generally, and gently, about what happened in the first days after the attack. The question turned as to who was really getting off.

In late July 2001, police posted a Northern Territory record $250 000 reward for information that would lead to the arrest and conviction of Falconio's killer. Holding up for the cameras a copy of the reward poster, which bore a photo of his son's smiling face, Luciano broke down again. He knew by then that he would never see his boy again. He had always known.

In August it was learned that police had obtained security footage of a stooped man who matched the description Lees had given of her attacker, and of his vehicle. This person had entered the Shell Truck Stop on the north side of Alice Springs and bought $136.65 worth of diesel, paying cash. It was shortly after midnight on 15 July. Police had initially denied any such footage existed.

Assistant crime commissioner, John Daulby, by then called in to handle the public face of the investigation, said the reason they had taken over three weeks to release the images was because they had been sent on to Queensland where what he called 'technical' police – in fact, the Australian Federal Police – were trying to enhance the poor-quality footage in order to try and decipher the numberplate on the vehicle. The photo should have been out in the public domain at the earliest possible opportunity. Daulby knew it. In vain he tried to defend the police position.

Lees had told police she thought the man seen in the truck stop footage was her assailant. I had already confirmed that in a phone call to Lees' mother, in England, who said Lees 'thought the likeness was very good of the man'. Why hadn't they released the grainy stills? At the very least, Truck Stop Man could have come forward and been ruled out of the investigation. Valuable time had been lost.

In a tense press conference with mostly local journalists, Daulby and the media lost patience with each other. Reporters had been on their best behaviour up till then, treading lightly around the senior cops and the police media in order not to be spited on some major break in the story. I put it to Daulby that a photo enhancer – even a kid with a computer – could have retrieved for police their best-quality image in half a day. Or less. 'Do you want us to put up crap and say, "Have you seen this person?"' he snapped. 'Or do you want us to put up the best image available?' What the police released three weeks later was of no discernible improvement on the original.

Daulby was asked whether they had delayed releasing the images because they knew the man's identity and were trying not to alert him. It was an attempt to try to find something positive in the inexplicable police stance. Maybe he was being arrested right now? 'That is absolutely wrong,' said Daulby.

The story went quiet.


Jasmin Afianos, editor of Tennant Creek's weekly *Tennant & District Times*, always kept an ear to the ground. In her town, 215 kilometres north of the Barrow Creek crime scene and with a population of 3500, she knew it was not always good for business or her own survival to run a hard-campaigning, small-town newspaper, chasing every rumour down every drain. She still had to do her shopping at the local food barn. She rang me with something she'd heard. Local cops were talking about a stuff-up with the truck stop footage.

A few days later, there was a page-one lead story in *The Weekend Australian* headlined: 'How desert killer case was botched'. Botched is an ugly word. Bungled is jauntier, but the editors knew what they were doing.

Bungled suggests clowns at work and leaves room for goodwill. Botched is meaner. It suggests incompetence. The story told how Territory police had thrown away their best chance of getting good images of the number-one suspect in the first twenty-four hours of the investigation. Instead of confiscating the truck stop's digital hard-drive and examining the contents, as had been recommended by the man who installed the service station's security system, police declined his help and dumped the images onto a domestic video cassette recorder. Digital footage does not lose quality when transferred to digital media, but it loses quality, dramatically, when transferred to video tape. The police spent weeks trying to enhance an inferior second-generation copy.

Police thought the man who entered the truck stop at 12.38 am was wearing sunglasses. They thought this because as he stood near the counter paying for fuel, he made a motion as if lifting a pair of dark glasses so he could see properly. But the footage they had salvaged was not clear. It was so poor that police could not be sure whether he was wearing thongs. The man who installed Shell's security system, Shane Ride of Alice Springs, said police had lost their chance to get Truck Stop Man's numberplate, and face, by dumping onto VHS. The original hard-drive digital footage was recorded over almost immediately afterwards and was gone forever.

Shell staff had alerted police on 15 July that they had pictures of a man who might interest them. '*The Weekend Australian* understands police backed down from seizing Shell's computer hard drive – which contained digital images – after service station management complained they would be left without security.'

Shane Ride had reluctantly revealed to me a secret of his trade: that service-station security cameras were generally of such poor quality they tended not to show any fine detail. Footage was often good enough to convict an unmasked armed robber who turned up at the counter with a sawn-off shotgun, but the cameras were not designed to capture in sharp resolution the numberplate of someone who had driven off without paying for their fuel. They were ostensibly installed as a bluff. Still, for someone who had parked his vehicle as Brad Murdoch had done, next to a diesel pump, close to and in full gaze of a security camera, Ride agreed the numberplate would have been captured. Police should have seized the digital hard-drive and taken it away for analysis.

Territory police did not admit to the stuff-up. They said growing criticism over their handling of the investigation had been morale-boosting and strengthened the resolve of Task Force Regulus. It was the talk of press-brutalised football team. Regulus was the twenty-fifth brightest star in the sky and was, according to the ancient Persians, one of four 'royal stars'. It meant 'prince' in Latin. But for police purposes the provenance of Regulus had no pertinence to the Falconio case. It was just a name chosen by a wistful copper, same as the Bureau of Meteorology christened cyclones Tracy, Max, or Monica.

I took a call from an Alice Springs filmmaker, Chris Tangey, who was having a battle with Territory police. Tangey told how, in the weeks after police had seized Falconio and Lees' Kombi van, they asked him to film as forensic examiners dimmed the lights in a police shed in Alice Springs and sprayed the Kombi with Luminol. Luminol, when applied to a surface in a darkened room, causes blood to glow bright and ghostly. They asked for Tangey's help because he was the only professional cameraman in Alice Springs with a Sony PD-150, which could record in very low light.

Tangey told me that the video he shot appeared to show police ignoring evidence in the form of a glowing handprint. He admitted he was unqualified to form this opinion but he wanted his theory checked out. Tangey ran off a copy of the tape for the police but kept the master. Police were now threatening to come and seize the master tape, but Tangey was stubbornly hanging on to it. He accused police of ignoring the 'handprint' he had seen glowing on the back of the Kombi, and thought it further proof of Northern Territory police incompetence. He would only hand over the master to an 'independent' policeman from another state.

I was grateful for Tangey's call but I thought it was all too overdramatic and took the view that the police knew more about what they were doing than Tangey. Still, it was worth putting a call in to Daulby. And the footage had spooky resonance for another reason. There, among the white-suited staff wandering around the gloomy Kombi spraying Luminol, was forensic biologist Joy Kuhl, still on the job two decades after she had infamously declared that the sound-deadener sprayed on the firewall of the Chamberlain family's Holden was fetal blood. Azaria's blood. Mrs Kuhl was a lovely woman who had worked in Territory police forensics ever since. Her burden had been a very heavy one, all over that one mistake, although she has never once conceded she made a dreadful error. Instead, she believed that science was not sufficiently advanced to back her claims. After all, when she made her call about the fetal blood in 1981, DNA was not even an acronym.

When I called police media about the Tangey angle, the response was surprising. It was put to me that if I sat on the Tangey story, they'd give me something better. There was no demand that I not report the Tangey angle, just a request not to do it right then. I never found out why. Maybe they thought me obnoxious and wanted to get me onside; perhaps they were tired of being beaten around the head by the national media and all the so-called experts on the street; perhaps they wanted something to take the heat off them. It didn't matter to me. I was never convinced by what Tangey was saying but was interested in something else: in the video dub he had provided me of the Luminol session were the first-ever close-up images of the Kombi. It does not, in hindsight, seem like a world-beating news break. But by then the story was dead and even an incremental development like this was something. All I had to do was publish this 'better' police-fed story first, and then I could do what I wanted with the Tangey material.

'What if you were to be told,' said the police media person, 'that Joanne Lees is back in Alice Springs with a film crew?' I was in the BP dunny in Katherine, having just re-entered mobile range after working on another story. I briefly lost unrestricted flow to the yellow urinal scent bar. There was no way Lees would have done this for free. She had promised via Paul Falconio in his Alice Springs media appearance that she would never make money off Falconio's death. And now it seemed she was. Not that I would blame her for that. It's just that she should never have made the undertaking in the first place. And just as curious: why were the police telling me? Didn't they like her anymore?

Daulby, a big, neat, angular-chested man in a creaseless uniform and standard police-issue moustache, was on the line from police headquarters across town in Darwin. He was angry with Lees. And me. 'When are you going to apologise?' he said.

'For what?'

'For saying we blotched the investigation.'

'We never said that.'

'Yes, you did,' said Daulby, 'I've got the paper right here in front of me.'

'We didn't say you blotched the investigation. We said you botched it.'

He should have laughed. He didn't. Daulby was an all right bloke. He could be testy but he could also be reasonable. But as the face of the Northern Territory police force, all the pressure for a result had settled on his shoulders. Calm discussion followed. The headline in *The Weekend Australian* on 16 February 2002 read: 'Lees returns to killing scene with TV crew'.

> Joanne Lees, the woman who said she would not take money to tell her story, has signed a contract with a British current affairs program and is back in Australia filming at the scene of her boyfriend's shooting and abduction.
>
> Ms Lees was in Barrow Creek, 200 km north of Alice Springs, on Thursday afternoon with a TV crew from *Tonight with Trevor McDonald*, a bi-weekly show claimed to be the most popular current affairs program in Britain.
>
> And Northern Territory police have found the manner of Ms Lees' unannounced return surprising.
>
> Police did not know Ms Lees was in Australia until she and the secretive crew turned up in Alice Springs on Thursday morning. Ms Lees phoned police headquarters from her hotel room and said she wanted to see Barrow Creek task force superintendent, Kate Vanderlaan.

Ms Lees wanted an update on the investigation into her boyfriend's shooting, but also tried to persuade police to co-operate in an interview with the TV crew.

Alice police referred the request onto Deputy Commissioner John Daulby, based in Darwin, the only police officer doing official interviews. He told the crew he would not be available until later this week.

'I guess we're mildly surprised at her return to Alice Springs,' Mr Daulby said. 'We certainly weren't aware of it but I must say Joanne Lees is free to go about her business. She doesn't have to tell us what she does.'

Mr Daulby said NT police had not kept in regular touch with Ms Lees.

'I must say that our contact with Joanne has been based upon [if] Joanne wanted information, she would call us,' Mr Daulby said.

'It's not like my weekly calls to the Falconio family. Joanne doesn't want that kind of contact, that's Joanne's position.'

David Mannion, editor of the joint Granada-ITV production, refused to confirm whether Lees was involved in a re-enactment of the crime, or how much she was being paid. Asked if his program, known for its exclusive interviews, paid people to appear, Mannion told me: 'It's not unheard of.'

Les Pilton was quoted in the story as saying he was surprised Lees hadn't stopped by. 'As far as I know, poor Jo's still in England,' Pilton said. 'If she came here, surely she'd drop in and say hello.' But Lees was not happy with the Barrow Creek people, particularly Helen Jones, and in the program launched her outlandish attack about Jones 'getting off' on her tragedy.

My story for *The Weekend Australian* was wrong in one respect – Lees had not returned to the precise killing scene. The TV crew had taken her to some anonymous stretch of the Stuart Highway to do her re-enactment. It would later be revealed that Lees was paid A$82 000 for the story, which aired in Australia in March 2002 and went down very badly. She told her interviewer that police 'more or less implied I was the murderer'. With all her unwillingness to cooperate, and with police having full knowledge of her yet-to-be-revealed secret, she was fortunate they had the good sense not to charge her with murder.

'Slap in the Face', said Sydney's *Daily Telegraph*, complaining that Lees had monstered those police and people who had helped her in 'her darkest hour'. Up till then it had been possible to have some respect for Lees' refusal to play the media game. Her fears of the overwhelming media creature were valid. But now she was playing the game, using the media to swipe at the media.

By late February 2002, Northern Territory police announced they would review their investigation. The idea was to fine-comb and see if taskforce officers had missed something. It was time. The investigation had gone nowhere. The review would offer nothing useful; it would only serve to embarrass or annoy cops who believed they had done all they could. What they really needed was for the killer to make a mistake.

The Tangey story came out. Police dismissed the 'handprint' Tangey had seen as inconsequential. And fair enough. There was no sensible reason they would ignore vital evidence. And despite their annoyance with Lees, police never once publicly cast doubt on her story. In order to clear up scuttlebutt about how Lees would not have been able to move her manacled hands from her back to the front when she escaped the gunman, and to clear up an error in the re-enactment Lees had performed for Granada TV, police revealed an exact replica of the handcuffs the gunman had fashioned out of black cable or zip-ties. A policewoman demonstrated how she was able, with no effort, to get her cuffed hands from behind her back to the front of her body, as Lees had described. It was convincing, for those who needed it. Daulby said the cuffs 'have been constructed for a unique purpose, and that purpose is to incarcerate and detain somebody'.

In July 2002, a year on from the crime, police released to the public photos of Lees' bloodied knees and hands, taken shortly after she was rescued. It was another attempt to get people, and the media, to focus on the reality that something actually had happened to Lees out there in the desert. I noticed Daulby's hands shook as he held the photos. Later I talked to some of his colleagues about this; they had noticed it too. Daulby had now done numerous press conferences so it wasn't as though he was intimidated by the media. I wondered if it was because he was reluctant to let this evidence be made public, and was angry at perhaps having been ordered to do so. Maybe it was because the public tendering of these images confirmed, finally, that police simply did not have a clue. And it was a painful admission for him to make. Maybe he'd had too much coffee that day. I never envied him his job.

The photos showed, up close for the first time, the blue t-shirt Lees was wearing at the time of the attack. It contained a lively DNA spot on the back – possibly blood, and possibly the gunman's. The t-shirt had a twenty-cent sized 'Hugs not Drugs' sticker still attached, which Lees had been given upon entering the Alice Springs Camel Cup, an annual event for tourists, earlier on the day she and her boyfriend were hijacked. And there was mystery DNA on the gearstick of the Kombi. Police had taken the DNA profiles offshore, to international databases, looking for a match. No luck.

The man police were searching for was closer to them than they knew. They already had his name, because several people had phoned in saying Murdoch was the man. And James Hepi, in particular, had told them all about Brad Murdoch. Police just didn't believe it.

# 6 THE HZJ75, A CAR FOR ALL REASONS

Following the hire-car lady's directions out of Adelaide, heading for Sedan and Swan Reach. 'Make sure you go past the Hilton Hotel,' she said, 'and you'll be on track.' I kept looking for a marble-walled palace but the dregged-out streets seemed all wrong for a Hilton. What she didn't tell me was that Hilton was a fucking *suburb* and the Hilton Hotel a one-storey corner pub.

First leaving Adelaide's outer reaches, it seemed about right, almost like Darwin, seeing Aborigines in ragged clothes and no shoes, crossing major roads without looking, maybe hoping a truck would solve their problems for them. Then the antique wine towns with Lutheran accents appear and disappear, replaced by tiny antique bush towns that can't come up with too many reasons for why they still existed, with a single pub, a single shop, a single garage and that's it. Waist-high rock fences ran for miles and miles, built by convicts for farmers in the pre-wire age, an age when they imagined this land could be a relocated Europe. It never was.

It was easy to see the trap for modern settlers. Beautifully decrepit old stone homes or deconsecrated churches going cheap in pin-drop towns, which for a bit of money could be done up and easily become home, places to maybe write that book or raise those geese or get the kids away from those computers. Then you start noticing the black Harley-Davidsons. You're in Confederate country.

I met James Hepi at the Sedan pub, a small stone building in a tiny barren town. Hepi lived closer to Swan Reach but this was where he preferred to drink and hang out with his friends. A very quiet pub. 'That's how I like it,' he told me. It was early 2006, several months after Murdoch's trial for the Falconio murder had finished. Hepi had never spoken to any reporter about his working days with Murdoch. We had a beer and didn't say much. In his court appearances Hepi had come with a reputation for fierceness, but he was a different unit to Murdoch. Hepi had mates, proper friends who could relax in his company, not people who trod carefully around him. Hepi even had a girlfriend he could keep.

We went over to a garage where one of his friends, Bruce, changed the points and adjusted the timing on Hepi's rough-running Holden ute. Sedan was such a desolate little place. I got the feeling Hepi missed the north and would be back there if he could. Especially Broome, his old town. When things cooled down, maybe he'd go back. We reconvened that night at the pub at Swan Reach, the next town along, some 30 kilometres east over the river. Hepi brought his girlfriend, Michelle, a pretty and intelligent woman who watched closely and expressed the standard misgivings about the media. Both were concerned that James not be portrayed as some kind of thug. There had been a line spun by Murdoch's lawyers that perhaps Hepi was the real Falconio killer, that he'd shopped Murdoch to cops to save his own guilty hide. It was not hard to assure them that I had no interest in that conspiracy. At the same time, there would be no avoiding the fact that Hepi had been a dedicated criminal, even though it hadn't paid off for him. His rickety old ute proved that. That night we drank and talked around the edges of things.

Hepi lived on hard land, a block of eighty acres somewhere between Sedan and Swan Reach. It was only 90 kilometres northeast of Adelaide as the crow flies but once you'd twisted through the back roads to get there it was twice that far. There was no ground water here; Hepi had to truck his in. The proceeds of his criminal activities – shifting great quantities of dope between South Australia and Western Australia – had once been considerable.

He was liquid to the point that cash had to be buried, laundered, invested and, hopefully, never explained. All that had now been spent or stolen from him. He worked on a potato farm these days, forklifting loads of spuds.

When, in 1965, Mick Jagger called Invercargill 'the arsehole of the world' after playing a concert there, it could be argued he was just showing off his geographical knowledge. At the base of New Zealand's South Island, Invercargill is one of the southernmost townships in the world. By the time James Hepi turned eighteen, he knew Jagger wasn't simply talking out of his atlas.

Invercargill, one of the coldest inhabited places in the southern hemisphere, was indeed at the very end of the earth. Hepi was a Maori in a predominantly white town, which made life difficult at times. But nowhere was it more difficult than in his home, where he experienced such violence as a boy that he learned fear was an instinct that was of no use to him. He had seen in his father about as much as a man could do.

'Brad Murdoch was a standover man. He could go all right but it takes all sorts. But we can all go all right when we have to. That's just life. I was brought up tough too. Hard and rough. I was dragged up. I marched my father out of the house when I was a young man. He was a violent, violent, violent man. He was extreme. Sometimes you'd fight to live. That's all right. I can be a very violent man myself but I tend not to be because it's so ugly when it happens. Invercargill is rough and tough. There's not too many Maori boys down there and I was one of them. I was all right, but I didn't want to be stuck there working in a meatworks and get some girl pregnant. There was very little opportunity for me in New Zealand. It was either the meatworks or shear sheep. So, get out of there. I chased a girl over to Australia. I knew people in Sydney so yeah, off we went.'

Hepi tried Sydney and Perth for a few years but it was Broome where things fell into place. He had a fiendish taste for the weed and beer – appetites the tropics well understood. Broome had the same sort of remoteness as Invercargill but there was none of the bitter weather and none of the attitude. People – Chinese, Japanese, Burmese, Aborigines – didn't seem to get on each other's nerves. The pressing ambience seemed to eliminate the franticness from people, slowing them down. The fact that many spent their days coned-out helped.

Hepi found work on the pearl farms. There was some drift diving, walking along the bottom of the sea gathering pearl shell, but mostly diving on the farms, attending to the shell which hung in rope nets, seeding them and capturing the cultured pearl. Men worked in teams, watching for each other's backs and making sure the hookers – the 200-metre airlines which pumped oxygen from compressors on the luggers – stayed clear and untangled. In this blue world – and sometimes, in the tidal north, a silty, stirred-up world where it was impossible to see more than a metre in front of your own hand, and hard to be sure some creature wasn't lining you up – Hepi found a dream job. It was a strange thing being around pearls, which were someone else's riches. 'There's millions of them. Pearls everywhere,' said Hepi. 'You'd find them lying on the bottom of the ocean where the shell has rejected them and spat them out.'

He'd work six months of the year for a year's wage. And even then, the diving work was only on the high spring tides, a few days every fortnight. 'They pay well because it's a high-risk job. If you look after yourself, you'll make a lot of money. Risk-for-reward. You put your life on the line at times with these guys, jumping into water where you know there are sharks. I had a friend I worked with who was eaten by a shark. In Roebuck Bay. There were six of us in the water and one of us went missing. And we found bits of him, so… He was a young fella, pregnant missus. That happens, you know.'

With time on his hands between tides, Hepi started sourcing marijuana from south of Perth and was then introduced to more reliable contacts in outback South Australia. Hepi had got to know a lot of people through diving, Aborigines and whites alike. Broome loved its dope. The more he bought the more he could sell.

In the end it wasn't the sharks that chased Hepi out of the water, or the money he was making from drugs. It was the bends. Hepi had gotten careless in deep water and surfaced too fast. Nitrogen bubbled in his veins and shot upward. The bends takes its name from the way divers double up in agony.

'I had a bend on the top of my spine, at the base of my brain. It stopped movement from my neck down and I didn't piss for a while. I had thirteen decompressions in the Darwin decompression chamber in the hospital. We were sometimes rough and quick and I'd come up too soon. The pain was beyond words.' In 1996 the bends – along with its sibling divers' torment, decalcification of the bones – put Hepi on a tractor, pulling a slasher for the Broome shire. Then he went into a taxi.

'The first time I met Murdoch was behind a yard in the industrial area. I was scoring some weed. He had a little caravan out the back of Brett Duthie's workshop at West Kimberley Diesel. I scored lots of other weed from everywhere and I didn't have any at the time. So, he was it. I'd heard about him through people where I drank, at the Satay Hut. She's a spot for rogues, the old Satay Hut. I got what I wanted, he got what he wanted – money for weed. That was the state of it. He knew what I did and he was quite surprised to see me there. But I didn't have any weed.'

At that time, around about 1998, the Coffin Cheaters motorcycle gang was a presence in Broome but didn't have a strong foothold. Hepi was a freelance dealer, beholden to no one. Everyone knew what he did and he had cornered the Aboriginal dope market. Hepi was black – or, at least, he wasn't white – and they felt comfortable dealing with him. Murdoch was dealing in smaller amounts, shipping to Broome from Perth through trucking companies.

'I'd see him at the Hut, seen him around,' said Hepi. The Satay Hut was an open-air drinking hole in Broome, close to the beach, no dress regulations, the type of place you'd stop in for a beer on the way home without having to worry about your thongs or singlet. You could sneak out the side for a joint and no one would care. 'He didn't seem to get out of that caravan much, he was flat out working for Brett on the trucks. I met him again when he was leaving town. He wanted to show me his Land Cruiser ute because he'd knocked off a motor and had a new, later-model Land Cruiser motor in it. It was quite a clever piece of engineering the way he'd fitted it up. He knew I had a Land Cruiser and he was off to somewhere upcountry with his little mate, Dags, and they were probably going to Kalumburu. I think they were going up to sell it to the blackfellas up there.'

Dags, or Darryl Cragan, was one of those who had to get up in court and talk about his long association with Murdoch. Dags had known Murdoch from Northampton, in Western Australia, where both had grown up. Knew him from before he even went to school. Murdoch and Dags ran into each other in Derby, about 220 kilometres north-east of Broome around 1997, and started helping each other out. Murdoch didn't have the personality to sell dope. Neither did Dags, but at least he knew people across the top of Western Australia. Murdoch was running around the edges of the real marijuana sales potential, unable to crack the code. Those KKK tatts on his arms might have had something to do with it. So too the disgust he had for Aborigines, which he was barely able to conceal. Dags was the face of Murdoch's drug dealing. A weathered, screwed-up face to be sure, shifty looking and older than its years, but that's what they were. They were the Ugly Brothers.

'There was no competition between Brad and me because he couldn't get the gear,' said Hepi. 'I had the gear, and I had the good gear in town for a long, long time. He really didn't get a lot of gear. And I just had lots and lots of weed. South Australian-sourced weed. I was living in Broome at Blue Haze, in the light industrial area as you come into town. I had a shed on a 200 square metre block with a bus that I rented out while I lived in the flat at the back. I was living there and coming here to Sedan once every six weeks. I'd do a turnaround trip in a week and buy fifteen pound and go home. I'd only be gone from Broome for a few days. People'd just think I'd gone fishing.'

By the late 90s Hepi had bought his block at Sedan, selecting it in order to be close to his suppliers, who also lived on bush blocks and grew either bush weed – scattered plants, cared for but tending to produce fewer of the heads that everyone wanted to smoke – or hydro. Bush weed could always be sold but hydroponically grown, full-strength, grown-under-lights whack-out dope was where the market was. Hydro, which by the time it reached the street market was sold as either a tiny $25 plastic bag or a foil-wrapped stick – a foily – was the go. Hydro was easy to compress and for those in the transport industry it made sense to move quality and quantity rather than just quantity.

It was in 2000, about the time of the Sydney Olympics, that Murdoch made his first critical contact with Hepi.

'I was on holidays in New Zealand,' said Hepi. 'I had bailed for ten months, went on holiday with my brother, blew a fucken shitload of cash and carried on. That's when Brad Murdoch rang me, in New Zealand, on me mobile phone. Four or five days prior to that, someone from South Australia had rung me and said, "James, I've got thirty pounds, can you help me out?" And I've gone, "No, I'm in another country, mate." And he's gone, "Ah, fuck."

'It just so happens a few days later Brad rang me, saying, "I'm in South Australia, I need to score some dope." So yeah, that's how Brad picked up his first load here, from something I'd organised. Really, I'd only seen him around the Satay Hut, mate. She was a place, the Satay Hut. Full of derelicts and whoever…

'Murdoch was being very nice to me because I had what he wanted. It was like, "I'll get you onto the dope, I got someone who's screaming to get rid of some, I know the cunt needs the money, you'll have to go and deal with him, and don't fuck him over, Brad, or he won't sell you the dope." That's it. And he did this maybe three times when I was away. Murdoch went to South Australia and bought dope from my contacts. I didn't give a fuck – I was out of the country. I didn't want to know. After that, I came back here and just lived for a while. Brad was dropping in. I was sourcing the dope again, and lots of it. I was also trying to do some work here, building a stone wall and fixing the place up.

'He was getting tired running around the country. He had another bloke with him at the time, bloke called Sheriff – Brian Johnston. Brian was the bitch.'

The Sheriff didn't show up for Murdoch's committal hearing. He just didn't come. The Crown lawyers couldn't say why. They were expecting him, he was on the witness list. He'd been subpoenaed. Maybe the Sheriff thought testifying in Brad's committal hearing was not necessarily something that would work in his favour. And perhaps he hoped no one would notice his absence, forgetting about him and letting him return to his weedy world.

'Brad wanted to know how I got around the country,' said Hepi. 'He followed me a couple of times across the desert. I'd been using the Tanami Track for a long time. It was just so easy. You turn off at Alice Springs, have a big line of toot [speed], and you nail it, you'll be across that desert in eleven hours. That's how I'd been doing it. You could also go across the bottom, through Kalgoorlie, across to Wiluna, cross the desert and come out just below Port Hedland. He was driving an F100 at that time.'

Hepi said that on a personal level he found Murdoch 'tolerable. He was doing a job for me. We spent a lot of time in passing. He could not sell the dope to the people I knew in Broome. People didn't like him. People were stand-offish of him. He didn't bother me but he couldn't deal dope, fuck, no way. That's why he needed his little gophers.' It might be thought that Hepi, as a black man, would have reacted against Murdoch's tattoos. 'I straight out asked him, "Where'd you get them, mate? That's fairly heavy work, Brad." He said, "They mean nothing to me now." I said, "You've got them tattooed on you. It must've meant something at the time."'

Murdoch never really explained and Hepi didn't worry himself about it. By the time they'd gone into business together, Hepi was using Murdoch as a delivery man and that was all that mattered. Hepi wore no tatts himself. 'It's something you want to be certain about,' he said. 'And Brad's were a fairly bold statement.' Hepi asked me what I thought they meant and I told him I didn't really know: 'I don't imagine he was *in* the KKK, just because he had himself branded with the insignia. I don't think there is a true KKK in this country. Just redneck wankers prancing about. It's a statement in support of lost causes. It's a warning, but it's also a symbol of loneliness.'

By the late 1990s, bikies were starting to move into Broome and wanting control of the drug market. They didn't like other criminals working their realm. They were a small but influential occupying force and didn't want Hepi making money that they considered their own. Hepi was forced to deal with the matter. 'I'd had problems with them but said, "Look, this is what I'm doing, but so fucking what? I was doing this before you were here, I was doing it for myself and I always have." Their concerns were that it was maybe bikie mull from South Australia getting in there. I went, "No. These are people I know who grow the shit, right from solo mums through to whatever. Not bikies." The concern was that if it was bikie mull it would be Rebels mull, not Coffin Cheaters. The money goes to another club. I didn't source from bikies. The weed Brad got, originally, was from his bikie friends.'

Murdoch carried with him the sense of bikie menace. Hepi would later learn, or come to believe, that Murdoch had been seen as an 'undesirable' even by the Gypsy Jokers, the outlaw club from which he had reputedly been excommunicated. Murdoch had a Joker tattoo – the evil, smiling clown – on his arm. 'Get asked to leave the Gypsy Jokers? That don't happen,' said Hepi. 'I didn't bother asking. So no, I don't know. Except that stuff went down and even they saw him as an undesirable. I learned that after I'd fallen out with him. What bikie gang does that?'

Word was that it had something to do with the way Murdoch treated women. That wasn't a bikie problem in a general sense, but it had to do with how he treated women attached to bikies from his own club. And he had a big mouth. He bragged outside the circle and that was bad for business.

Murdoch once showed Hepi some photos of himself in Gypsy Joker colours. He had a handsome sapphire-inlaid KKK belt buckle. Murdoch showed Hepi another photo of himself after he'd come off a bike. 'He'd lost half his face. It looked like bitumen bite.' Hepi saw it as crucial to his own success as a drug dealer that he remained free of bikie associations.

'I've never had any interest in bikies but Broome got to the point where they wanted to control it,' said Hepi. 'I had to sit down and explain this to them: "The people who are buying my dope wouldn't come up to you and buy dope. They *don't fucking like you*. They would go without before they'd buy your dope." This was the market I'd had and it was not imposing on anything they'd ever had.

'They were also worried about the toot. We had a bit of that going around, always carried speed. But really, it was all about the weed, that was it. So, in the end the bikies understood. It was just live and let live. I sold some of the dope myself and I also had a very faithful crew of good earners. I had one lady who was just brilliant – she was an old blackfella. I'd flick a couple of pounds a day to her sometimes. I'd sell it in ounces or sell as pounds to people, but mainly in ounces.

'As for the people doing all the foiling, I didn't want to know. That old lady, she'd sell a pound a day in foils. She was real good at it. I don't even know how many foils that would be. Not my area.'

Hepi was out for himself and did his job well. But it was tiring work being a courier-wholesaler and an extra driver made good sense. Despite Murdoch's implicit bikie baggage, he was not onside with the Coffin Cheaters. There seemed to be some sort of issue between Murdoch, the ex-Joker, and Broome's Coffin Cheaters. Hepi preferred to know nothing about it. He was prepared to overlook Murdoch's tatts, his unrepaired mouth and his looming presence which frightened people. Yet Hepi's functional, pragmatic greed in taking Murdoch on as a second driver would give him cause for serious regret.

Asked if he considered Murdoch a dangerous man, Hepi said no, he wasn't someone he considered a personal threat, because Hepi was not the kind to put up with intimidation. 'I'd consider him a nutcase. Dangerous? Yeah, dangerously cowardly. He'd shoot you – he wouldn't flog you. The only person I know he flogged was a 62-year-old man that he kicked the crap out of. The guy died of bone cancer. Old bloke called Nelson. Used to be a navy diver.' Nelson lived at what everyone called the Caravan Park, a backpacker and wanderer's home right next to the Satay Hut on Broome's Town Beach.

'Nelson was just an old fella. He'd try and chat up the chicks and the whole thing. And he copped a kicking. He didn't cop a slap. It was down on the ground, a 62-year-old man, apparently for talking to a lady the wrong way – some lady Brad was trying to fuck. And Nelson could be rude, but the ladies would go, "So what? He's just an old drunk." He was harmless. He didn't need to die from bone cancer from a kicking. The cancer started off in his shin, where he got stomped on. Nelson was a healthy, fit man, and ex-navy who had fought for his country. And he was a drunk but he was harmless, a Broome local, retired, living there by the ocean, with a pub across the road. Lived in a mobile home. It was a wander between the ocean, the pub and the shopping centre. That was about 1998. Murdoch wasn't charged because Nelson never said anything. Nelson come down and seen me and said, "Do you know this Murdoch?" I said "Yeah, I scored a bag of weed off him."'

The Nelson story was not enough to prevent Hepi working with Murdoch. He needed a reliable criminal colleague, and any person who was prepared to take such risks was unlikely to be a wholesome cleanskin. For all Broome's heart-warming multiculturalism, it came with the territory that some people had issues with Aborigines. Hepi once asked Murdoch straight out what his problem was.

'He said, "I just don't like them." I said, "Do you like me?" He said, "Yeah." I said, "Whatever, work it out. I like them, I deal with them, they're people I know. I've got to like everyone. If you can't like everyone, you can't sell dope. So get on the road and drive." And that was his job.

'I was the one who made the dollars. If I went away he couldn't sell the shit. People would not come and see him. I straight out said to him: "This is my show, man." Even though I was living in his poxy house in Forrest Street, in Broome, I had to live somewhere. This was my show. He didn't necessarily like it. People would come and see me. Not just to have a smoke, to see me. To do what I was doing – and I was liked for it – I had to be able to talk to all types of people. Brad didn't like it. He thought we were meant to be tough cunts or something. It doesn't work like that. I can get along with anyone. I can have a chat. In Broome, it was never like people didn't know what I was doing. They didn't see it as a bad thing. I was getting good weed and eighty per cent of the population were smoking it.'

When all Murdoch's bluster was set aside, it was possible, said Hepi, to have a beer with him, to talk about the things people like doing in the northwest, like sitting on a river with a live mullet on a line waiting for it to explode with a hooked barra. And Murdoch knew about cars. Murdoch's dad had been a qualified mechanic and while Murdoch did not have a trade certificate, he knew diesel motors intimately. And in the north, under many bonnets, beneath the deck of every fishing boat, and out the back of every community and cattle station was a diesel motor. Murdoch was useful.


Toyota initially tried to name their lightweight four-wheel drive trucks the Toyota Jeep. They were, as they still are, built tough to military specifications, but the company immediately ran into trouble with Willys, who made the US Army's Jeep. In 1954, Toyota christened their version the Land Cruiser and exported the first vehicle to Pakistan. The Saudi Arabians took an interest but Australians still showed allegiance to the British-made Land Rover for farm and outback work. And back then, in the 1950s, anyone who went bush was more likely to be working than adventuring and putting the vehicle to the challenge for the hell of it.

The early HJ45 series was popular in a limited way but by the mid-1980s, the HJ47 series Land Cruisers – like the HJ45, modelled to look like a truck with the fenders distinct from the bonnet and sitting over the front wheels, and little vents you could kick open to cool your feet – were taking off. By the end of the 1980s, Land Cruiser traybacks were the choice of bush engineers, station owners, Aborigines, miners, rangers, stock agents, geologists – anyone who needed a vehicle that could work all day and climb a wall if it had to. By the late 1980s, the Land Rover had lost its place: few who worked in the bush in north Australia were not doing it in Land Cruiser utes. There were only two colours, white or beige, but the vehicles still handled like tractors.

In the late 1980s, Toyota introduced the HJ75 and followed it up in the early 1990s with the HZJ75 – the 'Z' signalling a new, more responsive, higher-revving motor with an overhead cam. The 75 series was dressed up, squarer cut and came with air-con as standard. Some complained the new series was not such a good work machine. It didn't have the pulling power down low or the ability to crawl for hours over perilous boulders. But the 75 series could be driven high-speed on highways all day and the cabin came with new comforts, such as an adjustable steering column for big blokes. With an after-market winch on the front, the 75s came to rule the outback.

James Hepi's HZJ75 had a canopy on the back, beds, big rims and tyres, and dual batteries. 'It was jump in it and go,' he said. 'I've always like Land Cruisers, because you break down anywhere in the north you'll always come across another Land Cruiser. If you break down in a community you can buy a stub axle with a carton of beer. They're fixable and people know what they're doing. And basically, they don't fuck up. You get the oil changed or you drop it yourself on the side of the road. They are a hassle-free vehicle. Everyone's got one.'

Hepi fitted his ute with oversize rear springs for carting weight and always paid for the best shock absorbers. The bigger tyres gave slightly better clearance on rock-strewn dirt roads. He fitted a turbo-charger and oversize three-inch exhausts. 'When you do all the bits to them that we did, you could sit on a hundred and forty all day. And we did. In the Territory, it's legal to drive that fast. With the tanks holding extra fuel that we were carrying, people cannot believe that in ten hours – you've had a line of toot, you've got your fags, you've got your cool drinks beside you – ten hours later you're 1400 kilometres away. And in the north, if you're driving down the road with a gas bottle strapped to the back of your Land Cruiser, and especially me, looking like a blackfella, who's to wonder?'

Hepi carried his drugs in a gas tank strapped up against the back of his cabin. 'It was a forty-five kilo household gas bottle. I had a canopy on so it wasn't seen, but even if I didn't have the canopy on it didn't matter. Everyone else was driving around with gas bottles on the back of their Land Cruisers – that's how we carted our gas in Broome. Mine had a false bottom. No gas in it. Fill it with hooter, put a lick of silicone around the base, put it in the back and you're off to town to get some gas, mate. When I went to New Zealand for those ten months, I left my Land Cruiser with the RAC in Adelaide. I had thirty-five pounds stashed in the gas bottle. It cost me $900 for the RAC to look after the ute with thirty-five pounds of dope they didn't even know they had. They stored it. When I got home, I rang them, they charged up the battery and away we went.'

The remarkable thing is not that the Royal Automobile Club had unwittingly nursed Hepi's cache of weed, it was that Hepi's cash holdings were such that he could afford to stash thirty-five pounds and come back to it ten months later. 'I was making two dollars for every dollar I spent. When I first started off, I spent $15 000 and made $30 000. I'd come back, spend that thirty on dope, make sixty – taking $5000 out for costs. I came to sit myself on a float of about $85 000, which is what I spent on dope every time I came to South Australia. It's an awful lot of money – and look where we're sitting now.'

On a parched old bush block where fresh water needed to be trucked in.

'But that's the type of shit we did. A shoebox full with fifty-dollar notes will hold $250 000. I had money left, right and centre. That's why Brad was a boy. That's why he was here. He had never seen such money. He'd done shit for bikies and all he'd ever got out of it was a snort of nose candy and a stolen car now and then.

'I'd go on holidays and blow a hundred thousand fucking dollars. Just blew it. Had stuff in the ground here. It was a stash, forty-eight grand in a hole in case I ever got caught, to pay lawyers. That later disappeared – Brad knew about it. I bought pearls and paintings, flash paintings. Things a lady had bought for me. She'd said, "This is a good way for you to get rid of some money, buy this painting for $2500." Righto. That all got knocked off later. But I ate the best steak every night, had my dinghy and went fishing and wasted a lot of money.

'I was buying my weed in South Australia anywhere from $2200 to $2800 a pound. If I sold it in ounces, one pound would give me anywhere from $4000 to $4800. So you go back to Broome with ten, fifteen, twenty pounds, it starts to add up.'

During the trial, Murdoch's defence suggested that Hepi had at times carried a pistol on the road when he was working with Murdoch. The suggestion wasn't pursued, just left there to hang, something for the jury to ponder. A hell of a lot of stuff was left to hang. Hepi later explained: 'The Coffin Cheaters had said to me at one point, "We'll just take your mull". I said, "Well, you know where I am, but I'll tell you, I sleep with a gun so, yeah, if you want my mull, come and get it, but you better want it real bad". Yeah, I had a gun. It was Brad's .327.'

Witnesses also spoke of how Hepi would keep a pistol taped under his table at his Sedan block, easy to reach in case of unwanted visitors. There were times when he'd store up to forty-five pounds of dope in his shed and there were some who might have got the notion to just come and take it. 'And yes, I was prepared to look after my interests because there was a lot of money tied up in that. I also think the drugs we were taking helped increase the general paranoia – we took a lot of toot.'

Hepi had also had a falling out with one of his neighbours, a hydro-grower and talented amphetamine chemist whom Hepi had come to consider unstable. Hepi said he'd loaned a lot of money to this man, who was simultaneously being chased by South Australian bikies over a debt. Hepi told him it was time to pay up. When he couldn't, Hepi gave him a bitch-slapping. The man didn't like it. It was another reason for Hepi to keep a gun close by for protection. Trouble, Hepi knew, could come from any direction.

By March 2001, Murdoch needed to get himself into a HZJ75 Land Cruiser. He'd been crossing the country from Broome to Sedan in an F100.

'The F100 was real heavy on fuel and it's the type of car a bikie drives around the country,' said Hepi. 'It was big, lairy, it just wasn't the choice of car. It was a gas-guzzling thing which ran on fuel. You can get diesel anywhere, or roll a 44-gallon drum off the side of the road, hide it in the bushes in the desert and come back for it later. I had diesel stashed on the Tanami Track at one time. We needed compatible cars in case one car blew up a gearbox in the middle of the desert.'

Murdoch's and Hepi's relationship was necessarily civil. But there were no long nights weeping into beers telling each other what great blokes they were. Murdoch knew he was onto something big with Hepi and for the most part behaved himself among Hepi's friends. Hepi never saw Murdoch with any close mates. Maybe Pete Jamieson was one. Maybe Billy Gibbs, a Perth bloke with bikie connections. Jamieson ran a service station in Fitzroy Crossing, and would later provide Murdoch with a half-remembered, half-unsure alibi for his movements immediately after the Falconio slaying.

'Brad operated on the fact that he should inspire fear, but when someone doesn't scare he didn't know what to do,' said Hepi. Mostly, Hepi saw Murdoch with his bitches, quiet men like Dags and Sheriff, who seemed a little frightened of their big, toothless buddy. Later, when Murdoch started wearing a holster, he became the kind of guy Hepi couldn't take to a party in Broome. Or Swan Reach or Sedan. Not armed. Come to think of it, he wasn't the sort of guy you could ever take to a party. People would stand back, didn't want to know. Brad wanted respect and he thought it ought to come automatically, on account of his menacing presence. He'd somehow got the notion that society was limited to a few basic human types: bandits, sluts, niggers, desperados, faggots and cops. 'He'd go to the fucken Satay Hut with a holster fitted to himself,' said Hepi. 'It was like, fuck, we're in *Broome*. You take your thong off and slap someone, you don't shoot them.'

Now that he had a disposable income, Murdoch, according to Hepi, spent 'most of his money on his mum, his dinghy and the whores. Brad would have three to four prostitutes each time he went through Kalgoorlie.

So he told me. Got the impression it was the expensive ones because when Brad had money in his pocket it was like he had an urgent need to get blown, and it had to be by someone good looking.'

Murdoch and Hepi always had speed. It was as necessary to them as diesel to their Land Cruisers. The long desert crossings couldn't have been managed without it. They would have needed to camp out, or take a motel room, get sleep somewhere. Murdoch tended to drink his speed, in cups of tea, or iced coffee, or those little Yakult drinks that he used to try and manage his forever-aching innards, which were raw and ulcer-ridden from too much direct speed ingestion. They'd carry half-ounces of speed, or 14.5 grams. 'That's a fairly big bag of speed, but that's what we had,' said Hepi. 'We'd have a line and talk business, buy some weed, all done. Brad'd be in excess of seven grams of amphetamine a day.' They'd each take a gram in one go. That's a lot. A party user can get by all weekend on one gram.

It is difficult to overdose on speed, but it is possible to take too much. You run the danger of being taken to the far outer reaches of a car-cabin or lounge-room paddock where, in a state of teeth-grinding sleep deprivation and an eighty-a-day cigarette mouth, ugly little phantoms position themselves on the periphery of your vision and settle in to watch. You see them hopping about, making their moves. You can even smell them. They make you jump, at times, with all their hurrying about. 'You'd be awake for five days,' said Hepi. 'That's when Brad would be tipping tea and speed into his head. To drive here and back, it was never done in stops. We sometimes did it in vehicles together, but not in the same car.'

The amphetamine was mostly for personal use, although there were some small-time sales to the inner circle. Speed, as far as Hepi was concerned, was bikie business and better kept that way. Murdoch found speed could be used on women to persuade them to overlook some of the charm he lacked. And the hang-the-niggers tatts didn't help. The problem with taking seven grams a day was that it caused erectile dysfunction. No stiffy. And while the speed-taker could explain the pharmaceutical fallout to himself, he still wasn't able to do the job. That could lead to anger and embarrassment and, from her, unspoken questions about his manliness. Not that a smart girl would ever initiate such a discussion with Brad.

Hepi, when he bothered to consider his accomplice as anything other than a functional drug-shifting road android, felt something akin to sympathy. Not that Hepi would admit it, not now. Murdoch had left the tracks, long before he became Falconio's killer. 'I think he'd known a lot of hate, a lot of abuse. He was never a loved man, not ever. Look at the cunt. Could a mother even love it? It'd be hard work.'

They thought of themselves as criminals, technically, but more as tax evaders. The world needed them as much as it did policemen or doctors. The market they sold to was always unflappably buoyant, never subject to gluts or lows. Things were good.

# 7 DESPERATE MEN, DESPERATE WOMEN

In 1999 James Hepi introduced Murdoch to his closest bush-block neighbours: Freddy Everitt, his wife 'Laura', and their daughter, 'Jane', then ten years old. Everitt was ingratiating and slimy. He did some work for Hepi, clearing and slashing. Before that, Everitt had managed two brothels in Adelaide, one selling boys and the other girls.

Laura, Freddy's de facto, was one of his former prostitutes, now supposedly retired from the game although she could be prevailed upon by Fred to put out for the Swan Reach–Sedan locals when money was short. Laura was no looker but she had $10 000 breasts courtesy of a plastic surgeon. The boys liked that. 'Each one worth five grand,' was what they said in the area. Jane was raised in a cyclone of bad parenting.

Hepi would come to hate Fred Everitt, not just for his measly greed or his weakness, but for everything. Everitt was a lousy gambler who, when things started going wrong between Hepi and Murdoch, chose to sidle up to Murdoch. It was a bad bet.

In August 2002, a year after the Falconio-Lees hijack, Murdoch was charged with raping Laura and her daughter Jane.

'Fred was out here hiding out,' said Hepi. 'There's lots of weirdos out here in the bush, all hiding out. He was just away from the city. He'd had little boys you could root in his brothel. He was a deviate and a thief and a drunk. That was Freddy Everitt. He looked like a weasled-up old man.

'Before Brad was on the scene, they used to come over here [to Hepi's place]. All of them, Fred, Laura and Jane. And she was a nice kid. She'd say to me, "How come you're not drunk, James?" And I'd say, "I've got to cook your tea, Jane." And Fred'd be falling over in the corner, and Laura would be falling over in the other corner with her tits out.

'And I told Jane, "I've got to cook myself dinner, and you dinner, and that's how adults behave." She was a child who had to cook her own dinner at ten years old because the pimp and the whore had passed out. I just tried to treat her like a normal kid. "Jane, you can sit down and watch TV or draw, you don't have to wait around to pick up your parents' empty stubby bottles."'

Murdoch would later be found not guilty of the rapes, but Hepi had no doubt about Murdoch's guilt.


In the months before the Falconio murder, Hepi explained his business plan to Murdoch. There were to be another twelve months of intense trafficking between South Australia and Broome, then Hepi wanted to put away $200 000, bury it in a hole, and give the game away. The stress of criminality was becoming hard to manage, and the aim for Hepi had always been to go straight one day. All the amphetamines and the complementary obsessive-nervous cigarette intake did not make for a good long-term health outlook. The usual arrangement was that one of them would be in Broome while the other was on the road. During 2000 and the first half of 2001, both did trips but it made more sense for Murdoch to do most of the travelling while Hepi handled bulk sales in Broome.

Murdoch or Hepi, whoever was coming into town, would call the other from the Roebuck Roadhouse, just east of Broome, as they came into mobile phone range. The phone call was the signal to open the side gate of the Forrest Street house so that the vehicle could be driven straight into the high-fenced yard without dawdling outside.

Hepi had worked it out so he would arrive in Broome with the early-morning work traffic heading into town. It was a technique Murdoch adopted. 'It means you're coming into town with half a dozen Land Cruisers that are also coming in to work. You just slipped in right alongside them. If you sat on a steady speed across the desert, it was possible to know exactly where you would be in six hours' time. And if you were a bit ahead of schedule, you could sit in a little gravel pit 40 kilometres out of Broome, have a couple of pipes, wait for it to be perfect, then drive in, straight past the police station, and in through the open side gate.'

Hepi usually took seventeen and hours to cross the 1800 kilometres from Alice Springs to Broome, which was the toughest – and mostly dirt – part of the journey. That put Hepi's average speeds at more than 100 kilometres per hour, although Murdoch would later tell the jury at his trial that he always drove the Tanami Track at a steady 60 kilometres per hour, because he wanted to go easy on his vehicle.

Murdoch had – after disposing of Falconio – left the Shell Truck Stop in Alice Springs just after midnight on 15 July, and driven fast all the way to Fitzroy Crossing – a journey of some 1400 kilometres.

No one knows for sure what time he arrived in Fitzroy Crossing. His mate, Pete Jamieson, who ran a Fitzroy Crossing roadhouse, was vague about what time Murdoch turned up on 15 July. He wasn't even sure it was 15 July, but guessed it could have been anytime between sunset and dark on that Sunday, just before he closed the roadhouse for the night. Jamieson's testimony was useful to Murdoch because it suggested he had done the 1400 kilometres from Alice to Fitzroy in something like nineteen hours. That put Murdoch's travel speed at around an average 73 kilometres per hour.

A tape of a phone interception would be played in court. In it Murdoch, speaking to Jamieson from South Australia's Yatala prison, asked whether Jamieson had got the message about what to say in regards to the time he had passed through Fitzroy that day. Murdoch needed to slow his journey right down, because he had fashioned a careful story that he left Alice Springs and set off on the Tanami Track at about 3 pm on 14 July. That way, he reasoned, he could have been nowhere near the vicinity of Barrow Creek at the time of the murder, which occurred at around 8 pm that night. This meant, according to Murdoch, he had taken twenty-eight hours to travel the 1400 kilometres from Alice to Fitzroy Crossing, an average of 50 kilometres per hour.

Claiming such horse-and-buggy speeds was a dumb thing to do to a Darwin jury, whose members tend to be familiar with bush-driving conditions. It wasn't just that there were no speed limits on Territory roads at that time (the 130 kph limit was introduced in 2007), it was that no one, apart from geriatrics towing caravans, ever did 60 kilometres per hour on dirt. In order to eliminate corrugation rattle, standard policy is to go fast. Hepi described Murdoch's 60 kilometres per hour claims as 'a hunk of shit'.

'You got that much gear and you do sixty? At sixty, that's when you change from second to third, mate,' said Hepi. 'You're off across the desert. And we were set up in rockets. Air-con, windows tinted so the sun didn't get in, windows down now and then, windows up, you know how it is, comfortable bucket seats fitted from other cars. I showed Brad how to make an adaptor so you put a ten-speed bike changer in the car as a cruise-control so you don't have to put your foot on the accelerator.

'And you drive through the middle of the desert one-handed. And they're good roads. They run three-trailer road trains on them. There's nothing wrong with them. You have spotlights on the front of your car so you can see for miles. And at night, when your diesel's running optimum, it doesn't matter if you hit a roo – you just blow it off the road. And away you go. You're off across the desert at 130 kilometres per hour, at least, stop in the desert for an iced coffee and a toot and you're out at Fitzroy Crossing in the morning. No problem.'

Murdoch's post-murder imperative was to get out of the Northern Territory and deep into Western Australia as fast as possible. He knew there would be roadblocks – or, at least, should be roadblocks – on the state border by the morning of 15 July. As it turned out, there were none, but Murdoch wasn't to know that.

From Alice Springs to the West Australian border is 750 kilometres. Presuming he had disposed of Falconio somewhere between Barrow Creek and Alice Springs in the hours after the killing, as police believe he did, Murdoch would have crossed into Western Australia at about 6 am, then hammered the next 600 kilometres to Fitzroy Crossing and been there before lunch to refuel. He would have been driving like he'd never driven before and would by then have considered himself reasonably safe. He didn't arrive in Broome until early in the morning of 16 July – Hepi remembered him coming in at about 4 am. Somewhere along the line, somewhere close to Broome, he pulled over and killed time. Maybe he'd stopped at one of his hidey-holes, a creek or a river somewhere, to wonder at how he'd let that tiny little Pommy woman get away.

Hepi remembered when Murdoch rang in the early hours of 16 July he said he was over at West Kimberley Diesel, which was unusual. He said the car needed some work – gearbox again. Hepi said Murdoch seemed edgy, more so than usual. That day Murdoch shaved his hair and moustache. Hepi didn't ask why. 'Not that interested.'

In the grainy truck stop video footage Murdoch appeared to have a gimpy left arm. He carried it in a funny position. But no one – not Murdoch, not the defence or the prosecution experts on anatomical matching, who went through the fine detail of all Murdoch's other physical features – was ever asked about this in court.

By the time of his murder trial for Falconio in Darwin in late 2005, Murdoch had been acquitted of the rapes of Laura and Jane. The Falconio jury probably knew about this from the press coverage the case had received at the time, but in order to avoid any prejudice to Murdoch, nothing to do with the alleged rapes was allowed to be mentioned in the Darwin trial. When Murdoch was picked up in August 2002 in Port Augusta and charged with the rapes, he had a sizeable cache of weapons, including a nylon pistol holster. The strap of that holster had a hair tie attached to it, which the Crown said Murdoch had souvenired from Lees. While the Crown was able to discuss the hair tie, the holster was not allowed to be called a holster. The Crown just called it a 'strap'.

Most of the information about Murdoch's guns and holster had been ruled inadmissible at his Falconio pre-trial hearing because, in order to explain the weapons, the jury would have to be told of the context in which they were found when he was arrested on suspicion of the rapes. So the hair tie was left, like many other things, to hang in the air, disconnected from any context. It made no sense to anyone but the lawyers. It was another example of how a jury gets fed limited and sanitised information. Those witnesses who swear to tell 'the truth, the whole truth and nothing but the truth' are in fact led through a careful script whereby they only ever tell a partial truth.

Murdoch did not have a gimpy arm. The reason he carried himself in this manner at the truck stop is now obvious: he was nursing a holster and a pistol. He was anticipating making a last stand. He would later tell Laura and Jane during their ordeal that he intended putting an end to it all, that life wasn't worth living. He wanted to go back to Western Australia to shoot it out with some Coffin Cheaters and put a bullet in his own brain. But on the night he killed Peter Falconio, he'd left Joanne Lees hiding in the bushes and knew there was a chance that by the time he was refuelling his Land Cruiser at the Alice Springs truck stop, Lees might have raised the alarm. When he walked into that service station, Murdoch was prepared to shoot it out with anyone who challenged him. Crown lawyers later told me they agreed with the truck stop holster scenario – and while they would have loved to run it by the jury, they were not allowed to.

After Murdoch returned to Broome from that trip, things started going wrong between him and Hepi. There were more drugs to be sourced in South Australia but Murdoch had put his car in for drastic canopy modifications – even though he'd had a new canopy fitted to the vehicle only months before. Murdoch didn't want to go anywhere.

Hepi first saw the images of Truck Stop Man on the evening news in Broome, when they were first released to the public, several weeks after the crime. 'And yeah, that was Brad. But in that sense it wasn't too odd. Because he had to be there – that's where he was supposed to be at the time. It was like, "They caught you on a camera, Brad, they reckon you're a murderer". And he was like, "Oh no, you know I was there, I was on a run".'

Murdoch's reluctance to hit the road forced Hepi back onto it. He again had to become the main delivery man. It pissed Hepi off. He had invested in both vehicles, ensuring that they were virtually armour-plated for the punishing drives. And Murdoch was refusing to use his. Murdoch would sneak off to South Australia now and then, but always come back muttering that people were following him. 'I'd say, "Sorry? Who are these people, Brad? We're going across the desert at a hundred miles an hour. Who could be following? Good luck, try and keep up." He was suffering paranoia real bad.'

It was sometime in December 2001 that Hepi's girlfriend, Michelle, whom he had known for years but was just getting serious with, and who had moved into their Forrest Street house, took a call from Murdoch, who was on the road at the time. 'Bradley rang me up on my mobile and said, "Are you sleeping with James?" I said, "That's none of your business." He said, "It is." He said there'd be pillow talk and that I'd take James's side. Then he got pretty aggro. He said, "You don't know what I'm capable of. I'm coming up to Broome to kill you." And I said, "No worries, Brad, shall I leave the gate open?" But I must admit I didn't stay there that night. I went to James's friend's house.'

At the time, Hepi was also on the road, returning to Broome from Sedan with a load. Murdoch was supposed to be behind him, also with a shipment. He never showed. 'So I've got to Broome, rung him, said, "Where are you?" He said he was in Perth.' Murdoch was too scared to move. Everyone was chasing him. 'I said to him, "Righto, I'll come to Perth and pick the shit up myself."'

They arranged to meet in a hotel carpark in Perth. Maybe in Belmont, maybe Kewdale – Hepi can't be sure. 'I met the cunt in the carpark. He had a mate, a nasty little fella called Billy with him. Billy Gibbs.' Billy Gibbs wasn't one of Murdoch's bitches. Loosely known as a bikie 'associate', and as equally loosely known for being 'in the transport game', William Lacey Gibbs would be arrested and sentenced to four years' jail in 2002 on amphetamine and cannabis charges. He was Murdoch's Perth drug buddy, from back in the old days.

Gibbs could have provided damning testimony in Murdoch's trial. In a statement Gibbs gave to police from jail, he described the guns he knew Murdoch to have in his possession at the time of Falconio's murder. He said Murdoch had a silver, six-shot .22 revolver with a barrel of approximately four inches long with a wooden grip; a Chinese copy of a .45 pistol which was silver; and a .308 rifle with a scope and a five-shot magazine. Gibbs also said Murdoch kept the .45 pistol under his car seat and the .22 revolver at his side in a door pouch. Gibbs further said Murdoch had a .357 magnum revolver and two black Glock 9 mm handle-loading pistols. Of these last two, Gibbs thought Murdoch sourced them after Falconio's murder, but the others he had prior to 2001.

Joanne Lees had said she was menaced with a silver revolver, maybe with some scrolling running along the barrel. But it was night and she wasn't too sure. Several people testified that they had seen Murdoch with a small silver revolver in the months before the murder. One was Julieanne McPhail; another was Rachel Maxwell, who early in 2001 was going out with Hepi and recalled seeing Murdoch and Hepi at the Sedan block with what she thought was a 'John Wayne-type of gun – it was silver with a wooden bit on the handle. I did not notice whether it had engraving or etching'. But she didn't know whose gun it was. It could have been Murdoch's or Hepi's.

The defence argued that Murdoch's weapons of choice were a .38 Beretta pistol and a .357 magnum revolver – and both of them black. The person who could have settled it once and for all was Billy Gibbs, but by then Gibbs had been released on parole and was no longer feeling as cooperative as he had been when he gave his statement from prison. He let it be known he was not going to come to Darwin as a friendly Crown witness. The prosecution team decided not to call him and his statement never saw light of day in either the committal or the trial.

Hepi claimed he didn't go armed to that carpark meeting. 'No. I just went to say, "Where's the money, where's the drugs? It's taken me six days to get here, Brad, what's going on?". He was supposed to be coming to Broome with money that we'd earned and also a load of drugs. And he never turned up. I've got out of the car, said, "What's going on, Brad?". He's gone, "I've just spent three days hiding out in the desert".' And I've gone, "Yeah, from *what*, Brad?"' He didn't want to go across the border between WA and SA, from the fucken coppers at Norseman.' Norseman is at the West Australian end of the Nullarbor Plain. It's where Murdoch and Hepi would sometimes take a right and head north, up through Kalgoorlie and on to Broome. But they'd always mix it up between Norseman and Alice Springs, so as not to be seen as regulars on any particular route.

Murdoch told Hepi: 'They think I'm the Northern Territory killer.' Hepi replied, '"So what? Where's the money and drugs?" He would've had about $52 000 on him and about twenty-six pounds of dope, a large amount. We'd had two lots of real good dope. I had taken the first lot through but he got stalled at Norseman. And he said he didn't want to come across the border and he was sort of coming at it like I had put him in to the coppers for Falconio.' It showed the depth of Murdoch's paranoia. He wasn't even on the Northern Territory police radar at the time, nor was he of interest to any other police force. Why would Hepi have dobbed him in? It made no sense and would only have led to Hepi's own downfall had he done so. Murdoch was eating at his own entrails, as a fox will when it takes a bullet in the guts.

'I've gone, "What, Brad? This is all news to me, mate. I was across that border only three days ago myself". He said he didn't have the money or the drugs. But he had little Billy with him and Billy was armed. He had his hand inside his jacket the whole time – not that I ever saw a gun. The meeting finished with me going to my car, wondering if I should've turned up with a gun and shot him. But I would have had to shoot Billy as well. No one had put him in to the cops. His mind was unplugging itself. And that was the end of our relationship. I should've shot him but it was never meant to be about shooting anyone. It was about making money.

'I went back to Broome, collected up my money, spent five grand on my car and went back. I went back to work. I'd done three trips since my fallout with Brad, maybe four. I was going home to pick up Michelle, when I got busted on my way. Just outside of Broome.'

Hepi was arrested on 16 May 2002. 'Coppers pulled me over. I was coming in from the Roebuck Roadhouse. I'd come via Mt Magnet, through the desert, jumped out behind Port Hedland and come in on the bitumen. They got me at the roadhouse about twelve miles out of Broome. They said, "Acting upon information received, Mr Hepi, we believe you're transporting marijuana". And they went straight to the gas bottle, where it was. I knew exactly how the coppers knew about it, right then. I was arrested and taken to the cells in Broome. They pulled the gas bottle and the ute apart. They were looking for guns, drugs, lots of things. They were led to believe I'd be carrying amphetamine and arms. I had none. Apart from dope. All I had was a cheese knife on the dash because I'd been eating salami on the way in. I knew exactly where the tip-off had come from. All I thought was, "You cunt".'

It had been months since Hepi had seen Murdoch at the Perth carpark meeting. Murdoch had relocated to South Australia, shamelessly exploiting the drug contacts Hepi had introduced him to. They were now Brad's mates, too. And he was spending a lot of time with Freddy Everitt. Word was Murdoch was now using a trucking company to get his drugs across the border and up to Broome because he was too scared to do the drive himself. He was using a Broome woman with whom Hepi and Murdoch had briefly shared their house, to deal his drugs when they reached their destination.

One of Hepi's friends paid his bail. Hepi knew he was looking at a jail term – maybe up to a year. He'd been caught with roughly 10 pounds of dope – 4.5 kilograms. It wasn't as big as his usual shipments but it was quality hooch. He'd landed well within the trafficking category.

'I had an ace up my sleeve called Brad Murdoch,' said Hepi. 'And I used it.'

First, Hepi went to a public phone box and rang Taskforce Regulus, which was handling the Falconio investigation out of Alice Springs. 'I said I had information regarding the Falconio murder. The guy on the other end made some smart comment so I ended up hanging up on him. That's when I got in touch with Gordy.'

Gordon Bauman had represented Hepi at his bail application. Bauman was a craggy faced lawyer with a blokey accent who happened to get around Broome in a platinum wig and a skirt, which frightened his first-time clients but didn't affect his efficacy as a lawyer. He worked for Aboriginal legal aid and, for some reason, being a dark-skinned New Zealander meant Hepi qualified for legal aid. Bauman agreed to broker a meeting in his apartment between Hepi and Broome Detective-Sergeant, Peter Jenal, who had been Hepi's arresting officer over the drug haul.

Hepi laid out what he had: the details about Murdoch's weapons, how the man in the truck stop was a hundred per cent match for Murdoch, how Murdoch had been acting weird, how he had told Hepi the best place to dispose of a body out bush was in the soft dirt of a spoon drain. How he had seen Murdoch making cable-tie handcuffs in the shed at Sedan. Jenal immediately contacted Detective-Sergeant David Chalker at Regulus. Not too interested. 'Pete Janel could see the reality of it, but not the Territory cops,' said Hepi.

Still, Hepi's information would prove useful with his own forthcoming drug charges. Gordon Bauman put it to the judge, sitting in Broome, that Hepi was assisting Northern Territory police with the Falconio matter and could become a vital witness.

'There was never any deal that I was not going to jail for what I had said about Murdoch,' Hepi told me. 'It was only ever said to me that the judge may look upon my assistance favourably. In the end nothing about Murdoch was said openly in court. I think the judge had been filled in by Gordy but it wasn't openly read or said in court.'

Hepi was ready for jail. He'd had his pushbike serviced and had discussions with prison authorities about doing day work by riding out of the prison walls every day to work at the local golf club. But in the end Hepi was given a wholly suspended sentence. 'You could've seen my jaw drop on the ground. It was like, no, get fucked!'

For the sake of a South Australian mother and daughter, it was a real pity the Territory cops didn't listen to Hepi.

# 8  GUESTS IN THE DEN OF HELL

Senior Constable Michael: Right, the time is now 6.21 pm on Wednesday 28 August 2002. This conversation is taking place in the car park of Woolworths shopping centre, Tassie St, Port Augusta. I'm Senior Constable Robert Michael, Port Augusta CIB, also a number of uniform police from Port Augusta present. I'm Senior Constable Michael. I'm a police officer from Port Augusta CIB. Do you understand that?

Murdoch: Yep.

Michael: I'm now arresting you on suspicion of the offences of abduction and rape. Those offences I'll allege occurred at Swan Reach in South Australia. You are not obliged to say anything further, anything that you do say will be recorded and may be given in evidence. Do you understand that?

Murdoch: Yep.

Wednesday 28 August 2002, and South Australian police nabbed the 'outback killer', the best anyone came up with for Falconio's murderer. Murdoch never got a proper criminal outlaw name – or, at least, not a good one. He wasn't the Postcard Bandit, the Society Murderer, or Son of Sam. Backpacker Killer had already been taken by the drooling Ivan Milat.

South Australian police, when they converged on the Woolworths carpark in Port Augusta that afternoon, had an idea they might find Peter Falconio's killer. But they were there to arrest a man suspected of raping a mother and her twelve-year-old daughter. In preliminary statements the victims gave police, they told of being manacled in black cable-tie handcuffs, of being forced into the back of a Land Cruiser ute with a canopy, and of how this Murdoch had obsessed about Peter Falconio. He sounded like a good fit for Truck Stop Man. Given that, and the fact that this man was said to be mobile with an extensive personal armoury, police took a small army to Woolworths.

Murdoch was inside the shopping centre stocking up on supplies for a trip to Western Australia as police snipers took up positions under cars and on surrounding rooftops. Local residents and shopkeepers were ordered to stay low. As Murdoch exited the shop and walked to his Land Cruiser ute, he appeared not to notice that the immediate vicinity had gone unnaturally quiet. Bullet-proof vested officers with automatic weapons swooped. Murdoch offered no resistance. He was put on the ground, searched and found to be carrying an automatic Glock pistol – such as police use – down the back of his trousers.

A search of his vehicle revealed hidden compartments and a range of weapons – pistols, knives, a crossbow, night-vision goggles, and assorted implements of torture, including chains and an electric cattle prod. Also among Murdoch's possessions was an Australian Federal Police document which in 1999 had infamously fallen into the hands of outlaw motorcycle gangs in Queensland, Victoria and Western Australia. The document contained a list of some thirty federal agents and New South Wales state police, along with their codenames and contacts, who were attempting to infiltrate New South Wales bikie gangs at the time. Murdoch's copy was obsolete because that police taskforce had been quickly disbanded when the document was found in bikie hands, but it remained a trophy among bikies and their associates. That Murdoch was in possession of the document said something about the company he kept.

South Australian police immediately made the connection to Falconio and let their Northern Territory colleagues know. Initially they were not too interested. Several days would go by before they would say they were 'excited' by the apparent breakthrough. The real tragedy of the Brad Murdoch investigation is that Territory police hadn't become excited three months earlier, when James Hepi told Broome police about Murdoch. His statement contained all the information they needed to rapidly elevate Murdoch from a person of passing interest to someone they should have taken very seriously indeed. Others had phoned Crime Stoppers suggesting Murdoch was a fit for Truck Stop Man.

Had Territory police acted on Hepi's statement, the mother and daughter would never have been attacked. But Territory police had other suspects who were higher priority than Murdoch. They had actually been given Murdoch's name as early as August 2001, just a month after Falconio's disappearance, and they had in fact acted on that information, tasking Broome police to go around to Murdoch's Forrest Street address to look him over. The Broome police needed an excuse to visit and found one: there was an outstanding assault complaint against Hepi, which they hadn't bothered looking into. One cop went and had a chat with James while the other dallied with Murdoch, who had the bonnet up and was tooling on his engine. By then, Murdoch had changed his appearance and his vehicle. Murdoch came across as comfortable and chatty. The police reported back that Murdoch didn't match the wanted man.

Legally speaking, Murdoch was innocent of the rapes. The facts said otherwise. The jury – we have to guess – didn't like the mother because she was an ex-prostitute. They didn't like it that mother and daughter had stupidly thrown out the clothing they'd been wearing during the rapes, before complaining to police; and they didn't like it that it had taken them days to go to the police. Even worse, the mother had been caught lying to the jury. There were reasons for it all, but Murdoch's solicitor, Mark Twiggs, and his barrister, Grant Algie, did a very good job convincing the jury that the whole thing was part of a sick, three-state conspiracy to finger his client for this Falconio scandal which seemed to be occupying the nation. No wonder Murdoch would later insist that the same defence team should represent him in the Territory as he stood trial for Falconio's murder.

Senior Constable Michael: The recording equipment has now been activated. The time is 9.04 pm on Wednesday the 28th of August. This interview is being conducted in the video/audio room at the Port Augusta police station.

Other police who are present are introduced on the record.

Michael: Your full name?

Murdoch: Bradley John Murdoch.

Michael: And your date of birth?

Murdoch: 6.10.58.

Michael: And your address?

Murdoch: No fixed.

Murdoch is cautioned and again reminded of his rights. He is entitled to one telephone call and nominates his brother, Gary Murdoch, as the recipient of that call. He is told he could have a friend, relative or solicitor present during his interrogation.

Murdoch: How can I have a friend, relative or whoever? I have not made a fucking telephone call yet.

Police tell him they will not allow him to call his brother because in their opinion it might jeopardise the investigation. Murdoch elects to call a solicitor.

Interview suspended.

Senior Constable Michael: The recording equipment has now been activated. The time is now 11.54 pm on Wednesday, 28 August. I'm Senior Constable Robert Michael.'

Other police are introduced. Murdoch is again cautioned and is requested to undergo a forensic procedure. Police want a blood sample, penile swab and pubic combing. They warn the procedure is intrusive and that any information might be stored on a national database. Murdoch is asked whether or not he consents. He does not.

Interview suspended.


Senior Constable Michael: The recording equipment has now been activated. The time is 4.45 am on Thursday 29 August.

Police again introduce themselves, along with Whyalla general practitioner, Dr Jerome Connolly. Murdoch repeats that he does not consent. Police remove his handcuffs. He complains his wrist bone 'is that fucking tender in there' from when he was cuffed during his arrest. Asked about general illnesses, Murdoch tells Dr Connolly: 'Suspected diabetes coming on.'

Connolly asks whether Murdoch is a drinker.

Murdoch: 'I don't fucking drink. I'd get pissed as a maggot on one can, but bourbon, I haven't had a drink in a long time.

Connolly: Your teeth. Are they...?

Murdoch: Fucked.

Connolly: You have a few tattoos?

Murdoch: Yeah.

Connolly: How far? Are they all over you?

Murdoch: Oh yeah. Are they going to cause a fucking drama up here? These will give these boys a shake up when I fucking walk into that gaol.

Asked why, Murdoch says he will let his fellow prisoners 'work that one out, the story on my arms'. Asked if he has any tattoos on his legs, Murdoch says no. 'No, just me arms. See these people hanging around?'

The doctor tests Murdoch's lung strength with an oxygen meter. 'A lot of fucking cigarettes pass through there,' says Murdoch.

Told he is to have blood taken, Murdoch responds: 'Like I said, I am against it, but I'm not going to fight it. But my lawyer said to state my case on it that I am against it and through me stating it that I am against it, well, then you cannot use it in court.' Murdoch says that in pre-DNA times police would get an accused person to 'touch something' and, next thing, they'd have a fingerprint and the poor chap was found guilty. 'Now you're talking about DNA,' says Murdoch. 'DNA, all it does is give open slather. Who touches it after it's left here? Too many hands touch it. Not saying anything about these gentlemen here [police] or yourself, who else can get into that locked cupboard and unlock that cupboard? Everybody is supposed to be trusted.'

The doctor notes for the record that raising these concerns about DNA indicates Murdoch is in a state of mental alertness and fully cognisant as to what the procedures are all about. To punch that point home and in order to test 'memory function', Murdoch is once again asked for his birth date. He gives it, adding: 'For being a big surplus boof-headed person with tattoos I'm expected to be a fucking dummy and an idiot.'

Dr Connolly prepares the implements to draw blood, take pubic hair samples and swabs.

Murdoch: I fucking don't like those fucking things you've got in your hands, mate, I don't.

Connolly: I don't want you to get cross with me.

Murdoch: If you're going to grab my arm and stick a fucking needle in it and draw blood out of it, well, I've been told by the lawyer, state that you are not for any of this.

Connolly: Right, so you are not going to get angry with me for taking blood then?

Murdoch: Oh, I'm angry because of that needle. I don't like needles being stuck in me. I don't like junkies, but let what is going to happen fucking take place. Let it take fucking place.

Connolly: That all right?

Murdoch: I'm not going to get angry with you, Doc.

Connolly: Pop this thing around here, just around the arm – you need to stand up. This is just my tourniquet.

Murdoch: Shouldn't need any trouble.

Connolly: Pardon me?

Murdoch: I said you shouldn't need any trouble. I bleed like a fucking stuck pig.

Connolly: Just in case you do bleed, I want to get some tissues.

Murdoch: So what's your Port Augusta jail like, how many blacks in there?

Connolly: Oh, we've got a few.

Murdoch, to the cops: What's the matter, fellas? You've gone all quiet over there.'

Police do not respond.

The doctor has Murdoch raised slightly off the chair as he combs his pubic region, letting the hair fall onto a paper sheet below. The doctor complains that he can't get much of a sample.

Murdoch: Well, there is plenty of pubic hairs down there, down there on the fucking paper, now isn't there?

Connolly swabs Murdoch's penis, which he notes for the record is circumcised.

Murdoch: After all those swabs, *I* will wipe the fucking blower.

Murdoch continues: If I was supposed to have raped somebody, there's no marks [on his penis] whatsoever.

It is noted that Murdoch has 'normal male genitalia' although it is also noted that he shaved around his crotch area and around the back of his legs. Asked about it, Murdoch replies: 'It stops chafing, yeah.'

Connolly concludes the business of sealing and labelling sample containers.

Unsolicited, Murdoch comments: 'Twenty-three years ago at Port Augusta, blood samples in a bottle like that conveniently disappeared for police. Let's see if these ones disappear. Let it be known what I've said. Twenty-three years ago I had a dangerous driving charge, dangerous-driving-cause-death charge, and because I was a fucking boxer in Port Pirie, for fucking Alan Payne's mob, and the local sergeant down there conveniently disappeared [the sample] and I had to fight like hell. Fight you blokes with QC lawyers and I tore you blokes apart in a fucking court case and it fucking broke me, broke my fucking parents but I walked out of there with a dangerous-drive-fucking-cause-death charge and got fucking six months fucking good behaviour bond and that's as much as the fucking judge could fucking give me after a fucking bottle of fucking blood disappeared twenty-three years ago.'

He is referring to the time when he received a sentence of three months' imprisonment, fully suspended, for dangerous driving causing death.

Connolly: Don't lose it, please?

Murdoch: You see what I mean, Doc? You're the first set of hands to touch this [samples]. You see. And where do they go next? They go to this chappy, then to that chappy and then they go out the door and then they go to the next one and the next one.

The session terminates at 5.30 am.

Murdoch made a brief appearance in the Port Augusta magistrates court later that day, charged with two counts of rape, two counts of unlawful detention and offences related to the possession of firearms and a crossbow. Instead of being taken to the Port Augusta prison, as he expected, the following day he was shifted to Adelaide's Yatala prison and remanded in the high-security G Division.

It must have occurred to him that something was up.


By 2002 Frederick Everitt knew he was dying of lung cancer. His loyalties had been with Murdoch, grovellingly so, but not anymore. Not after what Murdoch had done to his de facto and his young stepdaughter. There was nothing stopping him now, not the fear he had of Murdoch, not anything. He was on the way out, fast. He told police everything. He promised to appear as a witness against Murdoch in the rape trial and, after that, he would testify against him over Falconio. Fred Everitt didn't last that long.

As a boy Fred didn't even make it through the first year of high school. He tried out as a jockey but joined the show circuit, manning sideshows and shovelling shit. He punched a bloke and got sent to a boys' home in Gosford, New South Wales. Still in his teens, he began running prostitutes at Kings Cross but was sent to Long Bay jail for living off immoral earnings. After prison he tried to go back to the Cross but was run out of town. Fred got done stealing in Tamworth, copped a suspended sentence, stole again and was sent to Dubbo jail. He headed to Whyalla and worked in the rolling mill, but steel didn't do it for him. He lasted three months before setting a course for Western Australia. He ran out of money on the Nullarbor and headed inland, working on a South Australian sheep station. After a year of that he returned to Whyalla and met his first wife. It probably says something about Fred that one of his two boys from this marriage would grow up to become a copper.

Fred bought the Whyalla Fish Factory, which worked all right for a few years but the marriage did not. He went to Adelaide and bought a brothel and an escort agency. The escort agency was, in his own words, 'a poofter agency'. The brothel was strictly girls. He met 'Laura', his de facto, thirty years younger than him, in that brothel. He was a lousy manager and had a snivelling way about him that some detected as weakness. He got out of town and went up to Swan Reach, inland mulga country, with Laura and her young daughter 'Jane', thinking he could run the businesses from his 86 acres in the bush by installing a manager. He quickly lost both.

In early 2001, 'Ben', who was living in the Swan Reach bush-block area, introduced Fred to another neighbour, a Maori bloke named James Hepi. Hepi's block was right next door to Fred's. Fred could smell money even if it was buried down a goanna hole. Hepi seemed to have lots of it.

Fred worked on Hepi's block, concreting, driving tractors, helping Hepi as he tried to turn his basic sheds into something more liveable. Fred didn't need it explained that Hepi was a drug runner. Ben grew hydro and was one of Hepi's suppliers. Ben was also an amphetamine cook of some note. The atmosphere around these drug dealers was sometimes intense but nothing Fred couldn't handle. He knew jail and he knew brothels from the inside. And then he came to know Brad Murdoch, Hepi's business partner.

Fred first met Murdoch through Ben. They sat around and knocked off a carton. Brad seemed like a good bloke to know, if you could stay on his good side. The sort of guy who wasn't scared of anything much. And Brad invited Fred to assist him in packing up his vehicle with drugs. Up to twenty-five pounds would go into a hidden compartment beneath the long-range diesel tank that sat in the tray just behind the cab of the F100 ute that Murdoch was driving at the time. Murdoch, Fred recalled, switched to a Toyota Land Cruiser in 2001. The F100 sat collecting cobwebs.

Fred Everitt was with Murdoch in early July 2001 when Brad bought a green camper trailer, designed – with its high-off-the-ground axle and big tyres – as a companion to a four-wheel drive. The tray at the back of Brad's cab, as Everitt remembered it, was arranged in such a way so that everything could be stored level, under plywood boards. Fluorescent lights ran along the ceiling. It was covered in tough green canvas. Fred also said he was there in July when Murdoch set off on a drug run to Broome towing that trailer. It was on this same journey that Murdoch was said to have killed Falconio. Fred had no reason to lie about the trailer, even though he never got to say it in court. He was dead by then. And police and prosecutors were perhaps quietly grateful for this because even though Fred was by then no friend of Murdoch's, the fact that he had seen Murdoch heading north with a trailer contradicted two key prosecution points: they would say Murdoch was not towing a trailer, because no trailer was seen in the truck stop video footage, and second, Joanne Lees had never said anything about a trailer.

The problem was compounded by the fact that one of Murdoch's mates, Pete Jamieson, would later claim that Murdoch had, on this same murderous jaunt north, turned up at his service station in Fitzroy Crossing towing the trailer. To those who saw Brad Murdoch as innocent, this trailer was crucial. To others it was a diversion. That Murdoch turned up at the truck stop without it meant nothing; he could have unhitched it, come south to Alice Springs, refuelled, rehitched it north of town and carried on. As to Lees never having seen the trailer, maybe it wasn't there. But even if it had been attached when he hijacked Lees and Falconio, there was no reason she would have seen it in the darkness of that night anyway.

Fred Everitt helped Murdoch pack for his July 2001 trip, yapping and fussing around Murdoch's feet as he pulled out of Swan Reach with Jack, his dog, in the front seat. As a dog, Jack was a disappointment to Murdoch. He wanted a wall-of-teeth protector dog but he knew nothing about animals. He treated it as he might a human, smashing and belting it into submission. The mutt turned cowering and frightened, desperate to be compliant but not knowing how. It was never an issue in court, but it was something people talked about endlessly: how come this dog had failed to track down Lees while she was hiding in the bushes?

Only a highly trained dog would have had the ability to snap into seek mode. All Jack knew was that if he did the wrong thing, he would cop a belting. And even if Jack had been able to set aside his fear and become alert to his surrounds, baying or barking at the woman hiding in the bushes, he would have had to somehow set aside the scent of Peter Falconio's blood, which was all over the road and now clouding and ramming into his every sense, filling his head and diverting his attention from the sheltering Lees. At best, a smart, untrained dog might bark in the direction of a person who was hiding. This dog had no sense at all. He was just sack of spotty confusion that knew the best way to avoid Brad's boot was to do nothing at all. Sometimes even doing nothing was the wrong thing. Jack was so thick and cowed by his conditioning that when a passenger tried to get into the front of Brad's cab, Jack could not be ordered out. He would turn to brick and would have to be physically pushed out of the vehicle. He would not object or snarl, just tumble out and stand perplexed, awaiting new orders to get the fuck into the back.

'Brad would always be armed,' Fred said in his police statements. 'He would always let people know he was armed. I have seen him pull firearms on people. He was armed all the time I knew him – I knew him for about two and a half years. When I first met Brad he had a .22 silver revolver. He carried it in his belt. After some time he bought a shoulder holster

and he carried the .22 in this, I think under his left arm.' Which is the side
Murdoch wore it on when he went into the truck stop after killing Falconio.
Brad was always changing guns. Fred remembered a larger silver revolver,
two Glocks and a rifle. Fred was of the view that when Brad left Hepi's place
in July 2001, he was carrying the silver .22.

Then came the Falconio killing and Brad fell off the radar for a few
months. He didn't come back to Hepi's block and Hepi took over the drug-
running side of things once again. When Murdoch did return to the block
he had a different canopy on the back of his ute. 'Brad seemed to have
changed a bit also,' said Fred. 'When he came back he appeared to be a little
bit different. He was always going on about Barrow Creek, saying things
about crooked cops and that it was a set-up by Hepi. He said to me the best
place to hide a body would be over the cliffs at Eucla, vehicle and all, and
let the sharks have them. Or in the grader run-offs along roads out bush.
He was always denying that it was him in the photo in the paper, the person
at the service station. He always denied he did the murder, saying he was at
Fitzroy Crossing at his mate's garage at the time of the murder. When I first
saw the photo of the person, I thought it was Brad. Though he didn't have
the camper trailer behind the Toyota.'

Later in the year, when Murdoch and Hepi fell out, Murdoch started
avoiding Hepi, hanging out on Fred's block. Murdoch got to know Fred's
missus and kid a bit better. For all Hepi's and Murdoch's strong-man
posturing, privately both were probably happier to avoid each other during
this period than to seek open confrontation. Because if that happened, one
of them would surely have died. Fred was caught between the two warring
big men. Freddy decided Brad was the better option.

Hepi now regarded Everitt as scum. According to Fred, Hepi once
came to Fred's block to borrow a generator which belonged to Murdoch.
Fred, protective, said Hepi shouldn't take Brad's generator. Fred said Hepi
hauled him off to the shed, threatened to cut one of his fingers off with a
pair of secateurs and smacked him about the head. Hepi told a different
story. He learned, some two years after the event, that Fred had come to

his house while he was in New Zealand and stolen his slow-combustion fireplace, smoke-stack and all, leaving a gaping hole in Hepi's roof. Hepi found this out from a young man who had helped Fred do it. But Hepi agreed with one aspect of the story: yes, he did drag Fred Everitt off to the shed and threaten to remove his fingers with secateurs.

Fred had backed the wrong man. Initially he took a bit of convincing from his wife and stepdaughter as to what Murdoch had done to them sexually. After all, were they really thinking this through? Instead of going to the cops, what about the media? Why didn't they go straight to Ray Martin and spin them this Falconio angle? Those people paid! But as his last decent act, dying Fred Everitt finally got up the courage to talk to the police about Murdoch and 'the atrocities he done here at Swan Reach with my daughter and wife'.

Murdoch had come to know Everitt courtesy of his relationship with Hepi. Like everyone else, the Everitts trucked in their water to fill their tanks. The pool in the backyard was a previous owner's bad joke – it was never any more than a green half-full idea. It was too costly to fill and maintain a pool in this country. Power came from the generator in the shed. The child Jane first met Murdoch in early 2001. He was friendly to her, always saying how she looked nice in whatever dress she was wearing. He'd come from behind and touch her on the shoulder. He usually did it out of sight of Mum and Fred, but that was all right – he was a family friend. Jane came to know that Brad and James Hepi had fallen out. It was over money, she thought. Whenever Hepi's name came up, Brad would darken and say that Hepi and some dirty judge over in Western Australia had set him up for the Falconio business. Brad told Jane that he was wanted for questioning over Falconio. In fact, Murdoch wasn't wanted for questioning at this stage, otherwise, police would have just questioned him. It was all in his head, and with good reason.

Jane noticed there was a two-way radio set tuned to channel 40 in Brad's Land Cruiser ute. Not that it was of any consequence. The guy was a road man who liked to keep in touch with the truckies. And liked to plan for every contingency. He had white PVC pipes running under the car in which he stored rainwater, in case he ever ran out. Brad was a real bush wanker.

Jane tried to play with Jack, the dog, but Murdoch didn't like that. Jack didn't need kindness. It would interfere with the dog's already messed-up psyche. Jane saw him thrash the creature with brooms or simply punch it out. Jack was pathetic.

Murdoch told Jane he'd once fired off a hundred and fifty rounds of ammunition at a group of Aborigines, saying he'd missed them on purpose. Aborigines were pretty much considered vermin around Swan Reach, so it wasn't as if the KKK tatts on Murdoch's arms bothered Jane's parents, let alone their daughter. They had no issue with the sentiment. It was just a rather more forceful statement than most would bother committing to. Jane didn't know what to make of the tattoo on his left arm, an Aborigine being lynched from a tree, with flames licking at his dangling feet. On his right arm was a corresponding tattoo of a Ku Klux Klansman pointing at the lynch scene. Murdoch's full sleeve tatts included what he called 'a garden of skulls' on his right arm and an evil-looking clown.

Murdoch liked to impress Jane with his toys, which included pistols, his night-vision goggles, rifles, his crossbow and an array of knives, both folding and fixed-blade. He also had a curious tool which seemed to be some sort of listening device. He explained to her how he could conceal the bug in a pot plant, trail a wire up to a kilometre away and listen in to people's conversations through what looked, to her, like a small radio.

Murdoch, who once gave Jane $500 for her birthday, always seemed to have cash in his pockets. He'd only ever stay a few days at a time, usually in the other house on their block – a broken down fibro job away from the main house and sheds. In mid-August 2002, Jane went down to the house to say hello and found the doors and windows covered in sheets of black plastic. Brad's Land Cruiser was reverse-parked in the shed with a green tarpaulin covering it, almost like he was trying to conceal the vehicle. Brad was always a bit mysterious, so she thought nothing of it. And there were bigger things happening – Fred, her stepdad, had taken a turn for the worse. He was on the way out and had been admitted to hospital in Adelaide.

When Jane and her mum got back from Adelaide a few days later, Brad was there. Jane was doing her homework when Brad came in and asked her if she'd come to the other house, the fibro shack, and help him unpack his shopping. The lights were on and Brad had lit a fire. He was standing in the kitchen cutting medical tape into strips. He did not respond when she asked what he was doing. When Jane asked why he had covered the shack in black plastic, he said it was so people couldn't see him with their spotlights. For Brad, that meant spotlights attached to helicopter gunships.

Brad's shopping was standard road stuff – baked beans, tuna, tinned spaghetti, long-life milk, sugar, tea, biscuits and a bottle of Jim Beam. Murdoch was wearing a black t-shirt with a glow-in-the-dark skeleton and 'Kununurra' stamped on the sleeve. He started rambling: 'I was wearing that t-shirt the night I pulled into the roadhouse. My mate owned the servo so I stayed at the servo that night then travelled the next morning. So how could I have killed Peter Falconio?' Jane went home to bed.

It had been just over a year since Murdoch had killed Falconio. He had gotten away with it, so far. He knew Hepi had been arrested, because he had dobbed him in. He had admitted as much to some other people he knew in the area, old family friends from Western Australia who had moved to South Australia. That was the Kotz family. In between drug runs, Murdoch was cannibalising Toyotas and helping young Ben Kotz rebuild a Land Cruiser trayback out of partially stolen parts. Ben Kotz said Murdoch came over to see him and his mum sometime in the middle of 2002. 'He was pretty distraught and said that he'd done something wrong and that he'd dobbed in his Kiwi mate.'

Murdoch fully expected Hepi to strike back, fingering him for the Falconio crime. But there was now plenty of distance between himself and the crime and besides, he could always turn it around and say it was Hepi who did Falconio. And Murdoch had overestimated the curiosity of the Northern Territory police, who stubbornly, stupidly, and tragically for Jane and Laura, failed to act. Murdoch was more free than he knew but was anticipating his arrest at any time. He had some things to do before that happened. That included shooting himself.

The next day Jane and her mum rang the hospital to see if Fred could come home. The hospital said no. They baked cakes. Packet mix. Laura knocked back a few cans of Jim Beam and coke. Brad came up that evening, a Wednesday, asking Jane to come to his house to help him sort out some maps. By 9 pm Jane was becoming tired. She said she wanted to go home. Murdoch turned nasty, fast, and ordered the little girl to sit still. He grabbed a pair of silver handcuffs from a backpack nearby and tried to put them on her. She struggled as he yelled at her to stay still and to shut up. He wrapped her eyes in what she thought was a wool-covered length of seatbelt and stuffed, she thought, cotton wool in her ears. She was pushed into the blackened bedroom, face down onto the bed and cuffed. The tape she had seen Murdoch cutting up in the kitchen went round her mouth and head.

Murdoch undressed the twelve-year-old girl and said to her: 'If you move I will give you brain damage.' The child was raped. She was shackled by the ankles and hog-tied with a chain that led from her handcuffs to her ankles, like a Guantanamo Bay prisoner. Jane lay there for an hour and a half. She felt a breeze crossing her body, as though a window had been opened. She started playing with a button device on the handcuffs and the left cuff sprang open. She did the same to the right. Murdoch hadn't used a key to override the release mechanism. She saw a fraction of hope but there was no scriptwriter on standby to help her escape. Murdoch, prowling the house, yelled: 'Oi! What are you doing?' He used heavy tape to cover the release mechanism and then dressed Jane, messily, her knickers on the outside of her stockings.

The girl was lifted into the back of Murdoch's Land Cruiser and chained, by the wrists, to a steel rung. Dazed, she saw her mother being rolled into the back of the tray alongside her.

Laura never liked Murdoch from the start. She had him pegged as a dangerous thug. He was Fred's mate and Fred was a pimp. Laura was working at Fred's brothel, 'Girls, Ladies, Girls', in Adelaide when they fell into a relationship. She didn't even like Fred. She was just going through the motions. All she knew was that she'd put out for her country and had nothing to show for it. Just a deadshit de facto husband and weasel companion, Freddy Everitt.

Laura had never really noticed Murdoch's missing front teeth, maybe because he didn't lisp. And the gunslinger moustache tended to conceal his black-scar mouth. What she did notice was that Brad tended to speak very deliberately – a small intake of breath, a pause before he spoke, as if he was collecting himself.

Laura wasn't in on the Hepi–Murdoch drug trade, but she knew about it. Fred, though never a long-haul man himself, was the beneficiary of a minor largesse that bought his silence and loyalty – beer, well-paid jobs, tax-free cash handouts and being in the rarefied company of big men. Being mates with Murdoch and Hepi put a spring in Fred's step when he walked into town. He was directly connected to the drug coven that operated in the backblocks of Swan Reach. Fred felt privileged and protected.

With all Murdoch's visible paraphernalia – his small-time weapons of war, his unkissable mouth, his self-important monologue – he wouldn't have seemed much of a catch. Yet there were a couple of women who hung around. Brad didn't take them to dinner. He chopped them up big lines of speed, saying, 'Get this into ya.' And there were endless joints to take the edge off the speed. When you've had enough of that, any bloke can seem just about passable.

When they were all still friends, the nights at Laura and Fred's place, and over at Hepi's, were long, pissy and drug-filled. She didn't like what her daughter was seeing. Of course, she didn't have to involve her daughter, but she did. Murdoch, who would tell police he was a non-drinker, just as a throwaway lie, usually drank port, Jim Beam and mid-strength beer. He'd mix his speed into whatever he was drinking.

On one of these nights, Brad got chatty, telling of a son he'd left behind when the boy was only small. He guessed he was now about seventeen – he hadn't seen him for twelve years. He once showed Laura photos of himself as a long-haired, bearded Gypsy Joker. Murdoch told Laura that his wife had suddenly got religion and had ordered him to leave the Jokers. He did so on the condition she leave religion, which she didn't. They left each other.

Talk of guns littered Hepi's and Murdoch's conversations. Laura came to know that Hepi kept a pistol strapped beneath his kitchen table with silver tape and Murdoch wasn't shy about walking around with a holster outside his t-shirt. She didn't know whether Hepi and Murdoch were expecting trouble or were just being tough guys.

She was not sure what had come between Hepi and Murdoch but knew things had started to go seriously wrong sometime around the beginning of 2002. Fred, with his loyalties to Murdoch, became scared of Hepi. Murdoch loaned Fred a revolver and a holster to protect himself from Hepi. Fred fired a few practice rounds but otherwise kept the thing under his bed, to be used only in case of emergency.

As Murdoch and Hepi fell apart, Fred grew closer to Murdoch. Laura was not included in their discussions but she knew it was all about drugs. She noticed that Murdoch, who had always been polite, began to lose his gentlemanly edge, treating her with mild contempt.

Laura didn't like what was happening but at least Fred wasn't bashing her anymore. He'd stopped all that when he found out he had cancer two years earlier. Still, she thought him a coward and would have left him if they had not signed a joint mortgage on their bush block. She had just wanted a place with her daughter and animals. Fred was the price. Fred, who'd always had cash in his brothel days, saw Murdoch as his final chance at money. When Murdoch was around, Fred began to speak to Laura as though she was a dog. 'Fucking pick that off the floor,' he'd tell her. Laura would tell him to fuck off; she knew he was only doing it to impress Murdoch. But she always ended up doing what she was told because it was easier than having Fred whingeing and yelling at her all day. Murdoch took Fred's lead, at least in respect of how he spoke to Laura.

Murdoch began standing close to Laura, or staring at her with his green eyes creeping her out. He didn't like her but she had those fabulous trophy tits, which Murdoch could not help wanting to touch. Once, with Fred out of earshot, Murdoch told Laura he 'needed some action down below' and stared down at his crotch.

Laura had stopped having sex with Fred altogether. The arguing during the day did not lend itself to affection at night. But there was something weird going on with Fred and Brad. Laura wondered if there was something sexual between them. It was the way Fred and Murdoch had spent four days holed up together in the other house. When Murdoch finally left, Fred burst into tears. Laura didn't dare ask him what was wrong because she felt sure she'd get a punch in the head. Maybe Fred was just feeling fragile after a bender on the speed.

When she was feeling brave, Laura would stir Fred about Murdoch. She told him how it was weird that Murdoch didn't have any hair on his arms or legs. A bit unmanly, a tough guy shaving himself like that, wasn't it? Fred got defensive, saying he didn't think it was weird. Murdoch was always taking speed and offering it to Laura. She didn't mind taking free dope but speed wasn't her thing. Fred was such a simpering crawler that he accused Laura of being rude for not taking what Murdoch offered her. Laura's feelings for Fred turned to hate.

Things got weirder. Murdoch would talk about how he'd wander in the night and hide up on the hill behind the Swan Reach pub, spying on the drinkers with his night-vision goggles. What was happening in this pub, according to Murdoch's dissolving reality? Cops and bikies drinking together, along with every whore he'd ever visited, not to mention pissed judges who couldn't wait for Murdoch to be tried in their courts, the whole lot of them in hysterics at Murdoch's expense and plotting his downfall through the joyful hysteria of clinking beer glasses. Everyone was out to get him.

Murdoch was losing it. And Laura had been slowly piecing together things about Murdoch. She remembered he'd left Swan Reach a day or two before the Falconio disappearance. On the day he left, Murdoch was making chains out of black cable ties, looping them together and testing them for strength. He didn't say why and she didn't ask. Fred had been helping Murdoch pack up his Land Cruiser for the trip to Broome. Afterwards, Fred told Laura to clean up after Brad. That meant going into the shed with a broom and dustpan and shovel. As usual, she complained but complied. Bits of tape, part of his cable-tie handcuffs, went into the dustpan and were burned in a hole in the ground along with the rest of the rubbish he'd left behind.

From the moment Laura saw the first images of Truck Stop Man, she knew it was Murdoch. The only thing that bothered her was that the pictures showed him in a baseball cap. She'd never seen him wear one before. He was a cowboy hat man. And sometimes when those searing summer days got the better of him, he'd even go for a white terry-towelling hat. Fred told Laura, 'Nah, it wouldn't be him.' She never discussed going to the police with Fred. Fred wouldn't have liked it.

In the months after the Falconio killing, James Hepi started doing the drug runs in Murdoch's place. Murdoch had dropped weight and was stressed and paranoid, saying the cops were trying to frame him for Falconio. When Laura got Fred alone and asked him about Falconio, it seemed as if Fred was no longer so sure about Brad. Fred warned Laura not to upset him because he was possibly dangerous. Murdoch told Laura and Fred he'd stolen Hepi's money – a lot, $150000 or $180000 – along with pearls that Hepi had hidden on his block. This, Murdoch told them, was his revenge for Hepi setting him up for the Falconio killing.

Murdoch had moved his belongings into the shack at Fred and Laura's and had given up travelling to Broome. He was now openly rude to Laura, treating her as Fred's hag. She told him to piss off. He moved out to a shed in Port Broughton, south of Port Augusta in the Spencer Gulf. Fred kept on ringing Murdoch, apologising for Laura, telling him he was welcome back at any time, but Murdoch only stayed at the block now and then, a few nights at a time. Hostilities with Laura increased. And Murdoch seemed to be going mad. He claimed that whenever Laura opened a beer, the sound of the can being opened was likely to bring the police to the block. Again, she told him to piss off. Murdoch lost it with her, got in his now rarely used

F100 ute and tore around the block smashing bottles and doing doughnuts. Fred tried to get it into Laura's head that the real person to worry about was Hepi. He gave her Murdoch's mobile number. If Hepi ever showed up, she was to ring Murdoch immediately and he would come around and shoot him.

Murdoch lost a lot of income when he fell out with Hepi. He was using trucking companies to shift his dope to Broome, weekly, in ten to twelve pound lots. He still had the potential to make $10 000 every week. Laura never knew exactly how involved Fred was, except that she believed he was helping Murdoch package the dope in Murdoch's rented shed at Port Broughton.

By mid-August 2002, Murdoch still came by, but less and less often. This made him, to Laura, passingly acceptable. As for Fred, fluid was building up around his heart and his system was beginning to shut down. After taking Fred to hospital on 21 August 2002, Laura and Jane returned to the block. Brad was there. With Fred out of the way, Brad didn't have much to say to Laura. She wasn't overly worried when Jane said she was going off to help Brad over at the shack. No matter how he'd treated Laura, he'd always been good to Jane. And besides, Laura was pissed. She crashed early, falling asleep on the couch while watching a gardening show on TV.

Laura awoke at about 3.30 am to hear the generator was still running. She checked Jane's bed – empty. As she went to have a look outside Murdoch came through the doorway wearing his holster. He did not respond when she asked where Jane was. He ordered her to change into warm clothes and walked her outside under a full moon, pistol now in his right hand, telling her she was a fucking bitch. She was led to the side of Murdoch's Land Cruiser and noticed he had his camper trailer on the back. Then she saw her daughter in the back, chained, mouth gagged with lambswool and medical tape, white with terror. Murdoch told Laura if she did not get into the back of his vehicle he would shoot her. She was having trouble getting in the cab so Murdoch gave her a shove. She saw chains hanging from the canopy. Murdoch handcuffed Laura to one of the chains and blindfolded her.

He told her that she didn't need to know where they were going – just that he was using them as insurance if the cops caught up with him. He zipped up the canopy of the tray and everything went dark.

As with Jane, Murdoch hadn't used a key on Laura's cuffs and she was able to slip her hands free and unwrap the tape from around her daughter's mouth. Jane told her mum she'd been raped. They were driving, somewhere, on bitumen and dirt. They went a long way, hours maybe. Jane was thirsty. Laura found a light switch, turned on a fluorescent light, found some long-life milk and gave it to Jane. She undid the restraints around her daughter's ankles. She had her Winfield rollies so she smoked. When Murdoch pulled over she saw dawn's first light through a vent in the canopy. She heard what she thought was Murdoch changing his number plates. They drove again, this time not far, on bitumen and down a dirt track. They stopped and Murdoch allowed them out for a toilet break, seemingly unconcerned that each had escaped the cuffs. There was no thought of running – each had to go separately, and alone. He then resecured mother and daughter in his specialty handcuffs made from black cable ties.

They drove again, Laura biting at the black cables, trying to chew through them, but this only caused them to tighten. Murdoch parked in some sort of limestone pit off the side of a track. Laura saw stacks of discarded tyres. He snipped free their cable ties, inviting Laura to run so he could shoot her in the back. As he cut Laura loose, she noticed his hands were shaking.

Murdoch smoked pot from a short straight-through pipe and seemed to calm down. He gave Jane a drink of water and made Laura a cup of coffee. He'd set up the camper trailer into a tent and arranged a bed for Jane to lie on. He began rifling through a bag of chains. Jane was told to come over to the car, where Murdoch began locking her wrists together, closing the links with a claw hammer. Laura, sitting in a folding chair, told Murdoch: 'You are fucking pathetic tying up a twelve-year-old when you have a gun.' Murdoch delivered a full-bottled slap to her face, knocking her back into her chair. Laura was shown a rifle with a telescopic sight and another large black pistol, different to the one in his holster. And a knife. Then he produced a cattle prod and sat for a while sanding its probes and testing its effectiveness against lengths of chain. Fleetwood Mac and Credence Clearwater Revival were mumbling out of the Toyota cabin as morning turned to midday.

'You were in the wrong place at the wrong time,' he told Laura by way of explanation for his actions. 'Everyone's using me for my money. I didn't do that Falconio guy, I didn't kill him. I know people in high places and I can do what I want.'

Murdoch blamed Laura for letting Jane get near him. 'That was your fault because you fell asleep and you shouldn't have let her come up in the evening and talk to me.'

'We trusted you like a friend,' Laura told him.

'Now you know, you don't trust anyone, whether it's me or anyone. Life's a bitch, isn't it?'

'I thought we were friends.'

'I've got no friends.'

Murdoch accused Laura of being involved in setting him up, claiming she'd let someone onto her property to snoop around when he was out. She had no idea what he was talking about. Murdoch told Laura that it was all coming to an end for him. 'I've been taking speed for about fifteen years,' he said. 'I've got a worn-out heart and a hernia. I don't want to live anymore. I'm going over to Western Australia to kill James Hepi and a couple of Coffin Cheaters and then I'm going to shoot myself in the head. I'm putting the rifle in the front. If any cop pulls me over, I'll just shoot them.'

He claimed it was all his ex-wife's fault – and God's. He said that when his wife turned to religion, it turned his life inside out. He said he hated religion, but didn't say why. Murdoch chopped himself two good lines of speed and snorted them – not his usual method. Jane was ordered into the front of the Land Cruiser, told to turn the music up loud and to stay there. Laura was chained to the fold-up chair. He laughed at her, saying: 'Now you can't go anywhere, can you?'

Murdoch grabbed at Laura's top and hauled it back over her head so her breasts were exposed. He grabbed a bottle of moisturiser and rubbed it over her, then disappeared for a moment. He returned, showing her the cattle prod. Laura began to scream and Jane, looking out of the cabin window, started to cry. Murdoch blinded Laura with a pair of black pantyhose and offered his victims an option: 'I want to have sex. Which one of you is going to be doing it?'

'I'll do it,' said Laura. Murdoch began running his hands over her breasts. The blindfold exacerbated her terror. She didn't know what the freak was going to do next. She was already hurting from the swipe to her left eye socket. She began to think about her death, wondering if she'd know when it was coming. She decided to risk getting angry: 'Go and fucking pay for it,' she told him. 'Take off my blindfold, please.'

Murdoch: 'I don't want to go to a brothel.'

Murdoch pulled off her skirt, underpants and blindfold. He attempted to have intercourse but after days on the gear, he couldn't get it up. He seemed embarrassed about this and turned his back on Laura to work on himself. Still nothing. Frustrated, he walked off to snort more speed. The sexual tension died in the roadside camp. By mid-afternoon, he was sulking. 'I've got no friends,' he told Laura. 'Everyone is against me, my family is against me. I've got no life at the moment, I'm always on the run. The coppers have framed me for this Falconio murder.'

August in South Australia is cold, day or night. Sometimes bitterly so. Murdoch produced a bag of Jane's and Laura's unwanted clothes that had been sitting out in the shack waiting for a Salvo drop. At about 9.30 pm, he began packing up and tried to explain to Laura the benefits of what had just happened to her and her daughter: 'You will make money out of this if you go to the media,' he said. 'From this day you are going to make a nice dollar out of this.'

'I thought you were going to kill us,' Laura said.

'No, I'm not. Why on earth would I want to hurt you and Jane?' He wasn't such a bad bloke after all. 'I'll drive you to Port Augusta, give you some money for a taxi and you are to go straight home, not to the police. I'll be watching you. If you get the police, I'll use the rifle on you. I can see 500 metres with the rifle.'

They drove. Murdoch pulled in to a service station on the north side of Port Augusta. Over a day and a half they'd travelled 300 kilometres to the northwest of Swan Reach and, true to his word, he dropped them off at the Shell servo and filled their hands with cash. Laura and Jane walked in, Laura showed the guy behind the counter her wrists, still bandaged in medical tape, and said she needed a phone. He didn't like it. He ordered her down the road to the public phone. Laura rang Fred, in hospital, who told her to get in a cab and come to the hospital. It did not occur to Fred that a police station was the more appropriate option. Laura tried to call a taxi but the phone was jamming and she couldn't get through. She and Jane walked back to the service station and this time the attendant reluctantly allowed them to call a cab.

The cab driver wanted his money upfront – $350 for the 300-kilometre drive south to Royal Adelaide Hospital. Laura tried to tell him what had happened but he wasn't too interested. Neither was Fred, not at first. When he was told about the rape his advice to his loved ones was to destroy their clothes, stained with Murdoch's incriminating semen. He had to think of himself, where he fitted in with Brad and what all of this might mean, and whether what had happened could be used to his advantage. Fred was terrified of Murdoch. But his main fear was that if Laura and Jane complained to police, Fred might lose the money Murdoch drip-fed him as payment for helping him package and ship his marijuana. 'They were living in absolute … fear. And I hope it is fear that killed Fred Everitt,' said Hepi. 'He was a rotten piece of work. The world's better without him.'

Still, that stuff about Jane, that sounded a bit rough. But no need to go to the police, not yet. Fred called Dags – Darryl Cragan. Like Freddy, Dags was a thief. He was also starting to have his doubts about Murdoch's sanity.

Freddy was discharged from Royal Adelaide on the morning of Friday 23 August. He, Laura and Jane got a lift back to Swan Reach with Dags. By then Dags had figured Murdoch was dangerous and his time with the big man was surely coming to an end. From Swan Reach, Dags drove them to a caravan park to hide out from Murdoch and think things over.

Dags was just as bad as Everitt – he only saw opportunity arising from the rapes. If his old mate Brad was to be arrested, Brad's money and possessions would be of no use to him in jail. Dags wanted to fleece Murdoch. There was no loyalty in this crew. They were so stupid. On the advice of Dags and Freddy, Laura threw the clothes Jane was wearing during the rape into a bin. Why? Probably to keep the kid out of it. Rape was adult business. Fred's advice was that they should just sit it out, listen to the radio news, wait to hear if Murdoch had kept his word and gone and done something shocking in Western Australia. It would be five days before Laura finally got Fred to agree they should go to the police. This, along with Laura's lies, would damage them fatally in the eyes of the jury.

Stupidly, when they finally gave their statements to police, Laura and Jane, as per instruction, didn't mention anything about Dags. They lied about him through omission, but later, even from jail, Murdoch had his feelers out and learned that Dags had ripped him off. Grant Algie, Murdoch's barrister, found out about it and put it to Laura, cold, on the witness stand. She stammered and admitted that Cragan had been present at the immediate post-rape scene. Why hadn't she mentioned Darryl Cragan before? She could not explain it. The truth was that she was to get kickbacks from whatever Cragan could find, and sell, of Murdoch's belongings.

In January 2003, Murdoch pleaded not guilty to two counts of rape, two counts of false imprisonment, two counts of indecent assault and one of common assault. Laura had injuries consistent with a sexual assault, but Jane refused to submit to medical examination. To the jury, the whole thing sounded implausible. They were living in a drug-tainted world, they were thieving from the accused, the so-called victims were pretty rough around the edges, and Murdoch's lawyer was banging on and on about how his client was being set up for the Falconio murder. And that was the only reason the media was in court – to link this to the outback killer. And why would Murdoch drop them at a roadhouse after raping them? It was a vendetta, nothing less.

Murdoch walked. But not far. Straight into the arms of South Australian police, who held him on behalf of Northern Territory police for the murder of Peter Marco Falconio. Grant Algie, for Murdoch, said the jury's verdict confirmed that Murdoch had been set up and was being framed for Falconio's killing.

# 9  THE ANSELL FACTOR

It is possible to get a clear idea of what speed was doing to Murdoch's head. Rodney Ansell, another Territory killer, provided the template. Ansell was shot dead by Northern Territory first-class Senior Constable Jamie O'Brien after Ansell had taken another officer's life on 3 August 1999. Ansell had crept up on a highway roadblock and snipered Sergeant Glen Huitson, a husband and father of two young children.

Ansell had always believed that John Cornell and Paul Hogan based their *Crocodile Dundee* film series on him. Like Hogan, Ansell was blond and handsome and had become a nationally known bush celebrity, long before crocodile man Steve Irwin invented himself. It was when English interviewer Michael Parkinson invited Ansell to Sydney to discuss his exploits that the Crocodile Dundee mythology really began. Ansell had reputedly refused to sleep in his bed at the Sebel Townhouse, preferring to unroll his swag on the floor. Like Paul Hogan's character Mick Dundee, Ansell professed not to know what a bidet was. Hogan's management later admitted the idea for the film – bushman Ansell in the big smoke – had come from the Parkinson interview. Ansell unsuccessfully demanded a royalty cut from Hogan's management. Still, it led to him – the 'real' Crocodile Dundee – taking talk-show tours of the United States, recounting his buffalo-catching, crocodile-taming exploits. But it wasn't a living. He tried to enter politics and failed at preselection, and he'd lost his cattle property largely due to his own neglect. That was years ago.

Now, totally wired and believing the government and police were out to get him, Ansell, 46, had hooked up with Cherie Hewson, a woman who, Ansell told friends, had a lot of bad stuff in her head and was intermittently suicidal. He claimed he was helping her recover repressed memories, but in the process he'd unlocked something else entirely.

Ansell survived out bush by growing drugs and later started to take speed in payment for marijuana. It was turning him inside out. When Ansell and Hewson left their bush camp at Urapunga, on the Roper River in southern Arnhem Land, to drive north to Darwin in August 1999, Ansell's mission was probably not of murderous intent – it just turned out that way. Hewson later said she and Ansell had been up for three days without sleep. Ansell believed Freemasons were trying to kill his sons. They were disguised as bow-hunters and wore night-vision goggles. They were circling his bush camp. They forced Ansell and Hewson to retreat to a nearby Aboriginal community for shelter.

Hewson seems to have unleashed the freemason angle during the memory-retrieval sessions. The twenty-nine year old had met Ansell three years earlier after she responded to his ad for someone to help him break horses. Territory policeman Stan Fensom, who interviewed Hewson in Brisbane several days after Ansell's rampage, found a woman who had gone totally wrong.

Hewson told Fensom she had come from a family of Freemasons in Warragul, Victoria. She had ceased contact with them and was now planning to expose them. Hewson said there were 'Freemason holes' everywhere in Australia; her whole family was involved. Asked why she was trying to get away from them, Hewson said: 'Because I didn't want to be a Freemason anymore, and be involved in sacrificing people, and killing people. Especially children.'

Officer Fensom: 'Have you ever sacrificed or killed children?'

Hewson: 'Yes.' She said she had been initiated into the cult at the age of eight. 'They take you to a Freemasons hall, and they make you watch a sacrifice and drink blood, and on penalty of death swear an oath,' she said.

Fensom: 'A sacrifice of who?'

Hewson: 'A young girl.'

Fensom: 'And how did they sacrifice a young girl?'

Hewson: 'They slit her neck. She's bound down to like an altar, and she's raped, and then they slit her neck, and they put it into a cup and other children are given it to drink.'

Fensom: 'And you drank?'

Hewson: 'Yep.'

There were bow-hunters operating near Urapunga; but they were common pig hunters, nothing more. According to Hewson, Ansell's two teenage sons, Sean and Callum, were staying at their dad's bush camp at the time. When word came through about the hunters, Ansell believed they would get at him by killing Sean and Callum. Ansell sent Sean to find Callum, who had driven to the local store. While Sean was looking for Callum, Ansell became convinced the boys had been captured and taken to Darwin. Ansell and Hewson left their bush camp and headed for Darwin, 600 kilometres away, to save them.

In Darwin, they stopped at several friends' houses and asked to borrow vehicles; they wanted to search for the boys in a car that the Freemasons would not recognise. In each instance, the friends refused. They went to the house of Geoffrey Stewart, a medical practitioner and friend of Ansell's. Finding no one home, they broke in. Hewson took a drink of water out of the fridge and said she felt odd soon after. Ansell drank some milk and concluded it was drugged. They borrowed two medical kits, hoping they might find Sean and Callum still alive after having been tortured by the Freemasons.

Their next stop was the residence of an acquaintance, Steven Robinson, and his partner, Lee-Ann Musgrave, who were caretaking a block off the Stuart Highway, near Kentish Road, some 50 kilometres south of Darwin. Ansell was disturbed to see a large grey van parked 300 metres back from the property. He told Hewson it was occupied by Freemasons. While warning Robinson and Musgrave of the peril, they ate some food and drank some Coke, which they also decided was drugged.

Ansell snuck outside with his 30/30 lever action to check out the van and returned, pleading with Robinson to leave the area, which was now thoroughly infected with Freemasons. Robinson, while shaken, stayed. Ansell and Hewson drove off and began arguing, Ansell claiming he had to go back and protect Robinson and Musgrave. He left Hewson in the car, travelling back on foot. Robinson – and Hewson, parked up the road – heard six shots ring out.

Hewson, in a fit of clarity, realised things were spinning out of control. She drove south to Acacia, hitched a ride to Queensland and never saw her boyfriend again. Meanwhile Ansell was concentrating on the grey van. At least one of his rounds hit the vehicle. After that, walking shoeless in the scrub, he travelled west of the highway along Kentish Road.

Brian Williams and his wife were in bed at home on Kentish Road when they heard two loud shots. Their neighbour, David Hobden, heard the shots as well. Hobden grabbed a shotgun and drove his truck next door to see if his neighbours were all right. While Hobden was driving along Kentish Road, a bullet smashed his truck's windscreen, a shard of glass instantly blinding him in the right eye. He 'sort of half-crawled' towards the Williams' house. Ansell appeared and jumped in the truck; but now Williams was on the scene as well, and furious at what had happened to his bloodied neighbour. He picked up a baseball bat and charged at the truck cabin.

'That's when he blew my hand off,' said Williams. Ansell knew neither Williams nor Hobden, and it is not clear why he targeted that area.

Ansell bolted and stayed low. Coppers were spread out everywhere in the area, using night-vision goggles and often just sitting, staring into the bush, watching for any movement. Ansell wasn't seen again until 10.30 am, when he opened fire with his 30/30 on a police roadblock manned by Huitson and Jamie O'Brien, who had driven up from their Adelaide River station to assist Darwin police. Ansell first snipered a citizen who was standing at the roadblock talking to the police. He took a shot in the backside. He would survive to make a near-full recovery. Huitson, thirty-nine, was fatally wounded.

O'Brien stayed with the injured men, frantically reloading and returning steady fire to keep Ansell, now wriggling forward to the roadblock, from taking potshots at the wounded men lying exposed at the roadblock. The only words O'Brien could discern from Ansell during those terrifying few minutes, were: 'You're all dead.'

O'Brien was only able to get a clear shot at Ansell when the police Tactical Response Group came tearing down the highway in two Toyota troop carriers, one of which clipped the other, causing it to roll. As the TRG jumped out of their vehicles, they still couldn't see Ansell and were calling to O'Brien to point him out. At that moment, Ansell, leopard-crawling through the dirt – throwing his shotgun and 30/30 ahead of him and scrabbling forward on his elbows, military-style – raised himself to fire on the TRG men. He exposed himself for the first time. O'Brien shot him dead. One policeman who stared at Ansell's corpse said he looked at 'the most miserable, pathetic creature I've ever seen'. Ansell was barefoot, skinny and grimy from days of madness.

A year or so later, O'Brien was promoted to sergeant. He told me, upon receiving a bravery award: 'I haven't really spoken a lot about what happened on the day. It's not really nice. Once that civilian was injured, he and his friend became the responsibility of Glen and me. We weren't in a position where we could retreat. We had to stay there and help the injured civilian.' That cost Huitson his life. He'd caught a bullet in the abdomen, just below his protective armour.

'Once Glen was injured as well – I didn't realise it was a fatal wound at the time, he was lying on the ground, not moving much – it was a very dangerous situation for him because he could be seen under the vehicle by Ansell. That made it absolutely out of the question that I could leave the area. I had to stay there for the duration and try and deal with things as best I could.' It was brave work.

Ansell's doctor friend, Stewart, later said the speed had gotten to Ansell: 'Within the last couple of months and that time that I spent with him recently, I sort of had some concerns, well firstly you know that he was using a lot of speed, and that I'd seen a gradual deterioration in his personality.'

Assistant Crime Commissioner John Daulby said at the time it would be speculation to say Ansell had shown he wanted to die by approaching the roadblock, but he added: 'He could have escaped – he chose not to do that.'

The circumstances were different but Ansell and Murdoch were alike in one regard: chronically overmedicated on speed, they believed they were the last righteous men on earth.

# 10  NORTH, SOUTH AND IN-BETWEEN

Two big men – both of them West Australians, both with a passion for guns, both raised in the sticks of the state, both strongly disinclined to take shit from anyone – arrived at Darwin airport two days apart. Warren Anderson came first, on 12 November 2003, and walked straight into an ambush. The media happened to be gathered in number, awaiting the arrival of Brad Murdoch from South Australia, who was expected at any time. On leaving the courtroom after being acquitted in his South Australian trial, Murdoch told the assembled media to report the truth of his acquittal and to fuck off, then grimaced as his hands were cuffed behind his back. He was taken directly back to a police cell in preparation for being bundled north to face proceedings over Peter Falconio and Joanne Lees. His arrival in Darwin had been temporarily delayed as his lawyers complained, futilely, that the manner of his arrest was illegal.

Anderson had purportedly come up to execute some animals. Or so the Northern Territory government took delight in telling the assembled media. Most of the reporters knew little about Anderson. He was only an occasional name these days, and his CV was not the sort of thing the mostly young reporters could quickly call to mind. They just knew that he was big, brash and rich and that whenever he spoke or moved, there was a chance of a story. And now that Murdoch's arrival had been delayed, the government's media people were happy to brief reporters on how Anderson, who owned a fleet of African animals on Tipperary station south of Darwin, was to these creatures what Pol Pot had been to Cambodia. The government reckoned it had spent $70000 of taxpayers' money feeding the animals because Anderson refused to.

Mark Colvin, presenter of ABC's *PM* radio current affairs program:

There were bizarre scenes at Darwin airport today when the millionaire property developer, Warren Anderson, arrived from Perth, amid reports that he was planning to shoot hundreds of rare and exotic animals at his private zoo on the remote Tipperary station. The Northern Territory Government was forced to feed the animals over a month ago, after Warren Anderson handed the station to new owners and the animal feed ran out. The Government has since sent Mr Anderson a hefty bill, and today the Supreme Court granted an urgent injunction prohibiting him from killing a single animal on the station.

As Anne Barker reports, the property developer today spoke angrily of shooting journalists instead.

Reporter: Mr Anderson, what's the condition of the animals?

Anderson: You don't know what's happening.

Anne Barker: The man who owns arguably Australia's most unusual zoo walked into a media circus when he arrived at Darwin airport this afternoon.

Reporter: Do you know what's happening, Mr Anderson? Can you tell us?

Anderson: Go away.

Reporter: Are you considering shooting the animals?

Anderson: Go away, I have cared for them for fifteen years. Now go away.

Anne Barker: Warren Anderson arrived in Darwin with a rifle bag, apparently to shoot his entire collection of rare and endangered animals at the private wildlife sanctuary he set up on the vast Tipperary Station. 2200 animals, among them giraffes, zebras, a pygmy hippopotamus, a scimitar-horned oryx and one of the world's rarest species, a white rhinoceros, have effectively been on death row since Mr Anderson abandoned them when he sold the station earlier this year.

The Northern Territory Government was forced to pick up the $13 000 tab for animal feed when the wildlife sanctuary manager Kevin Freeman complained more than a month ago that the food supply had run out. But today an angry Mr Anderson denied he'd neglected the animals and revealed he would pay the bill.

Anderson: It's a lousy $13 000, payable by the end of December.

Reporter: What's that for?

Anderson: Hay.

Reporter: For hay? And the figure of $70 000?

Reporter: Where does that come from?

Anderson: Someone has manufactured it in their minds.

Reporter: Where was the misunderstanding Mr Anderson, where was the misunderstanding?

Anderson: … like you people always do. Go away.

Anne Barker: But the Government's more immediate worry was Mr Anderson's threat to shoot the animals, rather than pay for their continued upkeep. When he sold the station the new owners gave him two years to dispose of his private zoo and Kevin Freeman today told the Supreme Court that Mr Anderson had rung him last night threatening to shoot the lot.

Kevin Freeman (court testimony of what he claimed Anderson had said): I'll be up there to sort it out tomorrow, I'll be bringing some big boys with some big guns and we're going to smoke everything.

Anne Barker: Almost as Mr Anderson stepped off the plane, the Supreme Court granted an injunction prohibiting him from shooting, killing or disposing of a single animal on the station.

But oblivious to the court order, Mr Anderson gave reporters no guarantees the animals wouldn't be shot.

Reporter: Sir, the Government's obviously concerned you're going to try and shoot the animals.

Anderson: So what? They belong to me.

Reporter: And will you shoot them? What are the guns for?

Anderson: To protect myself from pests.

Reporter: Will you be taking the guns to the property?

Anderson: I can't use them on the pests, because it's against the law. You're a grub. You're a grub.

This was indeed a bonus story on the back of Murdoch. It was also one of the Northern Territory government's shabbiest moments. They had orchestrated the wilful harassment of Anderson and the press had embarrassed itself by acting as the government's own attack dogs. It became completely farcical when a Channel 9 reporter, clearly enjoying himself, asked Anderson about his rhinos and hippos: 'How could you lose track of large mega-vertebrates?' Anderson didn't know whether to laugh or belt the reporter so did neither.

Anderson was later proved not to be an animal hater or executioner. The problem was Anderson's manner. He was not a bloke who tried to calm the waters or to explain things – especially when he was being chased around an airport with microphones by blood-scenting journalists.

In her story Anne Barker had said: 'But oblivious to the court order, Mr Anderson gave reporters no guarantees the animals wouldn't be shot.' That order had been taken in the Supreme Court that same day without his knowledge, or even his lawyers being asked to appear. It was served on him – along with the Hanuman Restaurant's famous claypot-lid oysters – at dinner that night. Police deliberately embarrassed him by walking into the restaurant and handing him the court order. The fact that the cops knew where Anderson was eating suggested he was under observation; it also proved how Darwin could sometimes be lousy in its smallness.

As for the bit about giving reporters no guarantees that he wouldn't shoot the animals, that was probably not intended to come across as sanctimonious. But it did. Anderson was given to deep, dark internalised moments and this throwaway line was the sort that could bring on such a mood in a hurry. Because where, in what book, did it say that he, Warren Anderson, had to provide any guarantees about anything to *reporters*, bucket-dwelling filth who wrongly imagined themselves an arm of the law or some perverted guardians of justice?

There were a dangerous number of assumptions in all the stories that came out about Anderson at this time, which was crazy in itself because Anderson was famous throughout the ranges as a quick-draw litigator. But the government was feeding reporters all sorts of helpful information – such as where they could tackle Anderson as he moved around Darwin – and they got the feeling anything they said was safe because it was government-endorsed.

Two days later, Anne Barker filed the story for the ABC's evening current affairs program *Lateline*, this time starring a different male lead:

Anne Barker: A team of police swarmed around Bradley Murdoch as he arrived in Darwin on a commercial Qantas flight from Adelaide ... In handcuffs, Mr Murdoch refused to answer the many questions from journalists ... He was then whisked to a police van which took him straight to police headquarters, where he was formally charged with murder, deprivation of liberty and unlawful assault ... This afternoon he appeared briefly in Darwin's Court of Summary Jurisdiction. Over the two-year investigation police have collected over 300 files of material and 600 witness statements. A committal hearing is unlikely to start until early next year.

Rex Wild, QC, Prosecutor: I wouldn't like to speculate on which ones will give evidence at this stage, but I would expect no less than 60 witnesses.

Barker: Mr Murdoch's lawyer is yet to receive much of the prosecution's material to prepare the defence case.

Mark Twiggs, Murdoch's solicitor: I think they'll go pretty smoothly. Mr Murdoch is waiting for the time when the evidence is out and we can have our say.

Barker: Mr Murdoch, clean shaven with glasses and wearing a green shirt and khaki trousers, sat motionless during the proceedings and made no application for bail.

Questions flew at Bradley John Murdoch as he descended down that airport escalator. 'Where's the body?', and 'Mr Murdoch, have you anything to say at all?' It was the only question he responded to. He said: 'Fuck off.' There hadn't been anything like these two days at Darwin airport since 1954, when Mrs Evdokia Petrov shook off her KGB handlers and fled a Soviet-bound plane to claim asylum in Australia.

The decision to lead Murdoch through the centre of the airport rather than taking him through a side exit was a calculating one. His hands now cuffed to his front, surrounded by police, it was a deliberate statement, designed to show the public they had, as they always said they would, got their man. Or rather, South Australian police had.

Detective-Sergeant David Chalker, standing directly behind Murdoch as the scrum descended the airport escalator, would later confirm he had received a call from Broome detective Peter Jenal, on 31 May 2002, relaying James Hepi's information about Brad Murdoch. He asked Jenal to take a statement and forward it to the task force in Alice Springs. But Territory police did not act on Hepi's statement. Had they acted, it may have seen the investigation brought to a close three months sooner and prevented two rapes.

A year after the Darwin airport showdown I was in Sydney on a work visit when Anderson returned my call. His anger over how he had been treated in Darwin was still with him and it didn't take much to bring it on. He wanted to be vindicated but didn't trust the press enough to talk about it. But he relented. 'All right, you can come out,' he said, warily. I took directions to

Fernhill, where Anderson had spent much of the last twenty years. Set on 728 hectares at the base of the Blue Mountains, it was 50 minutes west of Sydney, and another world.

Moments after exiting a frigid motorway, I pushed open Fernhill's wooden gates and followed a rambling rock fence by a disused mossy wooden-railed racetrack. It was stately, rural England. I pulled in at the big house only to find it was the stables. Bypassing some gardeners who looked like they might also have been bodyguards, I was waved on through, obviously expected. The sandstone Georgian mansion up the hill was Anderson's home. Derelict when he bought it, Anderson had spent $20 million creating an astonishing hideaway.

The mansion's wooden shutters were boarded up that day and, I suspected, on many others. Oil paintings glinted on high walls in a beautifully studied gloom. Marching me quickly through the many rooms, Anderson paused longest to reflect on a gold-framed photograph of a woman with permed hair, of no value to anyone but him. His mother. He was grounded in the past, partly through his exquisite art – there was nothing modern on the walls – and partly through his anger. He believed he'd done a lot for Australia but had been repaid by being branded a rich thug, forever doomed to attract the press's insinuating adjective 'colourful'. He said he was the rich man's Brad Murdoch. Or that was how he felt.

Anderson started out as a farm hand, picking up sticks and rocks on West Australian properties before acquiring a bulldozer and building himself a roadhouse. He got his first big break on a shopping centre project in Kalgoorlie. 'I made $200 000 and thought I was Rockefeller,' he said. He got rich building some forty-odd Coles shopping centres in Western Australia in the early 1970s; then Coles brought him to the eastern states to break the Woolworths' monopoly. Wherever there wasn't a Coles, Anderson built one.

He teamed up with billionaire Kerry Packer and built office towers. He built the Territory's Parliament house and Supreme Court – controversial because his friend Paul Keating, then treasurer, pushed for the funding so that the $160 million project could proceed. He was connected. The buildings were slammed at the time as decadent overkill for little old Darwin. No one said that anymore. They had settled into the city landscape and were viewed as functional and elegant.

There was a time when Anderson had mates. 'Who can you call friends today?' The question was directed not at me but at the last twenty years of his life. 'Have you got friends?' he said, returning to the present. 'When you're in the trenches with bullets flying around you, they'd stick with you?' I told him some might. 'You're lucky. Hang on to them.'

Anderson said he had few. His wife Cheryl, whom he had extricated from her despair living in tin sheds and caravans in the early wheatbelt days, was different. 'She's gregarious. She loves mixing. If people do something to her, it doesn't affect her. She forgives them. I don't forgive and never forget. It's the Swede in me.'

Cheryl was running a hotel at Perisher in the New South Wales ski fields and spent most of the rest of the year in Perth. 'We're very close but when you get older people have got to give one another a bit of distance otherwise it won't necessarily work out,' said Anderson. 'She likes to do what she has dreamt she wanted to do her whole life. She likes to run the hotel down there. She likes buying Armani dresses, she likes little gifts from me, all the nice things. I'm not the bad person people think I am. If I was, I would have killed half the people who have done these things to me. Not just this Territory business. Over the years they've dealt some really rotten hands.'

There's something about West Australians. They always cause more trouble than they ought, maybe because they dream big. West Australians own the better half of Australia. It's where the money is. In 2003, while writing a story on the anally fixated, sterile and, in certain circumstances, forgivable city of Perth, I rang Kerry Stokes, owner of the Seven Network who was then, as he probably still is if he hasn't bettered it, Australia's eighth-richest man. A Perth boy.

Stokes saw Perth as an extension of the entire state. As only a West Australian could. The citizens of other capital cities tended to be reminded of their bush cousins during periods of relentless drought, through affecting wide-angled newspaper photos of farmers shooting sheep or eating dirt. West Australians have always known there was a whole lot of land between Perth and Sydney. They never thought of empty, colourless desert. They thought wheat, sheep and cattle and the possibility of minerals. Stokes pointed out that the state contributed a third of the nation's export earnings through its mining resources. As such, he said it should have 'control of its own destiny'.

'Like most of my fellow West Australians,' Stokes said, 'you would rather you were part of a republic of Western Australia, rather than the [future] Republic of Australia.' Was he serious? Was he advocating secession? 'I'm very serious. Why not? Scratch the surface of any West Australian person and they'll say the same.' Stokes pointed out that WA held a referendum in 1933 at which 66 per cent of its citizens voted to withdraw from the Federation. Britain's imperial parliament refused to ratify the vote and decided to leave Australia intact.

Secession had been, I thought, the star-chamber after-dinner talk of loony right-wing politicians and their big-time mining mates. Stokes was different. He always seemed sober and sane, never a bully or a good old boy, but a politically inscrutable player who got into bed with no one. Not as far as I knew. 'Western Australia, together with Queensland,' he told me, 'are the major exporters of resources. Most of the head offices of most companies that benefit from these resources are in Perth. It should have control of its own destiny. It is the major exporter of iron ore in the north but don't forget the diamonds, gold, coal in the south, natural gas. There is a difference about Western Australia. The difference is remoteness. People tend to be more independent in the things they want in life. Most West Australians are always against centralised government as a matter of principle.'

I asked him why the rest of Australia should not benefit from Western Australia's riches, to which he replied: 'I'm still an Australian. But remoteness breeds its own uniqueness. We'd rather be ourselves than anybody else. A state-sized government is all we'd need to govern ourselves as a country. Financially, it would be a bonanza.'

I got the impression Warren Anderson might have liked to secede – to a one-man kingdom. Which in a sense is what he had done. But right now the horses were having the barrier doors shut behind them and Makybe Diva was going for her second Melbourne Cup win in a row. The Cup had to be watched, but Anderson couldn't tune in to the telecast on his office television, or on any other of the televisions scattered throughout the mansion. Too many remote controls and too many pay TV stations to flick through. The matter was becoming urgent. Warren Anderson was forced to permit a breach of his innermost sanctum, his bedroom, where he knew he could get Channel 7.

Anderson said he didn't let many people into his bedroom. I had no reason to doubt the claim. We were sitting together on his king-size four-poster bed, the customary 'don't try anything on me' cautions having been issued. But the race that stops the nation was just white noise to me. On the cloth walls of this darkened, cavernous, splendid room were five Norman Lindsay oil paintings. Naked women with lavish breasts were propositioning from every aspect. Lindsay knew his bosoms, or knew how he wanted them to look. The big mare Makybe Diva was home and hosed, again, but the bedside blonde – her name was Cecille – was summoning me to her sadness. She didn't have genitals. Nor did she have pubic hair. The artist had edited out all detail with a scribbly paintbrush. The woman had been rendered vagina-less. She was otherwise anatomically perfect. I raised the matter with Anderson. He explained those Lindsays were painted in 'the times'.

'You won't see anything,' Anderson said, grabbing a Maglite torch from a bedside holster and beaming it at the area in question. 'Lindsay laid the paint on very thick right there.' Despite the artist's ruthless expurgation, the paintings – to me – sent a sexual charge through the room. But Anderson, holding one of the most valuable collections of Australian art and literature, said he wasn't chasing that effect. 'It's not the nudity,' he said. 'It's just that they're very good pictures. And a very good investment. I had a lot more art...' he trails off grimly. 'I had to sell it.'

I was ushered back out to the kitchen, leaving behind a hysterical, blathering jockey and five silent, tragic but extraordinary women, to re-enter the real world, a world Anderson hadn't been enjoying much lately. Faxes studded with his pencilled annotations were scattered over the table. His world had turned inward. Anderson, one of Australia's wealthiest men and once its most powerful developer, no longer looked at Australia as a landscape to be subjugated with shopping centres and office towers. He saw wood-panelled courtrooms and grey-haired judges who just might give him justice.

Anderson must have believed in justice, because he told me he'd become a professional litigant. He was still doing big business but was fixated on the fine detail of the two issues consuming him: a court battle with the West Australian government to reclaim $50 million he loaned to the government in the late 1980s as part of its deal for Anderson to buy, along with Kerry Packer, Perth's Westralia Square site. The money had disappeared into Labor's WA Inc black hole. WA Inc took Anderson to the edge of ruin, forcing him to fire-sale some of his collection, most painfully his beloved antique guns; and it cost him his friendship with Packer. He would, in 2006, lose that case. And there was the fight with the Northern Territory government over his zoo, in which he believed politicians misused their power by engaging the Territory police force to humiliate him.

Kevin Freeman, a labourer who had the job of feeding Anderson's animals at Tipperary, had contacted the Territory government saying the animals had no hay and were starving. What the government didn't know was that Freeman – a disabled pensioner with a criminal record for dishonesty – was aware that Anderson was trying to sell his animals. Freeman had been nursing fantasies about persuading the likes of Elle Macpherson and Kylie Minogue to buy the animals on Freeman's behalf so he could start a celebrity zoo.

Anderson had already sold Tipperary for 'more than $100 million' to Melbourne lawyer and businessman Allan Myers, QC. The deal with Myers was that Anderson had two years to keep his animals on Tipperary before having to find them new homes. The deadline was getting nearer. Knowing this, Freeman started plotting his magnificent future. Macpherson, Minogue – someone, anyone, preferably not just rich but famous – would outlay the cash for the animals and he, Mr Freeman, of no means, would suddenly be rocketed into the red-carpet world as Zoo Director to the Stars.

Freeman contacted the office of the Territory's then community development minister, John Ah Kit, whose portfolio included animal welfare issues, relaying the sad story. Without investigating Freeman's motives or bothering to inspect the animals, Ah Kit thundered that hay must be trucked in. And he went to Darwin's *Sunday Territorian* newspaper complaining about Anderson's neglect and claiming that his gallant government just wanted to keep the suffering animals alive. Ah Kit initiated animal cruelty charges against Anderson's family company, Owston Nominees. It was only after going public with the claims that Ah Kit decided to send a vet to Tipperary, who saw no hay in stock but gave the animals a clean bill of health. It later turned out that Freeman, animal feeder, had in fact been over-rationing the hay in order to use it up and create the impression the animals were hungry.

A few days later, on 12 November, an irate Anderson flew to Darwin from Perth to investigate. A licensed gun dealer, Anderson carried a registered and authorised-for-travel .243 Mannlicher rifle. His animals' hay had been disappearing fast but at that point it had not occurred to Anderson that the reason for it might have been Freeman's dishonesty. Rather than looking for a logical explanation, and unable to raise Freeman, who was ducking, Anderson assumed his deer, which were breeding in great numbers, were eating all the hay. He planned to cull some of the deer, if it was required. The Northern Territory government preferred the word of Freeman over Anderson, bought the lie and on-sold it to the media – Anderson was going to undertake a wholesale slaughter of all his African curiosities at Tipperary.

Murdoch's airport ordeal was over in minutes. He was publicly paraded for the benefit of the media, led down the airport's central elevator through a mighty camera logjam and shoved handcuffed into a police vehicle. It was over in minutes. Anderson was hounded through the airport for forty-five minutes. Journalists would later call it 'fantastic' television.

Anderson hired a Land Cruiser at the airport and was travelling along the Stuart Highway, bound for his hotel in Darwin central, when three police cars swooped. He was ordered from his vehicle at pistol-point by a policewoman who grabbed him by the collar and stuck a Glock in his side.

It was a public and hostile roadside apprehension, most of it captured by a Channel 7 crew led by the excellent Jessica Adamson, the only reporter who'd had the wit to follow Anderson's car and grab herself a scoop. Police inspected Anderson's rifle and found it was legal. But Anderson was humiliated.

'I want to know who ordered that hit,' said Anderson, who sought under freedom of information laws a copy of all phone calls made from Ah Kit's office that day in order to attempt to trace the source of the scuttlebutt. He received only a heavily edited version. The airport footage that was broadcast around the country in the evening news said it all for those who'd never seen Anderson up close before: here he was, aggressive and bad-mouthed. Anderson's hate for the media escalated.

Anderson could not understand why he was not remembered for the things he had built; but when people go to Coles they don't tend to thank the building's maker, they stare aghast at the shopping bill. 'The person we read about was not the guy we knew,' said Shane Stone, once a Territory chief minister and later president of the federal Liberal Party. 'He's burned by the feeling no one remembers him. He's deeply aggrieved. But he's not forgotten by people who were around at the time. There wouldn't be a sporting club in the Territory that didn't benefit from Warren Anderson's support as a donor. We had never seen generosity on such a scale before.'

Tipperary station, just two hours south of Darwin, was Anderson's great statement, albeit one only ever glimpsed by privileged eyes. He maintained it was the best property in Australia. He bought it wild and broken-fenced in 1985, began acquiring the neighbouring stations and created a pastoral monolith into which he ploughed eighty to ninety million dollars. It had been described as 'one of the wonders of the pastoral world'. Set on the Daly River basin, Tipperary was a vast wetlands with 120 kilometres of river frontage – teeming with crocodiles, barramundi and bird life. Anderson built an indoor tennis court, Olympic-size swimming pool, school, equestrian centre, stud cattle pens and a 2200-metre airstrip. He began breeding endangered animals, building twenty-hectare steel-fenced enclosures for his rhinos, a seven-hectare lake for his hippos.

Tipperary's plains – inundated during the wet, but showing grass all through the dry – fed cattle in huge numbers for the flourishing live export trade. Tipperary excited Indonesian businessmen, who eventually bought in to the property when they began to see the great Australian–Indonesian dream. That would all fall to pieces, but never mind. Paul Keating related to the sentiment and to Warren, a man who could move seamlessly between a discussion of antique clocks and a bloody session on the pigs. Anderson told me, 'I've met about four or five people who've changed my life. If I hadn't met them, I would've remained an ignoramus. And I don't believe I am an ignoramus. I know a lot. I know a lot about art, buildings, furniture, silver, antique books, ethnographical objects, ornithology. I know farming back to front. My life would've been poorer only for knowing Paul. It's a tragedy to see what's happened. This divorce with his wife. It's hurt him a lot.'

Annita Keating had recently gone public in *The Bulletin* with columnist Jennifer Byrne, telling her version of how her husband had dumped her. Anderson mentioned, just quietly, that it was in fact Annita who left Paul. But do people – even Anderson, a mate of Keating's – really know what's going on between couples? 'No,' he snapped. 'That's why journalists shouldn't write the stuff they think.'

The public never understood Anderson, whose personal politics – judging by his friendships with politicians on both sides – were not easily defined. And it certainly never understood Tipperary. If it was really true there were all these wild African animals living just out of Darwin, why couldn't mums and dads take the kids to see them? The farm-born blue-collar bloke who started from nothing an elitist? That seemed partly the basis of the simmering discontent in Anderson v The People.

'You can't breed wild animals and have people climbing all over them,' he said. 'They need years to acclimatise, establish their territory and breed. They go extinct if people like myself don't do something about it. We've already got enough extinct animals, even in Australia.'

What the Territory government did not know when it won the court injunction to prevent Anderson from shooting his animals was that Anderson had that same day sold the animals to a Queensland animal sanctuary for $1 million. 'There's the good side of me and there's the commercial side of me,' said Anderson, 'and I'm not one that lets the commercial side of me slide. I've worked like hell all my life and I've made a lot of money because I work. I don't share-shuffle, I don't ramp shares, I don't rob public companies, I don't rob little old ladies. I build things. I've built a hundred buildings in this country. Those endangered animals, if you want to be very commercial about it, are worth $1 million. Now: why would I go and put a bullet in a million dollars?'

The government was determined to shake Anderson down. Why is not clear, but the basest of motives seems likely: class war. Anderson was seen as rich and arrogant and starving animals were a sure-fire PR seller. Territory government media staff revelled in the event. As he sat in the Hanuman that night with reporter Jessica Adamson (her presence showed Anderson's hatred of the media was not total; he and Adamson had struck up a conversation as the police dealt with Anderson on the highway at pistol point, crudely demanding that Channel 7 not film in a public place, a demand which was sensibly ignored; and, besides, after the media mauling he'd received at the airport, he was surprised to find himself glad that someone had filmed the incident, because it might be helpful in a later court case) her phone rang. It was a government press officer tipping her off as to Anderson's movements the next morning. Anderson was now certain the vendetta was real.

The government then managed to aggravate the Darwin legal fraternity by bypassing the local bar and engaging $7500-a-day Sydney silk Liz Fullerton to fly to Darwin to lead the prosecution of Anderson for animal neglect – which carried a maximum $10 000 fine. It was a blessing in disguise. The four-day hearing in April 2004 was an embarrassment. Freeman, the only substantial witness, was entirely discredited, to the point where the magistrate cautioned Freeman he might have incriminated himself and may need to seek his own legal advice. The case was adjourned till August that year, but everything about it stank. Fullerton never came back to Darwin to finish the prosecution. On the first day of the resumed hearing, the government hired a local barrister to walk into court and announce that the charges against Anderson were being withdrawn.

Despite this, the Territory's chief minister Clare Martin barged on, revealing the mysterious contempt her government had for Anderson. She said the prosecution failed on 'technical' grounds. It hadn't. It failed because there was no case. Martin told a reporter: 'Look, there was a case against Warren Anderson and we haven't been able to, we haven't been able to prove that in court but it doesn't mean there wasn't. He was not feeding his animals ...'

Threatened with defamation, Martin backed down with a fast public apology. The police likewise apologised for the gunplay, as did the RSPCA for its unfounded accusations. John Ah Kit, who had started the whole thing, initially refused to apologise and in turn became the subject of a defamation action. Ah Kit flew to Perth to try and cool things down in Anderson's West Perth office. He presented Anderson with a dodgy 'form of words' which might be used in a public statement. The form of words suggested both Ah Kit and Anderson had got a little het up, overreacted and were now both very sorry. Anderson told Ah Kit to jam it. The matter seemed to die away when Ah Kit retired unexpectedly from politics. Early in 2006 Anderson got his apology from Ah Kit and a $100 000 payout.

None of this really had anything to do with Murdoch. Except that in the north, people – killers and governments alike – sometimes had this idea they could get away with whatever they liked. They thought isolation would shield them. But isolation never works that way. If you want to disappear, best disappear in a city. If you want to hide something or commit a crime, do it in a busy place. The human traffic would unwittingly kick it down a storm drain from where it would probably wash unnoticed out to sea.

'You know,' said Anderson, 'they made me feel like Brad Murdoch.' And it's true that he got a harder time than Murdoch but, actually, it was me who felt like Murdoch. Like him, I had no front teeth. I was wearing a new denture and had still not got used to it. I sounded like Marc Almond and looked like the devil. Anderson's rambling estate, with its obliging November picnic weather, was a long way from Darwin, from which I had escaped for a few days. Anderson – who, unlike some other important men, was not wholly absorbed with the sound of his own voice – wanted to know what had happened.

I told him how I was at Throb nightclub with my girlfriend. It's the only gay bar in town and the one place in Darwin where no one hassles anyone else. My girl had asked me to request a song for her. On the way back to find my drink I saw a long piece of beaten meat. It was a woman I'd had a casual relationship with many years earlier. She waved wanly, as to a liberator passing the outer perimeter of her personal Belsen. She used to be beautiful but all that was gone. I sat down next to her, wanting to ask: 'What happened to you? Was it the heat or the boyfriend?' Instead I asked how many kids she had now. At that point I felt the briefest of taps on my shoulder and, way too late, saw a fist coming my way. I recognised the unsightly cruel-smiling face behind the fist: her mean Maori ex-boyfriend, who I'd never spoken to in my life. He'd been stalking his missus all night, waiting for some rube to talk to her. I was knocked half-senseless into a backward triple somersault. Security footage showed the boyfriend – and the two mates he had ready to back him up – making straight for the door. My front teeth dislodged and the following day an evil emergency dentist told me, as I was trapped in his chair, of his personal political ambitions and his plans to reinvigorate the Northern Territory's building industry. He wanted me to write a story about his vision. I wanted him to fix my teeth. The teeth were broken beyond repair and had to be extracted. The bill was going to be enormous.

'Are you sure?' asked Anderson.

'Am I sure what?'

'That's what really happened?'

'Yes, why?'

'Are you sure you were with your woman?'

'Quite sure.'

He didn't seem to believe it, couldn't accept that I hadn't been caught pants-down in a married woman's bedroom. I told him he ought to believe what people told him. I left him to his magnificent seclusion and headed back to Sydney, and then on to the insufferable furnace that was Darwin in November.

## 11 KILLING SEAS●N

It was the time of the build-up, Darwin's annual transition to the monsoon season. Grey storm clouds hung about but infuriatingly failed to deliver rain. Work rates had plummetted, imaginations stalled, tempers were blown. People were drinking hard and ending up at each other's throats. Methamphetamine use was rampant. It came in a liquid paste and was eaten in toilets. It was stronger and preferred over the traditional powdered amphetamine, which coagulates in the humidity and cannot be snorted unless you happened to own a pair of truly huge Arnhem Land nostrils.

The drugs replaced what energy levels the build-up had thieved. Serotonin levels swung erratically: joy one minute, black hate the next. The only people who ever looked sprightly at this time of year were the criminal lawyers. The 2004 crime figures were no worse than any other, but every Northern Territory year was bad. The Territory now cruised to a comfortable lead when it came to annual homicide rates and Alice Springs had become the per-capita murder capital of Australia.

The Northern Territory was on the cusp of wresting from Adelaide its reputation as the home of serious and sick crime. National newspapers were starting to base reporters here, to get the deaths as soon as they occurred. Murder was murder wherever it happened, but there was an irresistible evocative 'colour' to Territory death. It excited newspaper editors and, if their judgment was right, their readers: heat, distance, dust, madmen, crocodiles, lonely highways. Everyone was waiting for the Murdoch committal hearing.

Out in the town camps of Alice Springs and in the communities where tourists and the press didn't go, women were regularly being brained with logs and star pickets or hacked with knives by drunken husbands. The victims were always included in the annual homicide statistics but their deaths were rarely personalised. The media was not too interested in another dead black woman; besides, it was hard to put a face to dead Aborigines, and the media needed faces. Cultural protocols prevented the naming of dead Aborigines and a modern extrapolation was that photographs of the recently deceased not be published. Police and courts did not identify Aboriginal victims by name. On the one hand they were trying to show cultural sensitivity; on the other, it had the effect of making Aboriginal victims nameless and, therefore, unimportant. Non-Aboriginal deaths were of much more interest.

British and Irish parents breathed a sigh of relief once their holidaying offspring had filtered down from what they feared was disease- and drug-ridden Southeast Asia to their usual final destination before heading back home: like-minded Australia, with its broad beaches and infinite horizons where the greatest danger was a Pacific Ocean rip to drag the unwary struggler down to the black nothingness. We shared a more or less mutual language and had even destroyed our own pub culture in order to please the white people from the top of the world. There was now a fake Irish or English bar around every city corner in every capital. Even Darwin. Wolfhounds and glass-eyed deer stared down from the walls and breasty wenches pulled huge glasses of obscure-brand ales that were hot and vile by the time they were half drunk. And, for reasons that speak of either a lack of adventurous spirit or else loneliness, they could always be found full of genuine drunken Celts eating things they called crisps.

Backpacker murderer Ivan Milat did his bit to damage Australia's safe-haven reputation, as did the June 2000 fire at the backpacker hostel in Childers, in outback Queensland, in which fifteen young backpackers lost their lives. Childers was to deal a shocking double whammy, almost as if the fire was far from satisfied with the pain it had already wrought. As five young girls from the United Kingdom drove north to continue their holiday in Darwin after surviving Childers, they were near Emerald Springs roadhouse, less than 200 kilometres short of Darwin, when their old Ford Falcon sedan blew a front tyre. The driver didn't know the only rule about front-tyre blow-outs: never put your foot on the brake, just ease off or change down and let the car slow itself. Instead, the driver reacted and slammed on the brake. The sedan veered out of its lane headfirst into an oncoming truck. Four girls aged between twenty-three and twenty-nine were killed instantly.

And then came Murdoch. A visitor to Australia could not be inoculated against rotten people or infernos. But children were being sent off to holiday in Australia with their parents pressing them to their breasts just a little tighter as they said farewell.

It wasn't all one-way. Irish backpacker mates Trevor Stokes and Lee McLaughlin never became household names in Australia, which was strange given what they did. They were only ever big news in Ireland. In 2003, I took a flight to Karratha in north Western Australia, to visit the family of Greg Bebensee, who put on a very sad barbecue lunch for me. The Harleys, dirt bikes, engines, front-ends and unfinished mechanical projects scattered around the yard always reminded them of Greg, their boy who was into cars and bikes. Engines do not mystify everyday north Australians. Parts may be hard to get and patience may be required in waiting for them, but to long-time residents of the north, vehicles are life.

In the early hours of Sunday 6 June 1999, Greg, twenty, a beloved son and brother, was up in Darwin looking for work. After a night out drinking, he was taken down on the streets of Darwin in what forensic experts would call a frenzied 'blitz attack'. One sudden and furious blow from behind cracked the boy's skull, killing him instantly. There was madness to the attack because the killer did not stop there. Some seventeen blows to Greg's face, forehead and throat followed.

A then-record Northern Territory reward of $100 000 – which would be overtaken two years later when $250 000 was offered for Falconio's killer – was staked. Police did not have a clue. Nor would they until three months later when Lee McLaughlin's demons began to manifest. McLaughlin took himself to hospital in Broome, paralysed by a panic attack brought on by the strong weed he'd been smoking, which had in turn brought on feelings of guilt. He was anxious, short of breath and said he had been fighting with Stokes, his travelling companion. A nurse tried to calm McLaughlin and sent him home to the caravan park – the same one where Brad Murdoch had kicked the life out of old Nelson. But McLaughlin was not all right. He went to Broome police and told them his mate, Stokes, had killed 'someone' in Darwin.

By the time McLaughlin had done with damning his former good buddy, he would himself be exposed as a liar and a thief. But the Territory police believed McLaughlin's story from the start. They flew him back north to Darwin where he took them straight to a spot just south of town. Brushing aside some leaves, McLaughlin pointed to Greg Bebensee's wallet, the one his mother, Jacquie, had lovingly handcrafted with leather tools. In a police interview, McLaughlin said he'd been with Stokes when Stokes put the wallet in that spot, on the day they fled Darwin. A few days later, McLaughlin had a rethink and said he'd put the wallet there himself.

Stokes was tried but eventually acquitted by a jury. He flew straight home to Ireland. McLaughlin, too. All that could be said for sure is that one of them did it. I went out to Greg's grave with his dad, Karl. The man's grief was beyond words. The bare red earth cemetery on the outskirts of Karratha, not a skerrick of grass on it, only added to the sense of desolation. Closure? Not possible. 'That is a shrink's word,' said Greg's mum, Jacquie. 'That shuts the door. The door will never be closed. I don't care who they lock up and for how long. It will never be closed.'

In March 2004, two Thai prostitutes were murdered and thrown to the crocodiles off the Adelaide River Bridge just east of Darwin on the Arnhem Highway. The Adelaide River crossing is known as the place where tourists board boats to see the 'famous jumping crocodiles'. The normally secretive animals have been tutored to show themselves to tourists by launching up and grabbing bits of dangled meat proffered by tour guides. The animals must be overfed, because no croc in that crocodile-infested river laid a tooth on either woman, even though their corpses floated in the water for many hours. It was another great outback death. It had it all. Although it occurred to me that the friends or family of the dead women might not see it that way. *The Bulletin*, where I now worked, reported:

Darwin ABC television and radio management ordered reporters not to describe the two victims as 'prostitutes', because it was felt it would dehumanise them. The edict in fact showed a detachment from humanity. It carried the implicit high-brow assumption that a low-brow audience (Darwin) might think that the women 'deserved it' for being prostitutes. They were prostitutes. Essential-service workers. They operated with a posse of Thai women from a '70s-era redbrick motel on the outskirts of Darwin central. Shortly after the murders, I took an $88 room. To have a look at the scene.

Four middle-aged Thai women were working the joint. All of them on the wrong side of glamorous, the cleavages on their backsides bigger than the ones of their chests and all drinking red wine from a cask at 3.30 pm. But their phones seemed to be running hot. They lived in their motel rooms, apparently having some sweetheart deal with the management. Two very beautiful younger Thai women would rush in at times, sit a few seconds before their mobiles would sing an irritating Nokia preset ditty and they'd be off. The older women smiled at the fortunes of youth. They sat at their plastic table wearing plastic gloves as they pitched in to prepare a very delicate Asian dinner. Despite the Hep C overtones, a homey affair. When these women found out I was not a customer, instead of ditching me they invited me to join them for dinner.

They did not accept their friends' deaths; they adjusted to it. Nothing 'colourful' in these murders for them. They just felt the need to upgrade to driver-bodyguards. The famed frontier wildness had been traded for something sinister, universal and common – even if crocodiles were involved. It was a straight robbery-homicide and there was no charm in it.

The women's two killers were eventually bundled up and sent to Berrimah prison.

Word from the occasional exiting Berrimah prisoner was that Murdoch was pretty relaxed. He was telling people he'd get off. Old Stumpy Williams' hex from Western Australia hadn't caught up with him yet and he was talking to other prisoners of his innocence. He was certain he would walk away from this one, just as he had walked free from the rape trial in South Australia a year before.

# 12 WHITE LINES AND PEARL-HANDLED PISTOLS

Adelaide barrister Grant Algie upset the Darwin legal fraternity even before he got to town. The convention was that every accused murderer using legal aid got himself the best local barrister – preferably a Queen's Counsel if one was available. It was about sharing the work and the money around the local patch. The national profile wouldn't hurt either, win or lose. As Darwin barristers jockeyed for the job, Brad Murdoch was insisting he wanted Algie. Understandably so. Algie wasn't a QC but he'd gotten Murdoch off the rape charges and he was now going to get him off a murder.

Algie flew into town and held an airport press conference, maintaining his client's innocence and calling on the media to play fair during the committal hearing. He would be saying nothing more on the record until after the trial, when his man walked free.

Algie was blonde-haired, bearded and Custer-like. Physically, he gave the impression of being imperious, with his way of gathering himself up and looking down on people. But that was only a first impression. He was a southern gentleman, in both the Adelaide and American senses. He was a man who seemed to come with surroundings. It was as if, on approach, one didn't just encounter Algie but walked into a club with Chesterfield lounges and cravatted men who drank steadily but did not become inebriated. He looked as if he might carry a derringer in his sock.

Algie was backed up by Mark Twiggs, Murdoch's solicitor in the rape trial. He was also from Adelaide and a recent veteran of South Australia's infamous and revolting Snowtown bodies-in-barrels trials. Twiggs became known to most as 'Mister Twiggs'. It was an acknowledgement of his hefty Dickensian frame and very Dickensian surname. Mr Twiggs was a quick-to-laugh man whose most noticeable defect was his fanatical allegiance to the Adelaide Crows Australian Rules football team.

Algie and Mr Twiggs would set up shop after court most afternoons at the Deck Bar or Kitty O'Shea's, close by the courtroom. They'd drink big beers and members of the press were mostly welcome to join them. Except on bad days. It was not that they were trying to indoctrinate the media in the Murdoch side of things. One or two media-type suckholes did try and win them over by pretending Brad was a great bloke done wrong. But they didn't seem too impressed with that approach. It was more that they were out-of-towners and enjoyed the company. A person was allowed to talk about their client as an 'innocent killer'. It was no problem to suggest that when this was all over they could go into partnership with Murdoch by setting up 'Brad's Extreme Outback Backpacker Adventure Tours'. They'd been effective, or lucky, in the rape trial. They had a job this time.

The Crown, led by Rex Wild, QC, and Anthony Elliott, were not doing any public drinking but were sweating on the case they had to prove against Murdoch. Much was at stake. They were no hick-town lawyers by any means, but none of the outsiders knew that. There seemed to be a view among foreign media – a self-fulfilling view, because it helped add intrigue to stories doing the rounds – that Darwin was a frontier town full of wild men and society escapees. And it had been once. But not anymore.

Rex Wild and Anthony Elliott were backed up by two distractingly attractive junior lawyers, Ann Barnett and Jo Down, each of whom looked as though she could have worn Catwoman's costume with great success. They added a sense of sophistication and were, presumably, highly capable, but it was hard to know. Both were always Joanne-silent with the media, never giving away more than quick, mistrusting glances. Maybe they needed to fashion themselves as aloof lest the scumbags tried to get under their guard. They became known as the Rexettes.

The Crown, in an uncharacteristic outburst, went so far as to promise the media there would be 'surprising twists' to the case. Asked what these might be, they fell quiet. But the conservative Wild – no natural fan of the media – needed to say something. He was being surrounded, screeched at for news. 'Surprising twists' was the most his office could muster. This was to be a sane and level-headed prosecution, a comforting notion to all but the underfed media. Still, this same prosecution office – although none of the same staff remained – did not have a good case against Lindy. They didn't even have a motive. But they beat her. Would they say Murdoch had a motive to kill Falconio? Would it be said Falconio and Murdoch had had contact before 14 July 2001?

As for Joanne Lees, something about her was making otherwise rational people seethe. Which media outlet would find her hotel room first? Or would hers be a safe house in suburbia? The first photo of Lees would make a freelance photographer rich for months and a newspaper rich for a day. What every photographer really wanted was to catch Lees poolside, in a bikini.

The mystery woman arrived in court via the back door. She would be the first major witness. Rex Wild, the Territory's longstanding director of public prosecutions and never given to histrionics, began to outline the Crown case. It sounded as though he had taken some of his introductory statements from a tourist brochure: 'Barrow Creek is an isolated township in the red centre of Australia. Joanne Rachael Lees became aware of that isolation when she was the subject of a terrifying ordeal on the Stuart Highway just north of there on 14 July 2001.'

Murdoch pleaded not guilty to three charges: the murder of Peter Falconio, depriving Lees of her liberty, and assaulting Lees.

Paul Falconio took the stand, essentially to establish that his family had not seen or heard from Peter since his disappearance. Then came Lees. Given her overall slightness, she proved a surprisingly awkward-striding woman. Her physical appearance had changed markedly in the three years since Australia had last seen her. Or maybe we never really did see her. There was just that one carefully controlled media moment in Alice Springs and that D-grade documentary. Her face had lost its youthful fullness and had been angle-ground by worry. Lees wore convent black and white and had barely touched her face with make-up. Any suggestion of the glamorous court widow had been firmly culled.

Joanne Lees' testimony got weird well before she was embarrassed into admitting she'd had a secret lover. Lees described the scene that took place in the early evening of 14 July 2001, as she and Falconio trundled north out of Alice Springs in their old Kombi. They'd smoked a sunset joint at the town of Ti Tree, after which they came across low scrub fires on the side of the dark highway. Lees said Pete, at the wheel, wondered whether he should pull over and extinguish outback Australia. 'They looked unusual,' Lees said of the fires. She had a nervous courtroom tic, coughing and clearing her throat every few seconds. 'And they looked as if they'd been started deliberately. I said it could be a trap or a trick and I asked him to move on.'

Traps and tricks in a bushfire? This was still an hour or so before the encounter with the Barrow Creek gunman. At that point Joanne and Pete's world was, supposedly, open and untroubled. But Lees herself was neither open nor untroubled. Her evidence and demeanour at the committal hearing revealed a strange person. Feeling fearful on the highway could have had something to do with the joint she'd just smoked, which in unfamiliar country might have ushered unwelcome phantoms of paranoia into the Kombi. And they were in the vicinity of Coniston Massacre country, where in August 1928 Mounted Constable William George Murray shot down an estimated thirty-one Aborigines. It was a reprisal mission for forty long years of Aboriginal refusal to accept the white presence, spearing settlers, miners, and telegraph staff at Barrow Creek itself. Not that Lees or Falconio knew Barrow Creek's bloody history. They were just there to update it.

What Lees was saying jarred with the picture she otherwise portrayed: that of two young people setting out dauntless into the night in a slow, shaky old bomb of a Kombi, with no timetable, prepared to pull over and camp anywhere whenever they got tired. Lees spoke of 'just one long road headed north'. They were happy, she said. Why was she worried about an ambush? When they had set out from Alice Springs, Lees had taken the wheel while Falconio slept in the back. She played one of her favourite tapes, by Texas, fitting road music given the band's uncluttered steel-guitar soundscape. Wild did not pursue the Lees' ambush scenario, instead steering his star witness onto even dodgier ground.

In 2001, Lees had been assigned a police chaperone in Alice Springs who discovered her secretly deleting messages from a secret email account – 'Not a secret email account, a second email account,' said Lees, unpersuasively. Wild knew this from interviews Lees had with Alice Springs detectives at the time. Grant Algie knew it from the case notes the prosecution was obliged to provide to him. Thrown to Algie, as it were, Lees floundered, foolishly denying that she knew anyone called 'Steph', which was her lover Nick's email pseudonym.

Forced to admit it, Lees came unstuck. She denied that she and Falconio had fought the night they left Alice Springs; she admitted they had cable ties in the Kombi – such as were used by her alleged attacker to fashion handcuffs. Asked whether she and Pete were getting along, Lees gave Algie a frigid, 'Yep.' She became unhelpful, defiant, and half-smart. It was not a pretty sight. Yet Algie was barely laying a finger on her, saving the real savaging – or so we imagined – for the future trial.

In Alice Springs, she'd been emailing a guy called Nick in the days after Pete went missing. Asked whether she had been in a sexual relationship with Nick before leaving Sydney, while she was still seeing Falconio, Lees replied: 'I am going to answer yes, but I wouldn't class it as an affair or a relationship.' Lees was doing a Bill Clinton. The discovery that Lees had 'made suggestions' that Nick meet her in Berlin after she'd departed Alice Springs deeply bothered detectives at the time – and briefly elevated her from victim to suspect. But police had to focus and remember that people were complicated. Lees was naturally embarrassed about this revelation.

While some saw it as final proof of her involvement in her boyfriend's death, of a complicated conspiracy involving Nick, Lees and Murdoch, anyone who stepped back could see it explained much about her strange behaviour. It was why she could not look the Falconios in the eyes when they first arrived from England after the killing; why she had been so stupidly defiant towards the press; why the cops had needed to be sure and had therefore grilled her so repeatedly in Alice Springs.

The drugs – the dope and her admission that she'd taken half an ecstasy tablet back in Sydney – and the affair with Nick constituted the biggest story since the killing itself. For most. A mate of mine who had been filing to Reuters in Bangkok was trying to brief one of his editors on the hot breaking news of Lees' drug-taking and affair. The editor was not impressed, telling him: 'If an English backpacker had come to Australia and *not* taken drugs and *not* slept around, then *that* would be a story.'

The affair explained why Peter's brothers, Paul and Nick Falconio, wanted nothing to do with Lees anymore. The Falconios and Lees were not talking or sitting near each other. I had written an article describing the brothers as 'an open-faced pair who have a soldierly sharpness about them'. The article was not that flattering to Lees, talking of her severe appearance and the distance she and the brothers were keeping. At that point I had not approached the brothers. They had enough to worry about. Instead, they approached me. They wanted to know what I had meant by 'open-faced' and 'soldierly'. I explained how they were neat people who always looked permanent-pressed in comparison to me, a shambolic character who, even if I'd ironed a shirt ten minutes earlier, still managed to look like I'd been sleeping in it; and how, with their foreign legion haircuts and high-set prematurely receding hairlines (mine, ape-like, was *pro*ceeding) they looked kind of unconcealed and open. 'Yeah,' one of them said in his soft Yorkshire voice, 'that was all right, that story, that was.' Jesus, I thought, they must really hate Lees.

And we all did by now. She was just not likeable. She – and this was not her fault, but it somehow added artillery – had a Sloanish upturned nose which seemed an accurate genetic reflection of her superior view of herself.

She tossed her head like a thoroughbred. Attempts to feel empathy for her – beyond the fact that her boyfriend had been executed and she'd had a terrible time – went nowhere. To put it badly, I wouldn't have wanted to be her boyfriend. She looked like someone who wore the pants. And she did wear pants, sometimes, badly-cut culottes that crawled and wedgied. Christ, you'd think someone could *have a word*. She would look down that nose and flick her hair in apparent disdain for all in the sweep of her vision.

Lees had been arriving at the Darwin court every morning in an unmarked silver Commodore with darkened windows. She was hiding in the middle of the back seat, between two minders, with a shirt or jacket over her head. Neither the DPP nor the police would admit to organising this charade. With no cameras allowed inside the courthouse, it led to ridiculous scenes every morning, with cameramen and photographers desperately lunging at the car windows as it hurtled down a driveway into the underbelly of the court. It was the realisation that a chopper hired by a television station had been hiding way out in Darwin harbour, ready to swoop on Lees' car and follow it to her secret hideaway (it failed), that led Lees to offer a deal: she would pose, at a location of her choice, for one still-camera photo which would be pooled among all media. After that, the media would have to keep their distance. The assembled press rejected the offer because the TV stations – and indeed newspapers –
couldn't do much with one staged photo.

Lees came back, upping the ante to one still photo plus a brief 'walk' for a TV camera, both to be pooled, and a request that the media donate an unspecified amount of money to an unspecified charity. The media, some of whom will never pay for material even if the money goes to charity, baulked and threw back two options: the first, that those willing to pay ($500 was a commonly agreed amount) could get to use the images; or that she just come and do it for free. Lees' answer came back fast: no way.

The media was certainly bloody-minded in this clash of wills. So was Lees. She just wanted someone to pay, and didn't care whether the money went to a cattery or a women's refuge. It seemed, on worst-case scenario, that both Lees and the police were enjoying this exercise of power over the British and Australian press. Another possibility was that Lees' life since 14 July 2001 had become so strange that she had become unrecognisable even to herself. To relinquish anything that was not under her total control would be to lose herself, in her uncertain state, to the world. She might have been thinking that she'd lost enough already.

Lees had failed to conceal the now confirmed obsession and paranoia that were part of her. She seemed to think she owed nothing to anyone, but she could have thanked truck drivers Vince Millar and Rodney Adams, who picked her up on the Stuart Highway roadside after the attack. As Joanne fled Darwin for England after giving her evidence at the committal hearing, the straight-up truckies gave unadorned, no-bullshit evidence – and in doing so reasserted the hearing's focus. They rescued her again.

Millar told of being at the wheel, looking forward to a shift change with Adams, who was asleep in the cabin behind him. When Lees appeared on the night highway, Millar had to swerve the three-trailer Bull's Transport truck. Millar cursed at this startling apparition, thinking he'd collected it. Pulling up a kilometre down the track, he jumped out to inspect the damage. 'I was looking for a body, whether it be an arm or a leg or a bit of clothing,' he said.

Lees charged towards Millar. 'She threw herself at me and, being a bit reluctant to sort of know what was sort of happening at the time, I'd sort of grabbed her and thrown her back away from me, like sort of protecting myself if she sort of had anything on her' – he meant, for instance, a weapon – 'because you just don't know.'

Millar had already told the sleepy Adams he thought he'd hit a woman – but this was apparently not enough to entice his companion from his bunk in the truck. Millar saw the handcuffs. '"Oh jeez", I said. "Hang on a minute, just stay here". So I went to the driver's door and I sung out to Rod. I said, "Hey, Rod, I've got some sheila out here all bloody tied up".'

Adams put on his thongs and clambered out. 'It was cold, it was black,' Adams said. 'There wasn't a star or nothing out there. It was just a dead night.' They disconnected the trailers and took the prime mover for a quick look around for the girl's boyfriend. Then Joanne said something about a man with a gun. Millar: 'I just said: "What the bloody hell are we doing here driving around in the bush looking for a bloke with a gun?"'. Adams: 'Let's go.'

The men sat the shivering Lees on the warm engine cowling between them and drove south to Barrow Creek roadhouse, which was still alive with the last guests celebrating a mid-year New Year's Eve, which comes a week after the annual Christmas-in-July party. 'She was showing signs of terror,' said Adams. 'She kept saying "Pete". We couldn't work out who this Peter was. Through her sobbing, it was hard to decipher a sentence.'

Lees developed a potential problem because of her obsession with the media. She was always monitoring the press to see what people wrote. So when she learned that a suspect had been arrested in Australia in late August 2002, she went straight to a BBC website to take a look. She was working in Sicily at the time and said she 'wanted to see what people were writing'. She denied she wanted to see if there were any photos of the man, who was named as Bradley John Murdoch. But of course, she did. There was one photo of the shaven-faced Murdoch. When Northern Territory police flew to the United Kingdom in November 2002, they carried a photo board which bore twelve pictures of suitably crooked-looking men. She went straight to the Murdoch mugshot, in which he had a beard, telling police: 'I think it's number ten.' It was not the same photo the BBC had published but, in a case where impressions and circumstance counted for so much, was there a chance she had convinced herself that Murdoch was the man?

Algie did not pursue this matter in the committal hearing and would only give it passing mention in the trial. The fact was, the man Lees had described in the Comfit, the man with the moustache, was a very good likeness of Murdoch. He could shave his moustache and cut his hair, he could grow a beard but she knew who had assaulted her and Pete that night.

Along came Hepi, paying off the first instalment of his debt to society. He had come to do damage to Murdoch. And judging by his size and the way he refused to shrink from Murdoch's hateful glare, Hepi was capable of it. He was the first of Murdoch's former mates who did not seem to be praying for a trapdoor to open up beneath him and take him to someplace else, anywhere else, to a world without questions.

Hepi aside, Murdoch's former mates would not turn on Murdoch in court. But nor would they go out to bat for him. They knew he was a good fit for Falconio's killer in every respect. It was just that Murdoch, the man feigning disinterest and fake-yawning behind his perspex-shielded seat in the dock, was someone – of all people – they would prefer not to discuss. They had been subpoenaed to appear. The truth was they'd all been smoking Murdoch's drugs and hoovering up his speed, some of them helping him to traffic it. And one of them would sleep with him in exchange for her steady supply of speed. That was what they thought they would be asked about when they took the stand – the drugs, the sex. They weren't to know that the prosecution was not interested in such detail except as background: they only wanted to know how Murdoch looked, or acted, at certain key times. They feared that wigged judge and the coat of arms above his head; the bank of prosecutors who were ready to expose and embarrass; they feared Murdoch and his own lawyers. It was not just the formality of the setting, or the exposure. Nor had they been threatened with conviction for failing to testify. They had not been promised immunity. But the missile had been launched and they were sitting astride it as unwilling passengers. They simply told the frightened truth. None of them knew any longer where they stood with Big Brad. He'd been arrested for murder. Who was to say he had not fallen into a powdery heap, singing about how all his friends had led him off the path, about all the drug deals, about some grubby sexual indiscretion in the past? He'd stayed silent, of course, but they weren't to know. Brad was in jail and out of contact. And none of them were such good friends that they'd been desperately trying to visit good old Bradley in Berrimah prison. But they had no choice but to meekly reveal everything they knew. Brad wouldn't understand their position; he'd see them as traitors. And he could, after all, be found not guilty. He was not a person likely to forgive. Life could get difficult if he walked free.

Hepi saw things differently. He was to be the last witness before a two-month break in the committal hearing. Everyone knew the nature of Murdoch's and Hepi's drug-running partnership but the whole subject was legally pussyfooted around and never openly discussed in court. All the public heard was that each man had a Toyota Land Cruiser four-wheel-drive ute fitted with long-range diesel tanks that allowed them to move vast distances while keeping pit-stops to an absolute minimum.

Hepi and Murdoch lived between their shared house in Broome and Hepi's bush block close to Swan Reach, from where Hepi had very good contacts to source a seemingly endless supply of dope. The 7000-kilometre Broome–Sedan–Broome round trip was usually completed within one white-knuckled week. Murdoch had dobbed Hepi in to the police for drug-running after they fell out, but that was never said in the committal hearing. It was infuriating to listen to the lawyers and the magistrate, who all knew this background information, pretending for the benefit of the public that this unexplained 'partnership' between Hepi and Murdoch could just as easily have been about shifting carnations across state borders.

The defence, in particular, was not interested in painting Murdoch as a drug trafficking reprobate – not in the committal, anyway. They'd do that at the trial, in order to show that Murdoch was a businessman, albeit an illegitimate one, who had more pressing business than Joanne Lees and Peter Falconio.

*The Bulletin* decided to push the boundaries and report the real relationship between Hepi and Murdoch:

It is a matter of record that Hepi was busted in WA in May 2002 while transporting a large amount of marijuana between Sedan and Broome. But Hepi, jilted by Murdoch's sell-out, had an exit strategy. He told Broome police that Murdoch fitted the profile of the Falconio most-wanted. Hepi ended up with a fully suspended jail sentence in return for a promise to testify against Murdoch. He began making down payments on that promise last week.

Murdoch's defence lawyer, Grant Algie, put it to Hepi that he saw Murdoch as his ticket out of jail. Hepi did not equivocate for even a second. 'That's correct,' Hepi said. 'I would say I would be involved in getting my own skin off the line. That's what happened.' Asked if he would be interested in the unclaimed $250 000 reward for information that led to a conviction, Hepi said: 'I imagine I would.'

Several days after the Falconio abduction story broke, Murdoch returned to the Broome flat. Hepi said Murdoch shaved his hair and moustache and sent his Land Cruiser in for drastic modifications. Hepi said Murdoch had two revolvers, one a .357 magnum, the other a smaller .22. Lees had told of being menaced by a man with a revolver. Hepi said Murdoch was on edge and had gone to his local Broome pub with the .22 holstered beneath his flannelette shirt. He also kept a gun and holster taped beneath the kitchen table at the Sedan property.

When Hepi told the court he'd seen Murdoch in the shed at Sedan fashioning the same kind of zip-tie handcuffs that were used to restrain Lees, Murdoch shook his head in what was either disbelief or disgust. Sometime between July and December 2001, Hepi said, Murdoch gave him an unsolicited lesson in corpse disposal. '[It was about] how to get rid of them, to put them in a spoon drain on the side of the road. Just cover them up with soft digging dirt.'

Hepi's view: 'I didn't think I needed to kill anyone to carry on doing what I was doing.'

There are supposedly two codes of the road in the outback: the one for harmless travellers who'll always pull over and lend another a hand; the other a convention of silence among the dodgier ships of the desert. As it stood, both were now worthless. Hepi nodded to Peter Falconio's brother, Paul, as he left the stand, as if to say: 'There, I've done it.' Falconio could be heard to say: 'Thank you.'

And then there was Julieanne McPhail, a chance acquaintance of Murdoch's in June 2001, just a month before the Falconio killing, and certainly the strangest of all to take the witness stand. She was fairy-like, the type that made people wonder whether she really was of this earth or had come from a parallel universe. Whether she had a belly-button. Her name was not to be published at that point. It was suppressed. McPhail claimed to be worried for her safety.

McPhail was a tiny slip of a thing, quite pretty, with long and carefully tended flowing hair, forcefully well-spoken, mature-age jewellery around a young neck. Demure. Or such was the look. Then she told of a day in June 2001 when she set off alone from just outside Perth to drive to Adelaide. On that day, she drank perhaps eighteen stubbies of beer, stopped in at various pubs for top-up 'roadies', smoked numerous joints and hoovered up quite a few lines of speed. After twelve hours of this, she said, she went to sleep clear-headed.

Years before he was appointed the Northern Territory's administrator, Ted Egan sang a song that went: 'We've got some bloody good drinkers, in the Nor-theern Terr-a-tree...' This petite woman from Western Australia had finally, thankfully, silenced that song. She claimed her mind was unclouded by alcohol or drugs on the day of her road journey, 19 June 2001, because she was a heavy drinker in those days and could take it. If anything, she said her senses and memory of that trip were 'heightened' by the speed she said Bradley Murdoch gave her on their many roadside stops across the Nullarbor after they met each other on the road.

The purpose of her testimony was to describe the physical appearance of Murdoch and his Toyota 4WD in the weeks before he killed Peter Falconio, and how he had offered to sell her a small silver pistol – such as he would use on Falconio and Lees.

By 2.30 pm on the day she set out from Perth, McPhail had reached Norseman, some 700 kilometres east of Perth, where she bought a six-pack of beer and cigarettes. She drove, drinking, through the afternoon. By early evening, she'd knocked over a dozen beers. Just before she reached Caiguna, about 370 kilometres east of Norseman, at nightfall, she noticed a bloke pulled off the side of the road with his dog. She stopped in at the next pub to have a few. The man she'd seen on the road earlier appeared, introducing himself as Brad. They chatted. She had worked in Broome at one stage, and Brad was on the way down from Broome to South Australia. They talked of mutual acquaintances.

McPhail wanted to drive through the night, to get as close as possible to Adelaide before daybreak. Murdoch suggested she follow in the slipstream of his Toyota. He had powerful spotlights and her own headlamps were weak. By hanging behind Brad she could avoid kangaroos. She said Murdoch suggested they stop somewhere just up the road from the hotel because, he said, 'I've got something for you.' She did a line of Murdoch's speed, smoked a joint and had another roadside drink. Asked by prosecutor Rex Wild, QC, whether she drove side-by-side with Murdoch's car on the highway, she seemed horrified. 'Oh no,' she said, speaking in a teensy Marilyn Monroe voice for the first time. 'That would've been *dangerous*.'

They stopped intermittently for more lines and drinks until the night got the better of her at about 2 am. She needed rest. They pulled over at the head of the Great Australian Bight where she laid a swag on a flat rock. The two sat up chatting; she mentioned she wouldn't mind obtaining a small lady's pistol with a pearl-inlaid grip.

Murdoch's sexual awareness must have been heightened having a pretty woman in his vicarious care. However, McPhail said Murdoch had been 'a complete gentleman' that night, and showed her none of the wild violence he would turn on for Falconio and Joanne Lees a month later.

She had slept for a few hours when Murdoch woke her with coffee. They travelled on and she said he signalled her to stop somewhere near Whyalla, in South Australia. 'He pulled a small [revolver] out of the car and said he had one for sale,' she said. He offered her a shot – she declined. 'I didn't feel comfortable there at all.' Besides, the revolver was not pearl-handled.

McPhail failed to understand that she was a Crown witness. She thought she was helping out Brad's defence, talking about what a gentleman he was. It didn't seem to occur to her that all that stuff about the gun was part of a gathering circumstantial Crown case. Algie found McPhail a dubious specimen and quietly set about gnawing at her throat. She had mentioned, earlier, that she had worked in a bar in Broome. Asked what sort of bar it was, she said it was a private 'bikies' club'.

'What?' said Algie. 'A trail bike club?'

'Oh no, an outlaw motorcycle club,' she said, with that sweet, teensy smile. 'It was the Coffin Cheaters' clubhouse in Broome.' She turned, beaming, to the jury.

Algie made her look silly. Asked why she had raised with Murdoch the subject of wanting a lady's pistol, she thought hard and replied: 'I just wanted to take up shooting as a sport.'

'With a pearl-handled revolver?' asked Algie. 'Perhaps you were thinking of entering the Olympics?'

She let slip a seriously pissed-off glance, the wholesome visage collapsing as she finally realised she was in an unfriendly place. Algie wanted it known that she was so addled by drink and drugs that nothing she said about pistols, or anything else, was reliable. She tiptoed her way out of the courtroom, through the crocodiles, thoroughly puzzled.

This whole committal hearing was a waste of time according to Robert Brown, a big, happy bloke from Bourke in outback New South Wales. Via video link from Bourke, Brown said Peter Falconio had walked into his family-run service station on 22 July 2001, asking for a Coke and a Mars Bar. This was eight days after he was supposed to have been executed with a Murdoch bullet. Brown described a blond-haired man – Falconio was dark – who'd turned up with two other people in a 4WD, the type of which he could not place. Brown's de facto, Melissa Kendall, rushed out the back to where Brown was washing up, saying that Falconio – whom they'd just been reading about in *The Sunday Telegraph* – was in the shop.

Prosecutor Tony Elliott scoffed at this man's story. Elliott tried, to no avail, to use the neutral term 'the man' when discussing the person who had entered Brown's service station. 'You mean Falconio?' said Brown, with disarming self-assuredness. 'I served Peter Falconio myself.'

Senior Sergeant Megan Rowe revealed that Falconio had not used a bank account or his passport since 14 July 2001. Nor did he have life insurance, which meant there was no disappearance scam afoot. Rowe said Northern Territory police had 2500 possible suspects that had been whittled down to thirty 'hot prospects' who met the criteria of the man they were chasing: a Caucasian male; aged forty to forty-five; of medium build; over six foot tall (183 centimetres); owner of a 1991–99 white Toyota Land Cruiser diesel ute with a chrome or silver bullbar and a brown or khaki canopy, and with front-to-rear access. This access passage was important because Lees said she had been pushed from the front cabin of the ute into the back. Murdoch's Toyota did not have such access. Even so, Rowe said police were able to exclude all thirty hot prospects 'bar one'. Asked who that was, Rowe said: 'The defendant in this matter, Mr Murdoch.' From the dock, Murdoch mouthed 'bullshit' under his breath.

The magistrate, Alisdair McGregor – a gentle, folksy chap, possibly one of the last Territory public servants to favour a short-sleeved shirt with a tie – found there was a prima facie case and ordered Murdoch to face trial for the murder of Peter Falconio, and for assaulting and depriving Joanne Lees of her liberty. And that's the way these things go. No one ever expected to walk from a committal – it was just an exposition of evidence so that both sides had a fair idea of what the other had. Asked by McGregor whether he had anything to say, Murdoch replied: 'I'm not guilty of any of these allegations, your honour.' There was no application for bail. Trial was set for 26 April 2005, but there would be delays.

By the end of 2004, Murdoch was slipping from view. In the next few weeks would come Aceh. Wading ankle-deep in corpse water made that one little man's rampage seem pointless or, at least, infinitesimal in comparison. Nothing in the world would ever be the same again after Aceh. So it seemed. Having watched sad-eyed elephants picking through debris with their trunks feeling for bodies, I felt sure I was standing amidst the apocalypse.

One night, sitting in Banda Aceh, still rocking with aftershocks, were journalist mates Martin Chulov and Cindy Wockner, and photographer Renee Nowytarger. At varying stages all of us had been involved in the Falconio story, Renee spectacularly so. She had jumped on a flight to Singapore with Lees as she left Darwin after completing her evidence at the committal hearing. Lees, incredibly, had only been captured once by a photographer during her whole time in Darwin – and that was when she arrived at the airport for the hearing. Lees had won the battle with the media, although she did not count on Nowytarger's doggedness. Lees sat behind a curtain throughout the flight to Singapore. On landing in Singapore, she did not get off with the rest of the passengers but waited behind. But Nowytarger was waiting too, staring down a passenger tunnel with her long lens. When Lees flitted briefly into view, Nowytarger snapped and got a side-on shot of Lees. Worth the trouble? To the scorned media it was. But in Aceh no one ever mentioned the case.

Renee announced it was her birthday. She had a big bottle of vodka. There was even orange juice in the fridge. She asked if anyone wanted a drink. No one did. For journalists on assignment this was unprecedented, but that night a drink didn't seem right. Not that it was wrong, it was just that it wasn't needed. Encountering such grand-scale death had changed us all, forever. So we thought. So many to bury in Aceh that they bulldozed them into pits. And they hadn't even found a body in central Australia. But sure enough, that case about one death in central Australia did grow new legs and become important again. It would be nice to think it was because of something Aceh had showed us: that a single life, a newborn amongst the rubble, was special; or a single death, a wife stolen from her family in the diabolical tidal wash, was important and meaningful. But it wasn't that.

The truth was that it wasn't Peter Falconio's life that mattered, not to anyone but his family. He was gone and he wasn't coming back. The life in question belonged to Joanne Lees. Anyone who looked at her story, without emotion, could see she was innocent. Instead, her defiance had turned the whole thing into a cynical expedition. There was suspicion where there should have been none. The magistrate had warned at the start of the committal hearing that this was not to be the second Chamberlain case. Which, to extrapolate, meant Lees wasn't Lindy II. Maybe not. But most agreed on one thing: Lees had a way of coming over as a pain in the arse.

## 13 C/O BERRIMAH JAIL

Experts. They have their place. At a pre-trial hearing, Northern Territory Chief Justice Brian Martin ruled that most expert evidence would be allowed in open court. There were experts in forensic anatomical matching, experts in normal DNA testing, experts in unusual new methods of DNA testing, all of which pointed to Bradley Murdoch having bled, or opened a weeping sore, on the back of Joanne Lees' t-shirt, and having handled the gearstick and steering wheel of the Kombi as he shifted it off the roadside after executing Peter Falconio.

The experts, when talking of the likelihood of the DNA profile having come from one Bradley John Murdoch as compared to a person selected at random from the Northern Territory population, talked in terms of billions and quadrillions. You could tell they liked big numbers. You could also tell they were making them up. The big numbers were there to baffle, to overwhelm and convince. But the DNA wouldn't have convicted Murdoch on its own. What got him was Lees, who had finally turned up to court as a human being. It was Hepi and the Sheriff. It was Murdoch, who, with his lawyers, had weighed up, no doubt agonisingly, whether he should take his chances and give evidence on the stand.

It was Luciano Falconio, Peter's lovely, gentle, inconsolable father, who told the court through tissues that he had not heard from his son since that

14 July night, who buried once and for all the rubbish about Peter pulling some disappearing act, telling how his son, who had disappeared at the age of twenty-eight was to have turned thirty-three last month, was always a boy who'd ring home.

It was Bev Allan, a part-time lover who liked Murdoch's speed, who said he'd come home from a trip in July 2001 ranting about roadblocks and denying he was the killer. It was Rex Wild, who trusted his instincts and did not berate or shout at witnesses, but just tried to let the facts – human facts, not expert facts – do the talking. He asked Lees why she had taken money from an English television show. Lees said after 'having left Australia, I felt desperate and helpless. I wasn't receiving much help from police. I felt the taskforce had been reduced ... they'd forgotten about Pete ... this was my way of raising the profile.'

This sounded less than convincing but the judge, Brian Martin, ended all doubt. He was the only person who ever found the key to Joanne Lees' heart. Maybe it was because of what he stood for – this whole thing, the court, the event, the murder itself. Maybe it was that he just asked the right questions. Wild had been effectively gathering facts but was having trouble with the violin soundtrack. Martin interrupted with some questions of his own.

Martin: 'Now, Ms Lees, again this might be difficult. The jury have not had an experience of being stopped on the side of the road on a pitch black night in the middle of the outback. Would you please try and assist the jury with how you felt at the various stages as best you could. For example, you told the jury that when you saw the gun and the events that followed, you were supposed to turn off the ignition and your hands were shaking. Can you give the jury please an idea of how you were feeling emotionally and what was running through your head at the time?'

Lees: 'I just kept thinking, this isn't happening to me. I can't believe this is happening and I felt alone, I kept shouting for Pete. I thought I was going to die. But mainly I just kept thinking, I can't believe this was happening.' Lees was truly weeping. Everyone believed her. Everyone more or less always had, but now there was reason to. She looked liked she had really suffered.

What the judge's question had to do with the law, I didn't know. He should've been a journalist. And then he delivered the Ray Martin killer blow. 'And as the events went forward from there, are you able to tell the jury how your thought processes worked and how you were feeling emotionally? For example, after you'd been tied up and things moved on from there?'

Lees: 'It happened … it all happened quite quickly from being tied up to being on the ground. My main thoughts that I remember is just screaming out for Pete to come and help me because I was frightened so much I had just used all my energy and once he'd stood me up and put me in the back of his vehicle I just thought, that's it. I am definitely going to die. I've got no energy to get out of the situation, I just felt exhausted. The next thing, [the] emotion that I can really feel strongly about is when I asked him if he was going to rape me. I was so frightened. I was more scared of being raped than I was of dying and being shot by the man. And then when I asked him if he'd shot Pete, I kept asking, he didn't give me an answer straight away and just the realisation hit me that he might have killed Pete. I hope that helps you.'

It did.

Wild asked Lees: 'Do you see that man [who attacked you] here today?'

'Yes,' said Lees, raising her voice. 'I'm looking at him.'

Murdoch broke his Easter Island-statue countenance to shake his head in disagreement.

All that had been made of Lees saying she'd been pushed from the front of the man's cabin through to the back didn't matter anymore. None of Murdoch's cars had front-to-rear access, but that detail was unimportant. It certainly did not bother the jury. Why shouldn't she get that part wrong? Who had ever been through what she had and survived to recount the exact detail? As Rex Wild told the jury, she wasn't there taking notes.

Martin: 'And then, as you slid out of the rear of the vehicle …?'

Lees: 'After I'd asked him if he was going to rape me and if he shot Pete, I just got some energy from somewhere and some inner strength and my focus was escaping. And that's when I concentrated on getting out. Just getting out of there.'

The star witness, by then aged thirty-two, had changed her manner of entrance since the committal hearing. Lees was delivered each morning to the courthouse steps in a shiny black XR-6 Falcon cop car, Tickford-enhanced engine with a spoiler on the back. Lees was silent with the media but gracious. Photos? As many as you wish. Earlier in the week, as she arrived at court to begin her evidence at the opening of the trial, Lees had been unable to conceal her nerves, chewing anxiously at the insides of her mouth while staring bolt ahead as she ran the flash-bulb corridor.

For the first three days of her evidence and cross-examination, Lees wore her hair in a single, austere plait, pulled so tight she looked as though her head had been caught in a bus door. On Thursday, the final day of her cross-examination, she had graduated to mouthing slight, polite hellos to the press as she moved through the poking cameras. Lees had finally begun to relax into herself. She had also let her long hair go free and wore clothes that hinted that she might have a life and a personality beyond her victim status. Lees had clearly grown more comfortable in taking the witness stand; she was not going to be beaten into changing her story. And no one tried to make her do so. As she became human, she became Brad Murdoch's nightmare.

Earlier in the week, Lees and the Falconio family – Peter's brothers Nick and Paul, and parents Luciano and Joan – had barely acknowledged each other. By week's end, an understanding had been reached. All were exiting the courthouse as a unit, in a deliberately orchestrated portrayal of togetherness for the benefit of the media. At last, impressions did matter to Lees. They had always mattered. Someone had finally got through to her. Her suspicion of the media was well-founded – although she was wrong that all media wanted to lie and distort her story. One journalist, a real snake from England, had been inventing stories suggesting Falconio pulled an insurance scam and was still alive. No one followed up his stories because they were such blatant bullshit. They were also hurtful.

The *Sydney Morning Herald* had, after the committal the previous year, broken a story which identified Lees' secret lover, Nick, in a photograph, although there was no interview with him. It told how they would drink together in Sydney. When the story hit Sydney newsstands, it was borrowed from, heavily, and relayed on to London in a rewrite from a Sydney-based British reporter. Somehow, a new word had been introduced to that story. Joanne and Nick had been seen 'snogging'. It was a Pommy word and it was a lie. Another story emerged during the trial, from a more serious British broadsheet, that Rex Wild had addressed the judge as 'Brian' during the trial. No one but this one reporter had heard it. The implication was either that Rex Wild and the judge were in bed together, or that Darwin was such a Nowhereville that these best buddies got pissed on the weekend and turned up in court to thrash it out on Monday. The reporter's ears had misheard. It wasn't an act of reporting evil – even though it looked like it. It was a mistake. The paper apologised.

When Grant Algie, Murdoch's barrister, began his cross-examination, Lees acknowledged him with an expressionless stare. She was expecting to go through what she had in the committal hearing, all the detail about the boyfriend Nick, and the drugs, that joint she and Pete had smoked before the attack. Algie, surely, would say that it had interfered with her senses and rendered her description of her attacker unreliable? Lees was bracing for an assault that never came.

Algie had considered his options very carefully. There was no way the jury would think she had made all this up. As for the affair, it didn't mean she was a murderer. It had been raised with Lees by Wild in her evidence-in-chief as friendly fire. Anticipating an Algie onslaught, the prosecution needed to air this matter so it didn't look like they were hiding things from the jury. Lees had explained to Wild: 'He was a friend, a good friend, and we became close and were intimate at one time. We were just friends and we overstepped the boundary of friendship but that ended and we became friends again.'

And the joint? To try and pretend to a jury, particularly a Darwin jury, that one joint would leave a person incapable of remembering a life-and-death experience would be inviting them to regard him, Algie, as a beat-up merchant of the worst kind. It wasn't raised by Algie. None of it was. He didn't want to risk painting her as some horrible drug-gobbling slut. It was too chancy. The jury might instead see her for what she was – a young woman who was only doing what young people did. Instead, Algie pressed Lees, gently, on the detail of her recollection. He never once raised his voice at her.

Whenever Algie referred to Lees, he called her 'Joanna', not Joanne. Whether he did this deliberately cannot be known. But after all that time he might have been able to get that much right. Maybe it was a subliminal hint that back where she came from, in Yorkshire, she had a different name. Split personality. Algie used other affectations. The cable-tie handcuffs that Murdoch was alleged to have made and used to manacle Joanne Lees with were not, in Algie's lexicon, handcuffs or manacles. They were 'wrist bandages'. And the man who attacked Lees and Falconio was never a killer or assailant – and he especially wasn't Murdoch. He was the nebulous 'bad guy'. It was an attempt by Algie to acknowledge that *perhaps* Lees had been through a trauma while making it plain there was some other monster still roaming at will.

Algie: 'Did you grab the man's testicles and squeeze them?'

Lees: 'I think I … that's what I was aiming for but I just reached sort of his inner leg but it had no effect.'

Algie: 'I mean, from the position in which you've described, with your hands handcuffed behind your back, you wouldn't physically have been able to reach to grab a man's testicles, would you?'

Lees: 'Yes.'

Algie: 'But didn't you tell the police…'

The attack, in real time, had been over in minutes. Lees was dragged, for hours, through the fine detail of how Algie's bad guy had restrained her and held her on the ground. Algie found it strange that as the man led Lees to his vehicle, parked behind the Kombi, she didn't try to glance back to see where Peter was. 'I was concerned for my own life,' said Lees. Murdoch also had his hand on the back of her neck, guiding and forcing her to his car. As for the dog, which she would wrongly identify as a blue heeler when it was in fact a dalmatian-cross, she had, in fact, only seen it for a few seconds, in the dim cabin light.

Lees' strong belief had once been that she had been pushed into Murdoch's cabin and then shoved into the back of the vehicle through a passage. This was supposed to be one of her biggest hurdles. Lees knew, by now, that Murdoch's vehicle did not have front-to-rear access. She was now not so certain how she got in the back.

Algie: 'Can you ... are you able to explain how it would appear that your belief you had then you no longer hold?'

Lees didn't try to cover her tracks: 'Yes. The police told me that there is no such vehicle that has front-to-rear access and that has put doubt in my mind and I looked at other possibilities ... all I know is I got from the front to the back quite easily. I did not walk around the vehicle.' It was simple. She had a sack over her head. Murdoch had pulled her out of the front and shoved her in the back.

At one point, Algie said as a statement rather than a question to Lees that Murdoch was not the man at the truck stop. I looked over to the jury and saw one woman actually roll her eyes.

Algie: 'Whatever did or didn't happen at Barrow Creek, Mr Murdoch wasn't the man you've described as doing these things. Might I be right about that?'

Lees: 'No.'

Algie: 'Do you think you might be mistaken in identifying [photo] number 10 as the man north of Barrow Creek?'

Lees: 'No.'

Algie: 'I suggest that you are wrong when you say that Mr Murdoch or any image of him represents any man who might have been north of Barrow Creek. Do you disagree with that?'

Lees: 'He is the man who attacked me north of Barrow Creek.'
Algie: 'Thank you, Ms Lees.'

There were many reasons for the intense interest in the case, none of them singularly persuasive. It had become a juggernaut upon which everyone had clambered. There was no point getting off until the end. It wasn't just the media. Presumably there was an audience out there, taken by the notion of two harmless young foreigners, waylaid in a gracious land that had suddenly turned hostile. It was the questions about Lees and her remarkable deliverance, which some could still not accept as truth. And it was the unremarkable scene of the crime, just another stretch of the straight-through-the-middle Stuart Highway, which for some reason had been stirring the darker corners of the collective imagination. No one could really explain the fascination. It certainly wasn't a cautionary tale. Other English couples would continue to travel the Stuart Highway. Someone tried to give the fascination a reason, a logic, suggesting: 'It was just that this could have happened to anyone.' Perhaps, but it had happened to *them*. It seemed to me, more than anything, the story of an all-Australian maniac.

Funnily enough – although he didn't find it so – a man named Stuart Highway was being sentenced to three months in jail in the courtroom next door, just as the Murdoch trial got underway. Highway, a normally mild, usual-suspect activist around Darwin who protested about almost everything, had smashed the windscreen of a police car during an anti-drug prohibition rally in Darwin's Raintree Park in 2002. Attempts by Highway's mates to interest the national and international press in what they saw as a political jailing failed. He wasn't David Hicks.

At times the Darwin courtroom seemed to be directly transported to that bloodstained stretch of road, a long way to the south. The air-conditioning system in Court 6 was providing its own highway soundtrack, every few minutes rumbling deeply and sounding for all the world like a passing road train. Above the judge, on the coat of arms, two red kangaroos faced off between secret-sacred Aboriginal designs. A wedge-tailed eagle, Australia's supreme bird of prey, hung above it all, a magical Aboriginal tjurunga stone grasped in its talons. What the crest didn't let on was that wedge-tails had evolved into opportunistic birds that hang off to one side of the bitumen, waiting to feed on what the road trains and cars knock over. Roadkill was the business at hand.

Prosecutor Wild had said in his opening address that Falconio would turn up, or be upturned, somewhere down the track. 'He will be found one day, I'd suggest to you,' he'd said, offering no evidence for his optimism on this point. Murdoch had told Hepi the best place to bury someone was in a spoon drain. Anyone who knew those roads could tell you that those drains appeared every few hundred metres. And if not in a spoon drain, then where? Best ask the eagles and the dingoes.

After Lees concluded her evidence on Thursday, the foreign press began to consider leaving town. The whole week's hearing had been conducted in such a polite, restrained way. The expected fireworks had not arrived. With Joanne Lees cooperating with the media, walking to and from the court by the front entrance, no one was spending their after-court hours trying to find and photograph her at her secret location in Darwin. One day, inside the courthouse, Lees walked past me, smiled and said a deliberate hello. Things had changed.

The Falconio family were such neat, well-ironed people. They must have wondered about some of the Darwin locals who turned up to court. One big woman took a seat in the public gallery wearing a worn-out see-through sarong, her straining g-string tantalisingly cutting its way through two giant back boulders. One of the jury members wore boardies and reclined with his knees up on the bench in front of him. Darryl Cragan, Dags, bush pirate, dragged himself to the stand in thongs, stubbies and a black t-shirt. The prosecution did not, for this trial, do what it often would do when briefing witnesses – ask them to dress well in order to convey a good impression to judge and jury. This was Darwin and the message was: be yourself. It was what was said that mattered. What those witnesses were saying, overwhelmingly, was that the man pictured on close-circuit television in the truck stop was Murdoch.

Big things had been expected from Brian 'The Sheriff' Johnston at the committal. After his no-show, someone 'had a word' and made sure he got to Darwin for the trial. A mental picture had formed of a cool, resolute man, unwilling to pick up a gun but, if forced, ready to stare down the worst mongrel a dusty town can manufacture. Someone was having a lend. Why they called him Sheriff was never explained – but he talked real slow and was not completely on the side of law. The Sheriff made three trips between Broome and Sedan with Murdoch, knowing full well the purpose of the journeys. The reason he went along, it seems, was to keep Murdoch company.

On his first trip with Murdoch, the Sheriff was driving when – in the words of Rex Wild – he had 'a disagreement with a kangaroo'. Sheriff had broken the cardinal rule of bush driving by swerving to miss that kangaroo. As any experienced bush driver knew, you didn't risk rolling the vehicle by swerving for the national emblem – you keep going and collect it. Especially if you were driving a V8 F100 with a battle-strength bullbar, Murdoch's car at the time. After that incident, Murdoch did not let the Sheriff drive his car. The Sheriff was with Murdoch and Hepi at the Sedan block in March 2001 when Murdoch bought a second hand HZJ75 Toyota Land Cruiser ute. The Sheriff said he assisted Murdoch in cutting the tray off the F100 and shifting it to the back of the Land Cruiser. He recalled that the mesh sides were drilled off the canopy and chucked out the back of a shed at Hepi's place. That was four months before the Falconio-Lees attack.

In court, the Sheriff was wide-eyed and terrified. All he knew how to be was honest. He did not know what else to do. That bit about how he'd helped Murdoch cut the mesh sides off his Land Cruiser was vital evidence and would help see Murdoch convicted for murder.

Part of Murdoch's defence was that the lockable steel-mesh sides were still in place on 14 July 2001. The significance of this was that Lees, when she made her escape that night, never said she had to fight her way through a steel-mesh cage to exit the vehicle. She just had to push out of a canvas canopy. Algie wanted it known that she had identified the wrong man because Murdoch's vehicle had mesh sides on it in July 2001. Yet three witnesses insisted the mesh had been gone by then. It was Johnston – who had no reason to lie, and many good reasons to try and save himself from the wrath of Murdoch, should Murdoch walk free – who nailed Murdoch on this crucial aspect. He was there when the mesh sides were removed. He'd helped remove them. He also said that Murdoch always travelled with a gun and tended to average at least 110 kilometres per hour on dirt roads. He, along with Cragan, had not been promised any immunity from prosecution in exchange for their testimony, which would see them identified as participants in Murdoch's drug trafficking. Rex Wild would come to consider this otherwise unimpressive little 'Sheriff' man as having gone a long way to helping the jury in arriving at their decision.

Algie put it to the Sheriff that Murdoch tended to have 'quite an erect, upright posture' when he walked, unlike the stooped man in the truck stop footage. The meek Sheriff looked bewildered: 'Not really, not to my knowledge, anyway.'

Algie: 'Tell me this, Mr Johnston, might it be that the man in the video is not Mr Murdoch?'

The Sheriff gulped: 'I think it is.'

During the committal hearing, Algie had been unable to unsettle Hepi. Hepi had even agreed he'd testified against Murdoch to save his own neck. During cross-examination by Algie, Hepi was being asked to look at police photos from South Australia which showed Murdoch's belongings in the back of his Land Cruiser. Hepi told Algie: 'He's packed all his gear in there just after he had abducted and raped children and the whole likes of – so that's probably all his belongings stuffed in there.'

Hepi's reference to the South Australian rape case sent a silent bolt through the court. Algie didn't comment on it, nor did Wild or the judge, but it was immediately clear this could be grounds for a mistrial. Any discussion about the South Australian rape charges was strictly off-limits: Murdoch had walked free from that trial, and you couldn't have this jury being told Murdoch was a child rapist. Technically, he wasn't.

Later in the day the judge advised the jury to ignore what Hepi had said about rape. For the Murdoch team, that was not good enough. In a closed-court session they applied for the trial to be aborted because Hepi had deeply prejudiced his client's case. But there was no way the judge, Martin, was going to bring this train to a halt unless he absolutely had to. He refused, reasoning there had already been substantial publicity about the South Australian trial and that what Hepi had said 'did not materially add to the jury's collective knowledge of the South Australian proceedings'.

Rex Wild asked Hepi about the Murdoch meeting that went bad in the Perth carpark. Hepi replied: 'He met me in the carpark and at the time I asked why he was late and all that and he said he had trouble getting across the border because they were looking for the Northern Territory murderer.'

Murdoch half shifted in his seat and rumbled: 'You're a fucking liar!'

Hepi didn't flinch or hesitate for a second. He looked Murdoch straight in the eye and sent him a loud 'Fuck you', hard and straight as an arrow.

It's hard to know what the jury made of this but it was, in all likelihood, a pivotal moment for them. In a sense, Hepi released them from their fears. While jurors' identities are kept secret, and there is no history in Australia of jurors being hunted down in retribution for finding a person guilty, Murdoch cut an intimidating figure. They had never seen him standing upright, because every day he took his place in the dock before the jury entered the courtroom. And the jury always left the room before Murdoch. But they knew he was a big man – and would confirm it, the day after Hepi testified, when the chief justice called for everyone to stand for a minute's silence to mark Remembrance Day. Some of the jurors, I noted, took a peek at Murdoch.

Jurors are afraid of jailing people, and not just because they might be innocent. They're scared for themselves. Especially with a bloke like Murdoch, who gave the impression of being connected to an outback-bikie underworld. Murdoch sat through the entire trial grimacing, muttering and rolling his eyes. When disagreeing with a witness at one point, he made a wanking motion with his left hand. He also tried to offset all these instinctive gestures by pretending to be studiously taking notes. But if the Crown was right, he was an opportunistic killer, a drug runner, a gun freak and a bitter loose cannon. And Hepi had taken him on, said 'Fuck you' right back to his face. Hepi showed that he was not frightened of him. The jury must have taken courage from that.

A Darwin jury had jailed Lindy Chamberlain on dodgy evidence. And now, twenty years on the country's most major murder trial since Chamberlain, being played out in the same city, they had plenty of circumstantial evidence on which to convict Murdoch. But would they? This jury was on notice.


The fragile figure of Bev Allan, occasional sexual partner of Murdoch, appeared in court, desperately against her wishes. She was clearly frightened of Murdoch. Allan said when Murdoch returned to Broome in mid-July 2001, he'd come to see her. He was a mess, scattered and hungover on speed. 'He told me it hadn't been a good trip. Said there'd been a few dramas, he suspected somebody had been following him on that occasion and that he'd had to deal with it.' Murdoch didn't explain – and she didn't ask – what he meant by 'deal with it'. Bev Allan had soothed Murdoch's nerves by rubbing him down with Vicks.

Allan had been for a drive to Wyndham in Murdoch's HZJ75 soon after he'd brought it back from South Australia. She said it didn't have mesh sides. She also knew Murdoch to own a Pennzoil cap which, although it was indistinct, was very much like the cap Truck Stop Man had worn.

Algie: 'Now, that may not be Murdoch in those photographs, do you agree with that?'

Allan tried to shrug off her discomfort. 'Well, in my opinion, it is him.'

Murdoch had a confidante, Jan Pitman, who was taking the same seat in court every day, guarding it fiercely, shooing away interlopers. She had now come out to nail herself to Murdoch's crucifix. There is a phenomenon of women who attach themselves to murderers and lifers, although it has not yet been named. Maybe 'wifers' says it all.

When Bev Allan exited the witness stand she passed Pitman, who looked Allan up and down with disgust. Pitman, middle-aged and brick-shaped, once wore a t-shirt with 'Don't Even Think About It' emblazoned across her chest. She was on safe ground there. Pitman would slowly blink her heavily painted eyelids and chew gum. It was to Pitman that Murdoch would make his exasperation known, rolling his eyes, muttering at something a witness or lawyer had said. She would stare back at him, expressionless, but absorbing his frustration.

Joanne Lees was now taking a seat in court every day. So was Luciano and his wife, Peter's mother Joan. Paul Falconio had gone home but Nick was hanging in till the end. Nick was pleasant and talkative and certain Murdoch was the man. He told of life in village Yorkshire, where people lived in cold old stone houses and life, at least on the face of it, hadn't changed much for centuries. He seemed a good man.

Melissa Kendall and her partner, Robert Brown, took the stand, the wild-card Crown witnesses. With their claims of seeing Falconio alive at their service station in Bourke after the attack, claims which were not for one moment credible, they were only there so the Crown could show it was providing some balance by not ignoring so-called evidence, no matter how absurd it was. Brown had improved on his repartee from the committal, where he had called Falconio 'Peter'. He was now referring to him as 'Pete'. It was too much for poor Mrs Falconio, who got up and left the room.

Several police were asked by Algie whether they had planted Murdoch's DNA on items in order to gain Murdoch's conviction. One of them, Detective Sergeant David Chalker, let Algie know he found it 'very offensive that you suggest that'. And it was indeed just a shot in the dark by Algie. If the police had wanted to fit up Murdoch, they could have poured his DNA all over the Kombi, and on Lees' clothes.

Senior Sergeant Megan Rowe was the final Crown witness, there to 'sweep up' any outstanding matters and to put the finishing touches to the Crown case. She was a considerate cop who won the respect of all who got to know her. She said she had been on the trail of Falconio's killer since July 2001, and gave an insight into the difficulty police faced in trying to find their man. In the early stages, all the police had was a possible suspect – the man pictured in the Shell Truck Stop – and the DNA found on a blood spot on the back of the t-shirt Joanne Lees was wearing at the time. The public made some 8000 calls to the police and tens of thousands of pages of information were generated. They also had partial DNA evidence which they picked up from the gearstick of the Kombi van. It seemed to match the blood spot on Lees' t-shirt. They had a profile but not a person. Rowe revealed that four members of the public had, prior to Murdoch's arrest, rung in to say Murdoch was the Truck Stop Man. This, you might have thought, when taken together with Hepi's statement, would cause the cavalry to be raised to try to bring Murdoch in for immediate questioning. Hepi said he was never even asked if he knew where Murdoch was. Which was in South Australia, about to assault a mother and daughter.

According to information provided by Lees, some items were never recovered from the Kombi van. They included her denim jacket and a half-heart pendant. And missing, with Falconio, was his St Christopher medal. This saint was, bleakly enough, the patron saint of safe travel – although, even bleaker, St Christopher's name was struck from the Universal Calendar of Saints after it was discovered that he did not exist.

The Crown case, involving some eighty witnesses over six weeks, concluded in early December 2005. It was four-and-a-half years on from Falconio's disappearance. No one except the defence knew whether Murdoch would take the stand and speak for himself. It was his right not to say anything to the jury, but they might take his silence as guilty arrogance. And what if he lost his temper? That wouldn't help. Court rules meant that the prosecution would get to cross-examine Murdoch if he testified. But the whole thing had not been going well for Murdoch. The DNA evidence was damaging, Lees had proven unshakeable, Hepi had clashed with Murdoch and come off better, his old part-time Broome-based girlfriend, Beverley Allan, was completely convincing, and Sheriff was strong too.

The judge asked Algie if the accused intended to give evidence. 'He does, your honour, and, if your honour pleases, I'll call Brad Murdoch.'

As he had done in the committal, Murdoch wore long shirts to court in order to conceal his full sleeve tattoos. He stood, wrenched back his shoulders to conceal his stoop and, looking like a giant duck, took a short flat-footed walk from the dock to the witness stand. He made an affirmation and told Algie how he had been born in Northampton, north of Geraldton in Western Australia. He tried to sound straight up, like a working bloke, and gave the jury a bit of the vernacular so they could see what he was like. He'd left school at fifteen and had worked ever since. 'Maybe around the transport industry, pulling spanners, mechanical work. Bit in the fishing industry. Mainly around transport and pulling spanners and truck driving.' His dad had died sometime after this whole arrest fiasco and he wasn't able to go to the funeral. That had been hard.

Murdoch told how he loved his cars, a bit of an obsession, really. He talked of how he'd shifted marijuana with Hepi, large amounts, up to twenty-five pounds, hidden in an aluminium capsule compartment in his long-range fuel tank. He would take different routes, always with Jack, his dog, and always with weapons which were to be used 'as a protectant'. One was a .357 and the other a .38 Beretta. He agreed he had met Julieanne McPhail on the road but said he'd never offered to sell her a gun.

Murdoch claimed he had set off on his trip to Broome, which took him through Alice Springs, on 14 July. He had taken the trailer in order to look like 'Tommy Tourist' and 'You know, we were doing something illegal'. Tommy Tourist? Pulling spanners? It didn't sound like good honest bush talk. It was forced and too chummy.

One of the reasons he couldn't have been at the Shell Truck Stop, he said, was that he only used BP. 'They're convenient, they've got clean fuel.' I noted two jurors exchanging glances.

In his earlier questioning of Lees, Algie had dwelled, at length, on a visit to the Alice Springs Red Rooster that Lees and Falconio made on the afternoon of 14 July, just before they had set off from town. Why he was so interested in this was not, at that stage, apparent. He now asked Murdoch how he ate on the road. 'Yeah, yeah, well, a couple of tubs in the back, we've got all dry tucker, cooking goods, got a fridge for any small meats or carry a little bit of steak here and there if you want to have a feed, so generally you're independent but every now and then you feel like calling into the roadhouse and grabbing a steak sandwich.'

Murdoch said he rolled into Alice Springs at about 10 am on 14 July. 'First thing in Alice, pulled in to the Red Rooster, that's a bit of a spot we always used to sort of go to. Chicken roll, box of nuggets for Jack. Jack was a bit of a liker on nuggets. Full chicken for the trip.'

I would learn after the trial that Murdoch had, during the committal hearing and trial, refused to eat chicken in sandwiches – or in any form – at lunch. And that in Berrimah Prison, he had a standing-order medical certificate that he was not to be served chicken or eggs, ever. They upset him.

When Northern Territory detectives Colleen Gwynn and David Chalker visited Murdoch in Yatala jail in 2003, where he was awaiting trial for the rape charges, they had an unrecorded discussion with Murdoch. It was to be an off-the-record chat but, when they left the prison, they immediately took notes of the discussion. Under the heading 'Topics Covered', the officers wrote how Murdoch had told them of his movements in Alice Springs that day. He mentioned visiting Repco and refuelling at BP. There was no mention of Red Rooster. He had made it up, after hearing Lees say during the committal hearing how she and Falconio had been to Red Rooster that day.

Obviously Murdoch had needed to create a location where he might have crossed paths with Lees and Falconio that day. He needed a DNA transfer point. Anywhere that wasn't Barrow Creek. He couldn't easily say he'd been to the Camel Cup, which the couple had attended. He'd never seen a Camel Cup and might be questioned on it. As for rubbing up against Lees in Repco, or at Barbeques Galore which he'd also visited, that wasn't easy either – Lees and Falconio kept all their receipts, and they had not stepped foot in either place. Murdoch settled on Red Rooster.

In a pre-trial hearing, the prosecution attempted to seek permission to introduce the detectives' notes into court. At the time they weren't interested in chicken allergies, and in fact did not learn about Murdoch's aversion until after the trial had concluded. But they were interested in these new claims that he'd visited Red Rooster. These notes represented the only time Murdoch had ever talked to those building a case against him. The judge disallowed them into evidence because it had been an off-the-record discussion. Had the prosecution known of Murdoch's medical problem, they could have asked one question: 'Mr Murdoch, do you eat chicken?' It could well have sunk him. The whole thing could have been called off and everyone could have gone home. Or maybe not. Murdoch, so accomplished at fashioning lies, could have said it was a recently acquired allergy. I'd asked Hepi, without briefing him on the reason for the question, whether he could ever recall Murdoch eating chicken. 'Chicken? *Chicken?* I don't know. I can't remember. All I know is that we had so much money all we ever ate was scotch fillet.'

Even though he was a drug courier who always moved fast, stopping nowhere long except to refuel, Murdoch insisted he'd spent a leisurely day in Alice Springs. He said he went to the Toyota dealership to use a high-powered hose to clean the undercarriage of his vehicle of the white limestone dust of the Sedan–Swan Reach region. He said he didn't want to turn up in Western Australia with his car covered in white dust, because that would have been suspicious. Even though, by the time he got to Broome, the vehicle's undercarriage would be covered in the red mud of the Kimberleys. He did some shopping at Repco, stuck his head in at Barbeques Galore, fuelled up at BP, did a bit of shopping at Bi-Lo – 'I bought iced coffee, yoghurt, Yakult, some general dry goods, dry biscuits, bit of bread, small goods, meats, tomatoes, bits and pieces.' And then, he said, he left Alice

Springs. He said he turned left onto the Tanami Track, 20 kilometres north of Alice, at about 3.30 pm, and slowly headed northwest. He said he did not drive directly north to Barrow Creek – 'No, I did not' – nor did he have anything to do with what Algie called 'the alleged disappearance' of Falconio: 'No, I did not.'

Murdoch said he nursed his combat-ready vehicle towards Western Australia at a docile '50, 60 kilometres an hour. I'm a big one for letting my tyres down,' he said easily, explaining how it gave a softer ride and things in the back didn't get broken. Jurors stirred. Lunch break was called. The court doors flew open and people made for the foyer, brushing the heavy-settling bullshit from their shoulders.

Murdoch couldn't explain how his blood got on Lees' t-shirt. 'I don't know whether I crossed their paths or not.'

Murdoch's decision to take the stand, to charm the jury with his knockabout Aussie loner drivel, was damaging. Rex Wild did not waste time when he rose to tackle Murdoch. 'Where did you bury Peter Falconio?' he demanded. Murdoch looked wounded and indignant. Shocked. Hurt. He leaned back in horror. The question was distasteful, vulgar even. It was as if the very notion that this whole trial about him cold-whacking a bullet into Falconio's brain was a new one on him. Algie had to do something. His client was upset. He rose with a lame, 'I object.'

Wild asked Murdoch whether he bled easily. 'I do bleed easily, yeah,' said Murdoch, explaining that he had a non-specific medical condition.

Wild: 'Were you bleeding on 14 July 2001?'

Murdoch: 'I don't know.'

Wild: 'Do you remember any particular injury at that time?'

Murdoch: 'Don't know.'

Wild: 'Do you have nose bleeds?'

Murdoch: 'No.'

Wild: 'How did the blood, your blood, which matches the DNA found on the back of Joanne Lees' t-shirt, get there?'

Murdoch: 'I don't know.'

Wild: 'You do, don't you?'

Murdoch: 'No, I don't.'

Wild had Murdoch and would not let him go. He took him through everything, over and over, to the point where Murdoch was rolling his eyes in frustration, looking pathetically to the jury for sympathy they did not have, trying to get them to see what a waste of time this all was. But the jury was absorbed, totally. They knew they were listening to a killer trying to save himself.

Wild hammered on about the witnesses who had said his mesh sides were missing in the period including 14 July. Murdoch said he would have never have gotten rid of them because he wanted them for Jack, the dog, so he could ride safely in the cage at the back. 'I give my dog Jack more respect than all of those people,' said Murdoch of his former friends.

Wild: 'I suggest you pulled over the Kombi and met the driver at the back of the vehicle?'

Murdoch: 'No.'

Wild: 'And shot him dead?'

Murdoch: 'No.'

Wild: 'You had to, on the night, move the Kombi from the place it was?'

Murdoch: 'No.'

Wild: 'And as a result of that you left your DNA on the gearstick of the Kombi?'

Murdoch: 'No.'

Wild: 'You had to dispose of Peter Falconio?'

Murdoch: 'No.'

Wild: 'You're a fastidious man, aren't you Mr Murdoch?'

Murdoch: 'I am a bit meticulous.'

Wild: 'You didn't want any blood in your vehicle, did you?'

Murdoch: 'I never had Mr Falconio in my vehicle and I did not commit this, so.'

Wild: 'You used the denim jacket to wrap his head in?'

Murdoch: 'No.'

Wild: 'You ended up with a hair tie as a souvenir?'

Murdoch: 'No.'

Algie then called, on Murdoch's behalf, a DNA forensic science expert, the elderly Dr Katrin Both, to cast doubt on the validity of the new-fangled DNA extraction technique known as low copy number. Using this new technology, police were able to pull the black-tape-wrapped zip-tie handcuffs and find miniscule amounts of Murdoch's DNA. Dr Both said she had 'a large number of concerns' about the reliability of the procedure.

It would have been dull court time except that Tony Elliott got stuck into her. Elliott focused on her inconsistencies and managed to turn her from a comfortable DNA elder into a snappy and defensive person who may not have been au fait with the new techniques. She stormed out of court and was heard vowing she would never again give expert evidence.

Algie called another elderly expert, biological anthropologist Maceij Hennenberg, who was there to testify that the man in the truck stop was, in no way, Murdoch. His reasoning involved a study he had done comparing koala hands to human hands, and he discoursed at length on how central Europeans had 'round heads like a soccer ball' by comparison to Aborigines, who had elongated 'rugby ball' heads. It wouldn't have mattered if there was a breed of humans with light-bulb heads. The jury knew the man at the truck stop was Murdoch.

On Monday 5 December, Algie began summing up to the jury. 'Well, ladies and gentlemen, here we all are again,' he said, weary. He was only there to assist them with certain matters. The first matter he wanted to help them with related to a spot 10 kilometres north of Barrow Creek. But he couldn't actually help them with that – the location where Murdoch was supposed to have killed Peter Falconio and attempted to abduct his girlfriend, 'Joanna' Lees – because 'Brad Murdoch wasn't there'. The whole prosecution case was strange, said Algie. There was no blood on the Kombi van Falconio and Lees were driving. No brain or bone fragment found in the patch of roadside blood. No projectile – or bullet – was ever found. Why?

Algie admitted that the prosecution had made a case that the projectile might have lodged in Falconio's skull and never left it, which would explain why they never found the bullet. But it bothered him. Algie talked of the 'unknown, unrelated bad guy' who had done all these things. He couldn't understand the logic of someone shooting someone and then picking up the body and putting it in his car. Not a meticulous man like Murdoch, who fussed about and loved his vehicles and would not have abided any blood spill. He told the jury the absence of Falconio's body was 'cause for serious concern when you're asked to return a verdict of murder'.

'From time to time, some people disappear themselves for reasons that are best known to them,' said Algie as the Falconio family and Lees stared straight ahead in disbelief. The man seen at the truck stop 'could've come from anywhere', said Algie. 'It's just a guy at a truck stop with a moustache.' He said the most powerful, non-circumstantial piece of evidence in the case – the spot of blood on the back of Lees' t-shirt – proved nothing. There was no dispute that Lees, Falconio and Murdoch were all in Alice Springs on 14 July. There was not even any dispute that this particular DNA sample belonged to his client. But Algie said Murdoch could have 'got a cut or something' and left a small amount of blood 'on a seat, on a door, doorframe, something like that. She comes along and a secondary transfer takes place.' Jury members weren't looking at each other. Their eyes were downcast. It was borderline embarrassing.

Algie attacked the evidence of Professor Jonathon Whittaker, who had pioneered the method of low copy number DNA extraction and testified that he had found Murdoch's DNA from within the handcuffs from a sample sent to his English laboratory. But playing the man rather than the science, Algie went for Whittaker, who had possibly come across as a little pompous when he proclaimed himself the world's leading expert in his field. 'It may be, members of the jury, that you take the view that, you know, experts telling us colonials that that's the way it is because they say it is not satisfactory. I mean, many of you, ladies and gentlemen, would be acutely aware that some twenty-odd years ago up here in the Supreme Court in Darwin, experts gave evidence that it was fetal haemoglobin, fetal blood, on the inside of the car that led to another conviction for murder. No doubt because they were experts you should believe them. But they were wrong.' And there it was, full circle back to Lindy. What Algie was saying was, in its own way, a threat: a Darwin jury had got Lindy wrong – don't get this one wrong. They may not have liked that, but Algie had to do something. He was going down and he knew it. He now knew he should never have been a gentleman with Lees. He should have torn her throat out. But it was all too late.

Algie turned on the Northern Territory police force, painting a picture of a group of conspiratorial, dirty cops who were not interested in finding the Barrow Creek assailant, just fitting up Murdoch for the deed. There were two main strands to this argument: the first was that when police searched the spot off the Stuart Highway where 'Joanna' had hidden after the attack, they initially found only the lid of the lip balm. But months later, on a second search in October 2001, they found the lip balm container and bits of black tape she had spat out after trying to bite her hands free. How had they missed it the first time? Had they planted it in order to shore up Lees' improbable story? He wondered out loud if 'some kangaroo came along and took away the lip balm container for a few months and then brought it back'. No one in the jury laughed.

The other strand was that police had planted DNA in the handcuffs sent to Britain for Whittaker to examine. Although Algie did not accept that Whittaker's pioneering low copy number DNA extraction methods were valid, what if they were? 'There's another possibility, I suppose, members of the jury, isn't there? Could they have been contaminated intentionally, members of the jury? Could it be, to adopt the vernacular, a set-up, a fit? Would police do that, members of the jury? Do you think that's possible?'

Look at the royal commissions into police corruption in Australian states, said Algie. They do it all the time. If police were sure Brad Murdoch had done it, would they 'bend the rules, fabricate a little bit, lie a little bit, particularly if there's no harm done?' Somebody played around with the evidence, said Algie. 'Perhaps it was a dingo. Who knows?' Algie had misjudged the jury's willingness to do the task that it had been set. He presented an argument about history and politics and corruption, not about a specific murder. It was a bad move.

Algie told the jury to give Brad Murdoch 'some credit' for choosing to take the stand and testify on his own behalf. After all, Brad didn't have to. Murdoch was a 'knockabout sort of bloke, a man's man perhaps', said Algie, talking fondly about 'the Brad Murdoch we've come to know' during the course of the trial. He was admittedly a big-time drug runner who took speed and had armed himself on his travels, but was just in the wrong place at the wrong time. He just got caught up in this terrible mess.

'He was not at the Shell Truck Stop,' said Algie. 'He wasn't at Barrow Creek. He didn't go there. It wasn't him.' And so it went. 'Joanna' Lees had got so many things wrong. She'd said she'd made a lunge for the man's testicles as he was attempting to truss her up. Unlikely. What about her statement that her attacker's car had front-to-rear access, through which the 'bad guy' shoved her? Murdoch had no such car. Would a person such as Lees really have hidden in the bushes for so many hours before seeking help? Why not run straight out and flag down help?

Algie also made a brief remark – but did not expand on it – that Lees could have driven the Kombi van with her wrists manacled. The inference was clear: she was part of a conspiracy to kill her boyfriend, or to help him disappear. She could have been the one who shifted the Kombi off the highway and hid it in the scrub. Peter Falconio dead? Where was the proof? 'Thank you, members of the jury, for listening. On behalf of Brad Murdoch, thank you.'

'Corruption, conspiracies, this innuendo running through the case,' Wild told the jury. 'There is not one tittle of evidence to support it. Not one.' The cops could so easily have fitted Murdoch up good and proper, if they wished. But they didn't. They just went with the evidence they had. As for Algie raising the spectre of a notorious case from decades earlier, Wild advised the jury to be cautious: 'You're not interested in what happened in the Azaria Chamberlain case. You're interested in this case.' He counselled against those who would turn what happened on 14 July into a 'mystery'. 'I've heard it said at various times that this is "the Peter Falconio mystery". It's no mystery. Peter Falconio died on 14 July 2001.' Brad Murdoch killed him.

Joanne Lees might have got certain details wrong about the attack that night. Why not? 'This young woman was in a state of emergency – she was in fact fighting for her life,' said Wild. 'She was not there taking notes. She was having the most terrifying experience of her life or any person in this room could have.'

Wild noted that two of the three 'expert' scientific witnesses the Murdoch team had called were 'older' – they were in semi-retirement. They disputed the evidence provided by the Crown's younger scientific experts. Wild wondered if perhaps they weren't up with the latest methods, or were reluctant to acknowledge the skills of younger people coming up in their field. Murdoch looked at Jan Pitman and clearly mouthed the words: 'What a fucking wanker.' Pitman looked embarrassed and tried to shush him.

Here was a man, said Wild, with no loyalty to his friends. Even those who cared about him, like Bev Allan. Murdoch had said Bev Allan was nothing more than a woman who wanted to score drugs from him. Wild said Murdoch cared only for himself. 'This was a person who was obviously fond of him. He didn't care about her.' Wild said Murdoch had more regard for his dog than his friends. 'Very dismissive of other human beings. That's the nature of Brad Murdoch.' Pitman let go a major eye-roll.

What about the sunken-cheeked, sunken-eyed, mustachioed, thong-wearing bloke seen in the truck stop? 'Who,' asked Wild, 'does that sound like? It sounds like Brad Murdoch.' So it did.

Anyone who had sat through the trial had to wonder and worry whether the jury would be able to look past all the prejudice that had formed around Joanne Lees and see the black heart of Brad Murdoch. And it was a worry. He was a gun menace, a rapist and a killer. He was a man who thought, very wrongly, that being a road-warrior, tough-guy, KKK-tattooed outback kind of bloke marked him as a real man.

If Dave Fielder, Murdoch's old mate from Fitzroy Crossing, was right, Murdoch killed Falconio because Falconio had upset Murdoch. An argument over drugs, or perhaps the Falconio upstart had not shown the outback diehard due respect, maybe giving Murdoch the middle finger during one of those life-or-death roadtrain-coming moments so commonplace on the Northern Territory's inadequate two-lane Stuart Highway.

To take Fielder's line further, Joanne Lees was therefore merely a dividend, a war prize, someone to drag off and rape, a bonus he picked up while punishing Falconio for some infinitesimal offence he'd given. Police never thought any such thing. To them, it seemed most likely that the predator had seen Lees at the wheel of the Kombi van as she and her boyfriend drove out of Alice Springs on 14 July. Falconio was, at the time, lying in the back of the Kombi, reading and sleeping. Murdoch saw the attractive, jutting-breasted, long-haired Lees, apparently with no companion. He was out of his mind on speed and looking for release. It was Lees he was after. Of course, Murdoch would have known that she wouldn't have been by herself. Young women don't make those long road trips alone. He knew there'd be some bloke in the back, some weak Pommy or German. He could deal with him.

The jury took less than five hours to make up its unanimous mind. Guilty. On all counts.

Joanne Lees did not spare the media when she gave her victim-impact statement that Wild read to the court on her behalf before the judge passed sentence. She talked of the grotesque intrusions, having to move house eight times in order to escape the press. She said she had been watched and followed. Her hairdresser had been approached for an interview.

The judge told Murdoch something about himself, something Murdoch had probably never considered before: he was a coward. The judge also delivered a neat psychological slap, refusing to rate him among the worst of the worst killers lest Murdoch take pride in it. 'There are many adjectives that could be used to describe the cold-blooded nature and brutality of your conduct,' said Martin. 'I will not use those adjectives because I do not wish to encourage the perverse thinking within correctional institutions which ranks inmates according to the brutality of their crimes.'

The judge openly accused the defence of trying to embarrass Lees by dredging up an affair she had had with Nick before she left Sydney on her journey north. He said it was utterly irrelevant. And the judge was clearly angry that the defence had raised the hurtful spectre that Falconio was not dead, hinting, but only ever vaguely, that Lees could have had something to do with his disappearance. The judge slammed Murdoch, in a somewhat vicarious attack on Algie, for suggesting Lees was a liar and that Falconio was still alive. He said he agreed with the jury's verdicts.

When Murdoch had pinned down twelve-year-old Jane in 2002, he told her: 'If you move I will give you brain damage.' It was a vile threat, just about the lowest utterance conceivable. The modus operandi of this crime, a year after the Falconio execution, had the same telltale signs: women shoved in the back of a vehicle, bound and manacled.

Chief Justice Martin told Murdoch he would serve twenty-eight years in Berrimah prison before he could apply for parole. But, as the judge noted, he could well be dead by then. I wondered how Martin had arrived at that figure. Peter Falconio was twenty-eight when he died. Perhaps the judge gave Murdoch one year for every year of Falconio's life.

At Murdoch's sentencing, Wild disclosed that Murdoch had received a three-month suspended sentence for causing the death of another driver in 1980. He had served time in Western Australia for shooting into a crowd of Fitzroy Crossing Aborigines who were partying in a riverbed after winning a grand final. He didn't kill anyone but the judge in that case noted Murdoch had been motivated purely by his lifelong hatred of Aborigines. Chief Justice Brian Martin wondered whether Murdoch would one day tell where the body was buried. But he suspected Murdoch would not be capable of even one public act of kindness.

As for Stumpy Williams' hex, Aboriginal magic doesn't just travel through the air. What Aborigines call magic is hand-delivered, by courier of some kind. And, usually, it is not until the knife has been sunk, or the ground-up glass has been drunk, or the goose-quill dipped in excrement has scratched the skin and poisoned the blood and the person sickens and dies, that it is actually branded as magic. With no more than a shrug, Murdoch was taken off to Berrimah to live in a prison with an eighty per cent Aboriginal population, some of whom may well have some probing questions to ask about his racist body insignia.

As the door closed on Murdoch, I couldn't help but wonder: did Murdoch enjoy shooting Falconio? He must have. He didn't need to do it. It wasn't like having to shoot a beloved dog which had just taken a dingo bait and was writhing in agony. It must have answered some sense of purpose within him to pull out that revolver, put it to the back of Falconio's head and fire. Probably the back of the head, although it might have been the side. Or for that matter the face, so he could see the young man's short-lived terror, and watch his legs buckle, already a corpse before he'd hit the ground. But perhaps Murdoch never even gave Falconio that much thought. He was just an obstacle which needed to be removed.

# 14  THE END OF THE LINE

While waiting to give evidence, Hepi met Joanne Lees. Hepi was talking to
Nick Falconio at the time. Lees was off to one side by herself. 'So I talked
to her. She's … fairly vague. I said, "I'm sorry. I hope things go well and …"
That was about the extent of it. Politely nodded and, yeah…'

What was Hepi saying sorry for? 'The whole thing. She'd had a bastard
of a time. She was a bit flippant but what happened to her happened to
her. And I have no doubts about her story. So, sorry for that. I didn't really
know what to say to her, eh. I feel responsible. I gave the guy means and
motive for being there. And I could have been doing it myself, not have cut
in Murdoch to this whole thing, and no one would have been dead. So I'm
semi-responsible.'

Asked if he really felt that way, Hepi said: 'Yeah, I do a wee bit, Paul.
Maybe he would have been out there doing it for someone else, but – I don't
really know. I gave the man the opportunity to make money and showed him
how to go about it. We were running drugs, we weren't murdering people.
I was a liked person. And then this happens. It's something that doesn't settle
well with me. I feel sorry for her, I really do. She would have had five hours
of terror by some standover freak who is only strong enough to do it to a
woman, with a gun in his hands. It's real easy. And for my next trick I'll go
and rape a mother and a small child. You're joking. No way.'

Murdoch always wanted respect. He demanded it, but never figured out how to get it. The only thing he knew that worked for sure was scaring the crap out of people with his giant, looming, black-mouthed, tattooed presence. By all accounts, the judge's wish not to give Murdoch a rating, so he wouldn't be overvalued as an inmate, has not really panned out. He's got plenty of mates. He's the innocent killer.

'Yeah,' said Hepi. 'I reckon at the time he was full of speed and self-importance. He had everything he needed, as far as his limited vision went, so what's his next thrill in life? He had wound himself up into a state. But he had been planning something because he had these handcuffs made up. Instead of thinking, "How am I going to get myself to Broome, how can I get the drugs through?" he was thinking, "What can I do now?". He'd sit in a car for a long time. I think that front cab of his Land Cruiser was his den of hell where he sat there and surmised about what he could do next for a thrill. And it was, as it turned out, wanking his crank in the middle of the desert.'

When he came to summing up the case to the jury, the judge took a two-way bet on Hepi. He didn't seem to go for him much. He warned Hepi was not of 'good character' and that it was possible he had a motive to act out of malice towards his former business partner. But he also said once they had taken his warning into account, they could still find his evidence 'accurate and reliable'.

Hepi was back home in Sedan when the judge was summing up. 'I think that night we'd had some mates out and they'd gone, "Fuck, this judge has just slagged you off big time, James". And I said, "Yeah, he has, hasn't he?". He basically said, "James Hepi, piece of shit". I thought, "Yep". I was doing stuff outside the law, he's a judge and I'm a criminal. We know where each other stand. Still, what happened is the way it is, the way I told it. I don't think an innocent man is in jail.'

It was exhilarating being rich and reckless. That's over now. Hepi can't do it anymore. West Australian and South Australian police and prosecutors were not happy about a man who came out talking about his numerous drug runs, shifting huge quantities of weed. There was an attempt to punish him under proceeds-of-crime legislation but it was pulled at the last moment. There wasn't anything much left to take anyway. After Hepi's arrest in Western Australia, all his heavy equipment – including an eight-tonne Dodge tip-truck, a Massey Ferguson tractor, a slasher, his stashed paintings and buried cash – went missing. Hepi thinks Murdoch took it because Freddy Everitt was heard boasting about it around Sedan and Swan Reach.

'I'm gonna be a good boy because that's what I have to do. I'd love to go back and do this tomorrow. But I can't. If they catch me, they know James Hepi. Everyone knows James Hepi now. That's just it. But that's all right.'

'He's had his fun and the game's over,' said Michelle, from off to one side.

'Yes, dear,' sighed Hepi. 'I never looked over my shoulder – there was a time there when I did – but not now. I haven't done anyone in the back, ever. And the one time I did it was to the one person that deserved it. Fuck me? No, fuck you.'


A few weeks after the conclusion of Bradley Murdoch's trial, I received an email from Julieanne McPhail. She wrote that she had always thought Murdoch innocent until she read a story I had written which recounted the rape of Laura and her daughter Jane. The story wasn't what you'd call balanced – it didn't need to be. The word 'alleged' had finally been dispensed with. Murdoch was guilty and it was now possible to write what had not been permitted before: that Murdoch was good for the South Australian rapes. It didn't matter what the jury in that case had thought.

Now, with Murdoch in jail, McPhail was considering that she just might have been one of the ones who got away. Her encounter with Murdoch was only a month before Falconio and Lees were hijacked. She wrote to me that she had now become frightened 'to even drive off the main highway outside the city', even though she'd turned up in court and called Murdoch a 'complete gentleman'. Her written language was, like her, florid and precious. She said: 'I once described the outback night sky as being a truly beautiful thing, my own jewellery box with a lovely singing pearl and dancing coloured diamonds. I'm too scared to enjoy it again.' She invited me to call.

McPhail was no longer living in Western Australia, where she grew up. She was in another state, about to be married, and starting again, which is why her invitation to call was curious. Didn't she want to 'just get on with things'? Hadn't she been the one who had asked, in the committal hearing, that her name be suppressed? She said she wanted to debrief with someone who had closely followed the trial. I told her how she'd come across as such a strange creature, in both the committal hearing and the trial. She seemed unreal, like she'd floated down from the sky. She'd drop some minor bombshell and then give her trademark coy smile. I couldn't figure out whether she was up to something or was the real thing.

And she'd consumed some twenty beers on her journey between Perth and Adelaide in 2001, along with quantities of speed and dope, yet made it sound like just another typical day out. Somehow, she'd absorbed this into her small frame and stayed steady on the road. She really was 'quite pretty', as I had earlier described her. Her pristine presentation seemed at odds with the bush-pig lifestyle she was describing. Green patent leather shoes, green handbag, green dress and a mass of big, long, dark hair gave her the appearance of being expensively managed. She was carefully glamorous yet happy to stand knee-deep in the pig shit of a putrid personality like Murdoch. She was a conundrum.

I had noted in an earlier *Bulletin* story that she appeared to be running from a heavy past. She was, but not quite in the way I'd imagined. That is the thing with courtroom witnesses, especially fascinating ones who have been ordered by prosecution lawyers not to speak to the press: you only get so much and never their backgrounds or current life contexts, unless they're an expert forensic witness who will then be introduced to the jury as an envied master of his or her field. The people who really mattered were the ordinary people who had friendships or encounters with the accused. With them, all you ever got, and all that ever mattered in the courtroom context, was an oath that they'd tell the truth. Experts, by comparison, were peripheral. Necessary, but not the real thing.

By 2001, McPhail had sad reason for sometimes taking off on impulsive cross-country journeys in her little Suzuki Vitara 4WD. But in 1998, when she headed from Perth up to Broome, she was in her early twenties and just another young Australian checking out the north. She knew Broome to be a 'liberal, nudity-prone kind of place', and knew that taking off her top would give her the extra cash she wanted. It was not something she thought about, much. 'Heaps of girls do it.' She ended up serving drinks, topless, in a Coffin Cheaters clubhouse in Blue Haze, the light industrial area on the outskirts of Broome. The money was good and no one ever hit on her. So she said. I found it hard to see why anyone wouldn't have hit on her. 'The bikies were wonderful. I've had rougher nights working in straight bars. They just leave you alone, they know not to touch. Women are pretty well respected. They're maybe not considered equal but they're pretty well left alone.'

On Friday afternoons, guests would be invited to the clubhouse. She thought she remembered seeing Murdoch there but could not be sure. 'Yes and no. I think so, but there were that many people.' The clubhouse was the common ground McPhail and Murdoch found when they later met on the road to Adelaide in 2001. She also wondered if the fact that she had bikie connections had made her, in Murdoch's rapidly degenerating mind, an untouchable.

'Back then I was having a cruisy time driving around Australia, having a good time. People in the Kimberley, if you don't drink you don't fit in. They have these carton-a-night clubs. Once you can drink a carton a night, you're accepted in these rough, redneck circles. I also had a government job and flew up to these great, obscure communities that few people get to see, like Oombulgurri and Kalumburu. I was writing reports for the state government, just as a PA. Just because I was out there rednecking it doesn't mean it was going to be my whole life.'

Then she got to Darwin where she lived in the pink house on East Point Road, a Fannie Bay mansion overlooking the sailing club. The real difference from Broome was that now she was hanging out with rich people. She hinted at a surreal scene. Everyone was having a good time. Too good a time. 'My boyfriend owned the pink house,' she said. 'He ended up suiciding in 2000. He owned car yards in the Territory. I ended up finding his body. It was done with a shotgun. We were together for ten months before he did it. Manic depressive. He wanted to marry me, I didn't want to get married. There were major issues. That year, 2001, when I met Bradley, I was just driving around Australia trying to find myself. It was a tragic story and it took me a long time to get over that.'

Did Murdoch really offer you a gun? 'Absolutely. I could take you to that exact spot tomorrow where he let that bullet fly.' She didn't want it. It wasn't pearl-handled. And there is no reason Murdoch would have had a pearl-handled gun. Men do not carry pearl-handled pistols, as General George S Patton made very clear. An ivory-handled pistol, such as Patton owned, was acceptable, but, as he once remarked, 'Only a pimp in a New Orleans whorehouse or a tin-horn gambler would carry a pearl-handled pistol.'

Murdoch had given her the creeps. McPhail had felt a bolt of something akin to fear when she first saw Murdoch, but it passed. 'I found it creepy how he was parked off the side of the road then came screaming up behind me and really checked me out. But when I met him at the service station he was really quite nice. Along the way I was ringing [the man she was going to visit in Adelaide] at all the service stations. I think he saw that.'

McPhail had, of course, pegged Murdoch as a criminal. The way he dodged the South Australian quarantine checkpoint, heading bush and then catching up with her further down the road, suggested as much to her. Besides, their mutual Broome acquaintances were all heavy players in the Broome 'party scene'. She and Murdoch never discussed his work shifting drugs; McPhail just assumed he was doing someone's dirty work. His criminality was not an issue to her. She tended not to assess a person's character on where they stood with the law. Indeed, she became so relaxed with the bear-like man ushering her through the night that she was able to sleep in her swag with him nearby. The long drive and the many beers she'd had were telling her she was exhausted. The speed she'd taken was trying to tell her that she had more in her tank, but then the last joint before bed – and the world's purest air, blowing up from the Antarctic and washing her down – convinced her otherwise.

'I actually slept. I didn't feel worried about him at all. He was really nice. That's why I was freaked out later when I heard about the sex crime. I think I must be lucky. At the time, the only thing that was weird was his dog. It was just very stealth-like, very well-behaved, very wary. I couldn't touch the dog, couldn't give it a pat or anything.

'I did get freaked out when he pulled out the gun. I couldn't get out of there quick enough. Something just said to me, "Turn around, hop in your car and get out of there". Someone was sitting on my shoulder, telling me, "Get out. Really quickly". I turned around and got out of there. That's the last I saw him. I'm just glad to be sitting here now. What's even scarier to me is that I told Murdoch to go to the Barrow Creek pub,' she said. 'I'd met Les Pilton, the owner of Barrow Creek, quite a few times. I loved the place and had some really great times there.' Her car-yard boyfriend owned outlets in Katherine and Alice Springs, so they'd sometimes drive down from Darwin together. Barrow Creek was a mandatory beer stop.

'It was such a larrikin outback place, one that hasn't really changed since the 1930s. There'd be cats running across the bar rooting each other while you're drinking at the bar. I said to Brad, "Make sure you stop in at Barrow Creek". When I saw Joanne Lees in the court, I was pretty spun out. We do look pretty similar. We're the same sort of build.'

What McPhail was hinting at, or working on, was a story that the gunman had actually been after her the whole time. He'd thought it was her in the Kombi van. At the time I didn't pick up where she was heading with this. Anyway, Lees was much breastier than McPhail. Apart from the fact they were both probably about a size 10, that's where the similarities ended.

A few weeks after speaking to McPhail I was alerted to a story in *Woman's Day*: 'I Escaped the Outback Killer'. Julieanne had by then refined the story she had told me, and stepped on the accelerator. 'Murdoch knew I would be alone and unarmed,' she reportedly said, through 'tears'. McPhail had been chasing a media buck and had got one.

'I was easy, easy prey,' she was quoted as saying in the story. 'The last time I saw him he was really ticked off with me. Maybe he had a score to settle.' Hang on – hadn't she said Brad was a complete gentleman? 'We could easily pass as sisters,' she said of Lees. 'The hair, the build, the face shape – it's eerie.'

So, according to Julieanne McPhail, the whole thing was, after all, about Julieanne McPhail. I wondered what would have happened if Joanne Lees had ever felt the need to put herself in the spotlight this way, from the very beginning. Would it really have helped people believe her story? I didn't know. All that mattered was that the wet season rains had come, as heavy as they'd been in years. The old town got a good washing down. And it needed it.

## 15  NOTHING OF INTEREST

There was only one real question left: where was Falconio? Into which mine shaft was he shoved? What roadside spoon drain took him? Psychics, clairvoyants, diviners, pendulum swingers – at last count, eight of them – had all had a crack. Despite their claims of being able to see through to the other realm, they had no proven record of unearthing missing people. That was why Adelaide's Beaumont children were still missing, forty years on. It was why police hated psychics, but not as much as the families of missing people, who are understandably desperate to believe the claims but never seem to be taken to the place where the missing/dead person lies. And psychics never, ever conceded they were wrong. When the skeleton was not uncovered, they had an excuse: the body had been moved.

Psychics nonetheless hold great power over people: the 'what if' factor. Few have the strength to shield themselves from the enticing possibilities. The better-known Australian psychics are said to be in such demand that you need to make an appointment months in advance to take delivery of their wisdom. Some employ media controllers. I didn't have the time or patience. *The Bulletin* was a weekly magazine that needed the news yesterday. I went to see the always available Mr Nothing.

Mickey Nothing failed to keep his scheduled appointment with me on a Thursday morning on the main street of the Territory's Tennant Creek, some 225 kilometres north of Barrow Creek. This led to a search and some predictable car-window exchanges with locals.

'Have you seen Mickey Nothing?'

'Nothing.'

He was eventually located sitting under a scribbly bush with some mates out the back of so-called Drive-In Camp, where he lived, on the outskirts of Tennant Creek. This was not the time or place to worry about Nothing's living conditions, which were disastrous. Besides, the complicated truth is that if you told Mickey Nothing he had to go and live in a nice house in town instead of his tiny tin shack, it'd break his heart.

No one seemed to know where Nothing got his name. If he knew, he was not able to say. He spoke in short bursts of decipherable English but he was a true bush-bred man who'd come to Tennant Creek from the hinterland many decades ago to obtain the most basic of comforts. He mostly spoke his own Alyawarre language but age had had its way with him. Even his own people found him a little hard to interpret. Nothing spoke in quietly roared key points and he was all but blind. His age? 'Ninety, that's all.'

Around Tennant Creek Nothing had a reputation as a 'spirit man'. Some of his fellow Aborigines were a little spooked by him and considered that he might already have taken on otherworldly form. Word was he had certain 'powers'. Older Tennant Creek people remember Mickey Nothing as always having been small and ancient.

Nothing was not so much a kadaitcha man, or witchdoctor, as a 'clever' man who would reputedly appear at opportune moments – say, when you were lost out bush and panic was setting in. Nothing would materialise, on foot, dead snakes draped around his neck, and guide you to safety. Or he used to. He'd gotten too old for those epic cross-country wanderings through some of Australia's most inhospitable country for which he was deservedly famous. All he could manage when I saw him was the daily walk of several kilometres from Drive-In Camp to the main street of Tennant.

Asked if he knew where Peter Falconio was, Nothing said he did. Shown a photo of the victim, Nothing held it just centimetres away from his one, barely functioning eye and declared: 'That whitefella's finished [dead]. That cheeky whitefella finish him. He's at Hatches Creek, past the Murray Downs road. He's in the ground at Hatches Creek.'

'Cheeky' is not a mild word to bush Aborigines. It can mean anything from 'inappropriate' or 'unwanted' – such as a 'cheeky weed' – through to 'killer'. Nothing was most concerned that I not take him all the way down to Barrow Creek. Barrow Creek is on another tribe's land. 'That's Kaytej mob, we don't go to Barrow Creek, no. That's different law.'

Which road will we turn off? 'I'll choose it,' said Nothing firmly.

We turned east on the Murray Downs road, bypassing the Ali-Curung community towards Hatches Creek, Nothing's 'borning' place in the Davenport Range. This was slightly worrying. It's a fair hike from the crime scene. For Murdoch to have shot Falconio just north of Barrow Creek sometime after 8 pm on 14 July 2001, and then driven 160 kilometres northeast to Hatches Creek, on dirt, buried the body and returned to refuel at the Shell Truck Stop in Alice Springs just after midnight, he would have been pushing it. All up, a 610 kilometre journey in four and a half hours? Unlikely, yet not beyond possibility, especially in Murdoch's Toyota Land Cruiser trayback, fitted-out for punishing bush drives. The real question was why Murdoch would have gone all that way when he could have tossed Falconio out and buried him in a shallow grave much closer to the killing scene.

'Don't you worry, I'll show you where that fella is,' said Nothing. 'He's out at Hatches Creek.'

Nothing quickly proved that his excellent sense of place on his own home country came from feel and knowledge rather than his failing eyes. We had gone some way past the poorly signposted turn-off to Hatches Creek when Nothing emerged from his semi-slumber to scream: 'You're going the wrong way to fuck-all! You'll end up in Queensland!'

Retracing our path, we found the road to Hatches Creek and took it. Nothing suddenly became ravenous and made this loudly apparent: 'I'm tooooo hungry! I've got to eat! You've got to stop driving! Make me campfire! C'mon!' Wishing to avoid some sort of deprivation-of-liberty scandal involving an ancient Aborigine, we stopped.

Nothing could have eaten some sort of muesli bar concoction that was readily available in the vehicle, but he'd scoff at such pretender food. This man had never eaten vegetables in his life, unless they were served up to him in a stock camp many decades ago. He might have had a go at the odd bush yam or maybe the occasional seasonal bush orange or bush banana that grew around here. But meat was all that mattered. Snakes and kangaroos when he could get them, but mostly lamb chops and bread, which Angelo – Tennant Creek butcher-greengrocer – delivered to him at Drive-In Camp early every morning. Nothing had made it all the way to ninety on this diet, so he was doing something right. All he'd packed for our trip was a loaf of bread and several raw chops.

We had no barbecue plate, so it was clear what had to be done. A fire was made and the three huge chops landed straight on top. 'Any good?' I asked, once the half-burned specimens were stick-forked from the flames. 'Too good,' Nothing said, solemnly and painstakingly motoring through all three. Lack of tomato sauce was cause for passing disappointment. So was the sun, which seemed to be unnecessarily hurrying through its afternoon routine. It was 3 pm by the time Nothing had washed his hands in the red dirt and declared himself a happy man, now ready to continue the search.

As we got closer to Hatches Creek, site of an abandoned wolfram mine in an area riddled with deep shafts, the road became increasingly questionable. The entire wider Tennant Creek region had been rained on, hard, for weeks. A creek crossing appeared. It looked passable, more or less, but there were kids in the car. And a beloved, if slightly feared, geriatric Aborigine named Mickey Nothing, who might be missed. It would not do to get bogged, stranded and for him and the kids to perish. Especially as there's no money in the case anymore. Some had a go at claiming the $250 000 reward for information leading to Falconio's killer, but police had more or less let it be known that no one was getting the money.

We had told no one where we were going and it didn't look like the track had been travelled on for a while. There was water in the creek, but we had no real food – Nothing had eaten it all. And if it came down to a question of eating the weakest, Mr Nothing was the standout candidate. He didn't look appetising.

Peter Falconio? Nothing nodded his head to someplace beyond the flooded creek crossing: 'Over there.' He didn't care whether we found him or not. We turned back.

The Northern Territory police have tended not to discuss the ongoing hunt for whatever remains of Peter Falconio, except to confirm 'we still conduct searches any time we receive information'. Several weeks before the failed Nothing Expedition, a fleet of cops towing motorbikes on trailers passed through Tennant Creek, heading north. Word around town was they'd been for another look in the Barrow Creek region.

Police get annoyed when psychics contact them, and tend to ignore them. Yet they found it hard to ignore Leanna Adams, who had the rare distinction of being a psychic who had actually solved a missing-person case. Or so it seemed.

Thomas Braun, thirty-six, an Aboriginal man from Alice Springs suffering depression, disappeared in November 2001 when he walked out of his girlfriend's home. Braun's family were advised to contact Adams, an Aboriginal psychic who lived in Perth. She came to Alice Springs, drove west of town and was able to take family members directly to Braun's remains, a spot high on a ridge some 20 kilometres to the west of town. The Braun family had already tried and failed to convince police to do a search for them based on Adams' directions. The first question a curious police force should have asked was whether this was an elaborate stitch-up between the Braun family and Adams. But police never hinted at any such conspiracy; indeed, they would soon find themselves following a spectral mud map Adams provided on the whereabouts of Falconio.

According to a report in the *Centralian Advocate* in December 2002, Adams' own son had been killed in a car crash near the Aileron roadhouse, north of Alice Springs, in 1998. She claimed that her dead son had come to her in a vision along with Peter Falconio – both of them in animal form. Falconio's spirit, she said, was desperate for his remains to be taken back to his own homeland, in Yorkshire. Adams said she knew where Falconio was buried, only a few kilometres from the crime scene, on Neutral Junction station, just to the east of Barrow Creek.

Police have never confirmed that they got a bulldozer and went to the site, probably because they didn't want to start a psychic avalanche. But after Adams had found Braun, how could they not go? The what-if factor gets to cops too. They have never denied that they dug great holes in Neutral Junction looking for, but not finding, Falconio.

Frank Cuda was the first of the psychics to claim they know where Falconio was buried. He arrived in the Northern Territory just a month after Falconio went missing. Cuda had been swinging his pendulum over a map of the Northern Territory, he told me, asking, 'Where is Peter Falconio?' The pendulum said the answer lay in Renner Springs, 150 kilometres north of Tennant Creek – and an improbable 400 kilometres north of the crime scene. Cuda wanted the just-posted $250 000 reward but ran foul of an elderly pastoralist named Jack Chambers, who owned the land around Renner Springs. For Cuda to traverse his property, Chambers wanted half the reward money and, interestingly, insisted that he personally handle all inquiries from the soon-to-arrive media horde. Cuda claimed Chambers' hostile attitude interfered with the efficacy of his pendulum – and stormed back home to Queensland. But Chambers, aroused, found a patch of discoloured dirt on his property and thought it could be Falconio's blood. Police dutifully tested the patch. Not blood. Maybe engine oil.

Two water diviners from Toowoomba said Falconio was buried near the Aboriginal community of Yuendumu, 190 kilometres northwest of Alice Springs – and on the back road home to Broome that Murdoch took after leaving the Shell Truck Stop.

Then there was the Melbourne-based law student and psychic – a great combination: in theory she can tell you whether your case will succeed – who reportedly said that 'Peter spoke to me' and showed her where he was buried. He was four feet under, near a bridge north of Barrow Creek. She went to the spot but didn't have the tools to unearth him.

Clairvoyant-columnist Ann Ann said Falconio was down a mine shaft in the Barrow Creek area; clairvoyant-columnist Scott Russell Hill sensed that the body had something to do with the letter 'W' – spooky, because the roadhouse stopovers of Wauchope and Wycliffe Well are just over 100 kilometres north of Barrow Creek (and Wycliffe Well is the self-proclaimed alien visitation capital of Australia, as testified by the statuettes of the little green men out the front). Russell Hill also got something to do with 'Devil', another ripper insight because the Devils Marbles – a weird rock formation where giant boulders balance on a sea of granite – are just east of Wauchope.

But it was a non-psychic letter writer to *The Bulletin* who gave the most outlandish explanation for what had really happened to Falconio. She wrote: 'I believe that there was a problem with the Kombi van and that they did stop to check what the noise was. But I believe it was not where Lees says it happened. It makes more sense that they stopped way before that particular spot. Peter got out to check the back of the Kombi. Lees was asked to rev the engine. Lees did so, but she had not realised the Kombi was in reverse and has accidentally reversed into Peter.'

Bradley John Murdoch would have enjoyed that as an explanation for Falconio's death. But it did not explain his whereabouts. Rex Wild was wrong when he said Falconio would one day be found. He never will.

# AFTERWORD

It is with unyielding persistence that the Murdoch case has refused to shake its links to the Chamberlain case. Some of the links are real, some extrapolated by fanciful types like me, who find analogy and irony convenient devices by which to help make a point.

But you could hardly miss it when Ian Barker, QC, turned up to defend Murdoch in late 2006, on his appeal for his murder conviction. Barker was the man who led the Crown prosecution against Lindy Chamberlain, also in the Northern Territory Supreme Court, all those years ago. He had been effective then, devastatingly so, persuading a small-town Darwin jury to convict a woman for murder while never once suggesting what her motive might have been.

And here was Barker, 24 years on, telling the Court of Criminal Appeal that Murdoch had been badly served by justice. Barker's thrust was that all sorts of evidence should never have been allowed in by the trial judge; that the evidence of certain 'experts' was unsafe; that there had been a miscarriage of justice.

Barker, in what could only be described as a two-way bet, also said Murdoch's 28-year non-parole period was manifestly excessive. In other words, even if the appeal judges found all the evidence was properly admitted by the trial judge, then at the very least they should cut the man's sentence.

Not once in the Murdoch appeal was it suggested that the DNA found on Joanne Lees' t-shirt, on the gearstick of the Kombi and deep inside the cable-tie manacles was not Murdoch's. Not once was it even suggested that Murdoch did not kill Peter Falconio. Barker wasn't asking the court to release Murdoch. He was asking for a retrial.

And that was something we could have all done without. Fortunately, the Court of Criminal Appeal saw it that way, too.

'The core issue in this case was the identity of the assailant,' the judges said. 'In our opinion, the presence of the blood of the appellant upon the t-shirt of Ms Lees establishes beyond reasonable doubt the presence of the appellant at the time Ms Lees was attacked just north of Barrow Creek. When this evidence is considered along with the other evidence properly admitted at trial of events occurring at that location, the guilt of the appellant of the murder of Peter Falconio is established beyond reasonable doubt. The case against the appellant becomes overwhelming when the evidence of the identification of the appellant as the assailant by Ms Lees is taken into account. That is sufficient to conclude that no substantial miscarriage of justice has occurred and therefore to dispose of the appeal.'

As to reducing the length of Murdoch's sentence, they weren't playing along on that one either. They said they were 'unable to conclude that the period arrived at by the learned sentencing judge was manifestly outside of a reasonable range of sentencing outcomes in the circumstances. There is no basis on which this court might properly
interfere with the exercise of the sentencing discretion'.

Barker was just doing his job.

But in the space of those 24 years since Lindy had been convicted, Darwin had grown up. And by the time he stood up in court for Murdoch in that appeal court, the jury had already done what it was meant to do. They had, in finding Murdoch guilty, forced the little northern capital out of its sometimes too-pervasive apathy and made us look like maybe we weren't such a bunch of rubes after all. They reasserted the sometimes lost validity of the jury system – at least until next time. All links to Chamberlain are now permitted to end. They don't matter any more.

It cannot be known whether the jury came to their verdict by following the trial judge's detailed instructions on the law when reaching their verdict. All that mattered was they stood two people against each other, Murdoch and Lees, and found for the woman and, as well, for her long-gone boyfriend, the man lying dead somewhere, off to one side. To be able to set aside all the baggage that Lees herself had dragged with her on her journey required a good deal of forbearance and commonsense. They did well.

The way these things go, there might still be more to run in this case. It won't matter. We already know what happened. Exactly what happened. The jury told us.


I'd promised a guy in Broome I'd look into the Davey and Albert disappearances. I took a look but, with no bodies and no admissions, it was not possible to build a case against Murdoch. Northern Territory police have told me they profiled Murdoch as a cleanskin: a first-time, one-off killer. Western Australian police were more interested. They said that Murdoch was a possible person of interest in the Davey and Albert cases, but only because he was a confirmed killer who was in the general area when the girls disappeared and could – but only *could* – fit the profile of a serial killer. He remains a suspect, nothing more.

It had also been suggested Murdoch might fit the profile of Perth's triple-murderer Claremont serial killer, who operated in 1996–97. He did not. He was in jail for the Fitzroy Crossing shoot-up when two of the Claremont girls went missing. Police have discounted him.

The advertisement on the following page, from the West Australian Crime Stoppers, is included in the hope that one day someone is hauled in over the Broome disappearances:

### SARA LEE DAVEY

**Age:** 24
**Height:** 175cm
**Hair:** Black
**Eyes:** Brown

Sara DAVEY was last seen driving a four wheel drive type vehicle in Saville Street Broome on Tuesday 14 January 1997 at 5.00 pm. This is the last known location that she visited in Broome prior to her disappearance.

**Last seen:** Not known

### PETRONELLA ALBERT

**Age:** 21
**Height:** 160cm
**Hair:** Black
**Eyes:** Brown

Petronella ALBERT left her address in Broome area at 2030 hours 28/04/99, but failed to return home. All efforts by her family and the police have failed to locate her.

**Last seen:** blue dress, no shoes

# SOURCES

Paul Toohey relied on material from his own attendance at the Brad Murdoch committal and trial, and his subsequent coverage of the story in *The Australian* and *The Bulletin*. He also drew upon numerous interviews and police statements held as court records. Most of his sources do not wish to be publicly acknowledged. However, Paul does wish to thank James Hepi for his full and fearless accounts. Mr Hepi could have made a tidy sum selling his story but chose to risk telling it to Paul for no reward.